GOING

some

PLACE

GOING

some

PLACE

edited by LYNNE VAN LUVEN

COTEAU BOOKS
TWENTY-FIVE YEARS

Edited by Lynne Van Luven.

Cover photo, "Thunderhead near Grand Coulee" by Gary Robins, Available
Light Photographics & Design, Regina, Saskatchewan.
Cover and book design by Duncan Campbell.

Printed and bound in Canada at AGMV Marquis Imprimeur Inc.

Canadian Cataloguing in Publication Data

Main entry under title

Going some place: creative non-fiction across the prairies
ISBN 1-55050-137-2

1. Canadian prose literature (English) – 20th Century*
2. Reportage literature, Canadian (English).*
I. Van Luven, Lynne.

PS8373.G65 2000   C818'.54008   C00-920167-X
PR9197.7.G65 2000

10   9   8   7   6   5   4   3   2   1

COTEAU BOOKS   AVAILABLE IN THE US FROM
401-2206 Dewdney Ave.   General Distribution Services
Regina, SK   4500 Witmer Industrial Estates
Canada   S4R 1H3   Niagara Falls, NY, 14305-1386

The publisher gratefully acknowledges the financial assistance of the
Saskatchewan Arts Board, the Canada Council for the Arts, the Government
of Canada through the Book Publishing Industry Development Program
(BPIDP), and the City of Regina Arts Commission, for its publishing program.

contents

BREATHING SPACES

INTRODUCTION

IF SIMILES WERE TO BE STRETCHED WHIMSICALLY and the form of writing known as creative non-fiction were to be likened to a bird, it would surely be deemed a magpie. Like the distinctive, fractious, black-and-white bird with the iridescent feathers and the raucous voice, creative non-fiction operates on audacity and curiosity. Grounded firmly in "real life," it nevertheless swoops across the writing landscape, picking up the bright baubles and gewgaws of invention wherever it finds them. As long as the item glitters, the inventive magpie will seize and appropriate it to advance/enhance its sallies into narrative. Yet, despite its flights of fancy, the magpie of creative non-fiction is a hard-liner when it comes to actuality – it does not invent its stories, it simply tells them dramatically.

Because of its accumulative nature, creative non-fiction often causes literary arguments too convoluted and numerous to be completely articulated here. "What is it, exactly?" people ask, seeking a clear and exact definition. "Is it just a buzzword for a postmodern version of the personal essay? Is it fancy journalism? Is it travel writing with diverse destinations? Is it really *legitimate?*"

Obviously, one of the surest ways to find out how creative non-fiction is being defined is to turn to those contemporary writers themselves creating it. When Coteau asked me to edit an anthology on this subject, I advertised for articles centred loosely on the theme of location/dislocation – whether in a psychological or physical manner. I was looking for fluid discussions about the nature of being in the world today, about how people inhabit space, whether physically or psychically, and how they negotiate "geography" of both landscape and mindscape. As the manuscripts began to come in, I was impressed by their quality and also by authors' willingness to grapple with the physical and emotional *facts of life*. Unsurprisingly, I found that all sorts of writers commit creative non-fiction, and that submissions were arriving from writers known for their work in other genres. I found it perfectly logical that poets, novelists, and dramatists also felt a need to write non-fiction, perhaps because those three forms draw so heavily on "real-life bones" to support their inventions. In the end, choosing this collection's final entries from among such largesse has been an agonizing process. I had to turn away many excellent submissions because they did not rest comfortably within the framework set for *Going Some Place,* or because they were too long and could not be abbreviated without sacrificing too many of their essential elements.

I'd like to think that *Going Some Place* stands as one of many possible illustrations – I shy away from the word definition for a form so protean and evolving – of the different forms creative non-fiction can take. You will see that the genre includes poetic personal journals, meditations, memoirs, activist personal reportage, autobiography, personal essays on being an outsider, historical and literary travelogues, tributes to a particular person, celebrations of a distinctive place, and explorations of the past. Creative non-fiction can be a vehicle of investigation, rumination, discovery, and mourning.

Orchestrating an anthology as diverse as *Going Some Place* has proven challenging: the book is divided into three segments in which articles loosely similar in theme and mood are grouped in a genial synergy. "A Honeycomb of Memory" draws its title from Louise Bernice Halfe's fascinating exploration of contemporary storytelling, and begins with Caroline Woodward's "Choir," an exploration of the personal solace found in music shared within a community. Woodward's submission sets the tone for the entire anthology, which is an attempt to blend various voices into one harmonious, but varied, illumination of a difficult-to-define genre. In "Deaf Music," Margaret Hollingsworth explores the paradox of finding identity in music despite a hearing impairment. Writing in the playfully cerebral mode so evident in her novels, Kristjana Gunnars in "pensive nude," links the aims of art with human beings' place in the natural world.

Journeying is the theme for the subsequent four pieces: in "Counting the Rs in London," Nancy Mattson's poetic journals explore migration from New World to Old; in "A Guest of Karen Blixen," Betty Jane Wylie warmly re-creates the world of Danish writer Isak Dinesen; in "Not My Home," Daniel Coleman revisits his childhood in a missionary family in Ethiopia; and in "Of Remnants and Riches," Pauline Holdstock paints a vivid picture of Renaissance Italy.

The final three pieces in Part One bring readers back into the Canadian landscape: Eileen Delehanty Pearkes finds a solid narrative in the stones she collects in the Columbia Mountains she loves; Rita Moir and Shirley Scott-Bruised Head meditate upon their respective experiences of death in "Light on the Land;" and in "A Honeycomb of Memory," Louise Bernice Halfe pays tribute to the native storytelling traditions that shaped her.

The mid-section of the book, "A Question of Identity," explores that perpetual Canadian concern, identity, from a variety of perspectives. Ven Begamudré writes a sly and sassy autobiography in "Benny Hits the Big Four-Oh," while Kate Braid ruminates upon her feelings of dislocation in "The Born-

Here Immigrant." Nigel Darbasie tackles the historical roots of racism in "A Question of Identity;" Sue Walsh examines how fear is borne of racism in "White Girl Screaming;" and Caterina Edwards recalls childhood conflict with an "old-country" Italian mother in "Under My Skin." Looking back on the past enhances self-understanding for Joshua Frost in "Zaida," Rita Donovan in "Montreal Suite," and Barry McKinnon in "Wrestling the Alligator."

The anthology's final section, "Breathing Spaces," draws together a compelling group of articles which focus upon life and death as integral aspects of being human. Pat Krause's "Acts of Love" meditates upon the loss of a beloved husband; Myrna Kostash's "The Ballad of Frank Little" explores how the death of a union leader defines a certain period in Montana history. In "A Schooner in Memory," Don Gayton takes a trip with his father to trace the Maritime ancestors who shaped them both. Ann Charney's dismay at the "merchandizing of [Jewish] misfortune" in Czechoslovakia is palpable in "Strip-Mining the Land of Sorrow," and both Merilyn Simonds in "Breathing Spaces," and Wayne Grady in "Heart Failure," explore new awareness brought by death in the family.

When you read these narratives, you will be impressed, as I was, by the authors' incredible generosity and openness, by their ability to take us inside an event or an experience and share their deeply personal reaction to it so that we may appreciate its resonance and understand its relevance to our own lives.

HISTORIANS HAVE SUGGESTED THAT ONE OF THE earliest identifiable practitioners of creative non-fiction might well have been Daniel Defoe, whose version of *A Journal of the Plague Year,* published in 1722, advertised itself as a Londoner's report of the 1665 plague but was actually a melding of the author's childhood memories, family history and considerable research. Literary historians also note that people have always tended to read far more non-fiction than fiction. Journalists argue that creative non-fiction is simply literary journalism in less flashy personal costume than that flaunted by such sixties "new journalists" as Tom Wolfe, who noted, in *The New Journalism* (1973), the legacy of earlier novelist/ reporters Charles Dickens and George Orwell.

More recently, in *Imagining Ourselves: Classics of Canadian Non-Fiction,* British Columbia writer Daniel Francis observed that the word "non-fiction" only entered the language in 1907. Francis notes that early writers would never have so-categorized themselves. "Biography, autobiography, essay, memoir, cookbook, textbook, technical manual, all are 'not fiction,'" he observes. "Not so long ago everyone seemed to agree that the purpose of non-fiction was to convey information. It was writing which was empirical, fact-based. Fiction, on the other hand, conveyed experience. It did not describe things that had actually happened. But this distinction has never really been valid. Non-fiction writers have always leavened their facts with generous portions of dramatic licence." And, of course, novelists have always written from life, incorporating actuality into their inventions. For Francis, creative non-fiction describes "forms of non-fiction which employ fictional elements or strategies."

Again, not everyone would agree. Non-fiction author and journalist Heather Robertson vigorously rejects the term "non-fiction," insisting that there are only two kinds of stories – the true and the made-up. But over the past three decades, creative non-fiction has become increasingly recognized as both term and form. Robert Root and Michael Steinberg, the American editors of *The Fourth Genre,* a text of "creative nonfiction" (people cannot even agree whether the term should be hyphenated), maintain that this particular sort of writing is marked by five prevalent traits – personal presence, self-discovery/self-exploration, flexibility of form, facts/veracity, and literary approaches to language.

Since writers necessarily deploy "creativity" no matter what they write, the boundary-based arguments about creative non-fiction can seem alternately specious and precious. Nevertheless, it is fascinating to explore how many different forms of writing demonstrate literary approaches to narrative and storytelling. In the autumn of 1999, Charlotte Gray, author of *Sisters in the Wilderness*, a double biography about colonial icons Susanna Moodie and Catharine Parr Traill admitted in a *National Post* article that she writes in "the strange grey area of creative non-fiction: a genre that straddles the ever-more-porous border between stuff-you-get-from-records and stuff-you-make-up...." However, Gray assumes a position some might deem closer to investigative literary journalism than fiction. She explains:

> I put myself firmly on the "fact" side of the border. I don't invent. But I take known facts, and imagine. I imagine Susanna in the act of writing in her cold, damp log cabin. I picture the elderly Catharine struggling to tighten the screws of her flower press, her hands gnarled with arthritis. From the relatively little documentation available, I tried to read between the lines of those of their letters that have survived. I used my judgment in what to include and what to omit; what to emphasize and what to ignore; how to distill an untidy, sprawling mass of facts into a tidy package.

And that "tidy package" is exactly what most creative non-fiction writers strive to achieve, no matter what sort of "story" they are attempting to tell.

I'd argue that Gray is alluding to the two intersecting circles from which creative non-fiction draws both its vitality and veracity: the inner, intimate, private world of the writer herself, and the entire complex and multifarious public world beyond the writer's individual consciousness. Call them small-w and big-W worlds. You might illustrate this by drawing two intersecting circles, and note that creative non-fiction represents a collision, a fusion, a collusion – or perhaps even at times a confusion – between those two worlds. If the writer does his or her job properly and manages to link private understanding with an accurate portrayal of the external events, then she will create an artifact, a *third reality,* which brings inner and outer worlds together in a piece of prose which illuminates a larger issue, enables readers to understand a larger truth, or sparks a series of epiphanies from which new awareness comes. Creative non-fiction then becomes a way of linking the two states that mark the human condition – *private* and *public,* or *self* and *other.*

Picasso once said that "art is not truth. Art is a lie that makes us realize truth." The late W.O. Mitchell was fond of saying much the same thing, calling the best writers simply "damn fine liars." I like to think both Picasso and Mitchell meant that art in itself is not fact, but it may be a creation drawn from reality, incorporating pertinent veracities, to allow us greater understanding – that is, a fuller knowledge – of some actual, verifiable situation outside ourselves.

With that in mind, it is clear that the best creative non-fiction must communicate beyond a merely personal reportage: it must select information, data, details, emotions, images, characters, and situations and, deploying some of the literary techniques the genre embraces, make some commentary or spark some insight about the *wider world.* If the writing thus created remains utterly private in its terms of reference, it has not made the external connection required; it has not, in fact, transcended its making.

IT IS A TRUISM THAT A WRITER ALWAYS CHOOSES where to start the story: he can root his creative non-fiction in the personal and from that particularity draw connections to a wider situation outside himself; or she can base her narrative in a crucial event outside herself, and then from that make some personal extrapolations. The skilled creative non-fiction practitioner will adopt different strategies for different narratives, depending on what she has decided the "story" is and why she is telling it to us. It seems to me that the struggle facing all creative non-fiction writers is that which besets all artists: the grappling between Truth and Technique. Knowing that the story must be authentic, must be based in fact and the external, observable world, a creative non-fiction writer must decide what vehicles, what "tricks" of the story-telling trade, he or she may safely adopt to best convey that particular story. It is easy to see how *too much technique* could overwhelm, negate, or skew the truth, and how *too much truth* – too much detail, too many irrelevant facts about a particular situation – could totally smother the vitality of a story.

Going Some Place contributor Merilyn Simonds has long danced gracefully along the boundaries of creative non-fiction. Consequently, both *The Convict Lover* and her second book, *The Lion in the Room Next Door,* have upset some purists. In a review in the *Canadian Forum,* Alberta writer Nora Abercrombie praises Simonds as a good writer but maintains that the author creates needless controversy by describing her second book, based on events in her own childhood conveyed as subjective stories, as non-fiction. Simonds might reply that she is just being "accurate."

In his introduction to *Best American Essays,* Edward Hoagland writes, "Essays are how we speak to one another in print – caroming thoughts not merely in order to convey a certain packet of information but with a special edge or bounce of personal character in a kind of public letter. You multiply yourself as a writer, gaining height as though jumping on a trampoline, if you can catch the gist of what other people have also been feeling and clarify it for them."

So, since creative non-fiction adopts, expands and in some cases embellishes the personal essay format, is it fair to say that one of its aims is to amplify truth or truths by offering a personal or subjective lens through which to view a problem or situation? I'd say yes – with all the caveats about the power and necessity of veracity in whatever is written and purveyed as non-fiction.

On behalf of the wonderful writers herein, I invite you to explore this new version of the magpie's hoardings. And I hope that *Going Some Place* will stay in your hands long enough to serve as a record of what's happening with this fascinating hybrid genre, before flying off to provoke discussion and serve as a catalyst for dozens more such creations

– *Lynne Van Luven*

a

HONEYCOMB

of MEMORY

CHOIR: A TRIBUTE

Caroline Woodward

SOME BABIES CRY WHEN THEY ARE BORN, BUT I think I must have emerged singing. To the untrained ear, my yowling might have sounded like that of any generic baby, but I have never stopped humming, scatting or making my own versions of joyful noise.

I sang when I hoed the long rows of potatoes. I sang when I rode our Percheron horse along the fencelines of our Peace River homestead. I sang when I walked to meet the school bus, across the fields and through the bush, saluting the trees and greeting cattle in a singsong litany, delivering a bovine benediction.

Sometimes the adventurous teachers who came north to our two-room school in Cecil Lake could carry a tune, and a precious hour or two every week was spent singing. But except for rehearsals for the Christmas Concert and the Spring Talent Show, singing was not much of an educational priority in our farming hamlet. Many of the children were too shy or too stubborn, in the case of the boys, to sing properly in any case. The Christmas carols were a blur of mumbled verses, except for perhaps the first, but the choruses were enthusiastically hammered home by those of us who were not petrified on stage.

One winter my father came home from working away at a

construction site with an old pump organ, discarded by a church because very few of its white keys functioned. I learned to play the black keys, inventing a left-handed chord to accompany myself as I picked out with my right hand the melody to "O Susannah" or "Red River Valley." I had been coaxed out several times to sing solos in the community hall, "Silent Night" or "Danny Boy," rehearsing at home by standing in the farthest corner of the house and belting out the tunes for the musically discerning ears of my parents.

Sounds good.

Don't start off so high next time.

Can't hear the last verse.

Just stand up straight and don't fidget with your hands.

Bolstered by this heady praise, I'd made my forays to the limelight. I'd been too nervous to enjoy myself or even to look anywhere but up into the rafters, so I must have given sweetly wooden performances.

Then a red-haired Mennonite boy came to our school and my brief reign as a soloist mercifully ended. Johnny Siemens loved to sing. He smiled at the audience, he waggled his cute little head and waved his small hands in ways that gave extra oomph to familiar words and made even the grumpiest old-timers at the back of the hall beam fondly.

From the vantage point of middle age, I realize those retired schoolteachers with their shrewd, assessing eyes and the sour-smelling elderly bachelors probably smiled when I sang "Swanee River" too. But I was too busy keeping my shoulders squared and my fingers flattened by my sides to notice any such approval, while Johnny, our preteen boy soprano, observed all these good things, beamed right back and sang divinely, like the angel he all too soon became.

I remember quite clearly my last solo as a child. It was rumoured there would be cash prizes given at the Spring Talent Show. Unprecedented! Inspired by Johnny, whose piercing high notes had lately started to crack and nasally splat, and by the promise of rare hard cash, I commenced serious rehearsals. My parents, who could never be accused of being pushy stage-struck types, advised me that "Danny Boy" was out of the question since the histrionics required to hit the penultimate note were beyond me, no matter how low a note I started with. So I decided to stick to the tried and true: "Old Black Joe" and "Loch Lomond."

The term "show-off" was a black mark on one's character in my family, revealing a shameless and inappropriate need for attention. I was walking a fine line with this talent show hoopla, being twelve and all, which was too old for this sort of thing if I was interpreting correctly the silences and grunts and sighs around home. But I was determined. I had no money and I wanted some. So, forewarned of being labelled and knowing the hall would be jam-packed with the inevitable baby population, singers all, noisy toddlers, watchful peers, sharp-eyed mothers, and mumbling men, I made the short, heroic journey to centre stage.

I sang "Old Black Joe" to the back of the hall, where the farmers stood holding their suspenders and coughing up grain dust. I swung my head a little, from side to side, mourning my ancestors, all slaves down South, where my heart was yearning ever. Despite the fact it was February and nearly thirty below Fahrenheit, that we lived closer to Alaska than Alabama, and that I was the first-generation offspring of Dutch and Welsh immigrants, I did my best to convince the audience of my true musical roots. In fact, I received a decent smattering of applause before I moved along to interpret "Loch Lomond," a wee ditty I could have sung backwards in my sleep.

I trilled along the high road, shifting my gaze row by row from the back of the hall to the middle, where I encountered the frizzled home perm, glinting eyeglasses and frowning face of my very own mother. Row upon beaming row of friends and neighbours and then this, my anxiously poised close relative. I delivered!

On the bonny, bonny ba..a..angs.... I slid, spectacularly off-key, down the punishing banks of Loch Lomond. The hall was silent.

Oh, Gott! exclaimed the maternal voice and a nervous laugh was quickly stifled, but not quickly enough, by a gloved hand.

I took a breath and climbed back up the bank.

Sorry, I said and gathered air.

For me and my true love will never meet again, on the bonny, bonny banks of Loch Lomond! I finished triumphantly, nailing every pure, true note to the boards at the back of the hall, sending them out past the frost-spangled trucks and cars, some filled with men sharing rye whiskey. Up and out went my twelve-year-old voice, past the scrubby spruce and stunted pines and swamp tamarack, over the huddled willows in the muskegs and up to the indigo sky sequined with stars, there to vapourize among the northern lights.

The rest of that evening was a blur of the usual songs by the usual entertainers: the Scandinavian father-and-daughter accordion duo; Mr. Cuthbert, the Irish patriarch of Erin Lea, rising from the side bench to recite Yeats and Goldsmith to a hall for once silent; and the marvellously-disguised matrons of the Women's Institute presenting their collectively out-of-character skit of a louse-infested tramp claiming a park bench from all other comers. If there were fabulous cash prizes, I certainly didn't win any.

I joined the fledgling high school choir when I left home. I don't mean that I ran away from the homestead to join the choir in the way that the truly adventurous join the circus. I mean it was simply necessary for 120 teenagers to leave Metis, Mennonite, oil patch, cattle ranch or other just plain isolated places our parents had gotten themselves into in order to complete our education. We lived in the Fort St. John Dormitory run by Miss Lamb, a three-hundred-pound, sixty-something Englishwoman with platinum bottle-blonde hair and ice-cold eyes.

Gone forever were the morning sounds of wood blocks clunking into the heater, soon to crackle and spit sap, the kettle singing, the quiet murmurs of my parents, and gentle wake-up calls. Dad's Welsh baritone floated back to us as he made his way out to do the cattle chores; Mom sang comforting lullabies in English or Dutch or bits of both as she filled four lunch kits and made hot cereal and cocoa.

Instead, clanging electronic bells woke us up, called us to meals, started and ended study periods, signalled curfew and the final lights out. I adjusted to the hideous bells and the new regimes of dormitory and high school life – but I needed to sing.

What I sang for several months were two songs: "Bali Ha'i" and "Rolling Down To Rio." About sixteen girls were in the choir, fourteen of whom thought they were sopranos until Mrs. Pullan sorted the melody makers from the potential altos. I had a strong voice, so without benefit of formal musical instruction, I was designated an alto.

Oh dreary, droning alto! It just didn't sound right, and I struggled unhappily until one day when Mrs. Pullan whispered the best, most necessary advice in my ear: *Don't sing so loudly and listen to Helen.*

I was embarrassed and ashamed, but I listened to Helen, who could play piano and read music, as well as being blessed with a velvety alto voice. I learned to listen and to blend my voice with my neighbours in that choir. At the Festival we were commended for our strong altos and our songs, whose exotic lyrics meant more to tiny, pretty Mrs. Pullan, who immediately fled Fort St. John, than to me.

During my own first year of teaching back in Fort St. John, I was not content with working fifty or more hours a week on a pilot program with high-risk teens; I also performed as an alto shepherd in *Amahl and the Night Visitors* and joined my second choir. The Cardinal Singers (white frilly blouses, long red skirts) were accompanied and directed by one of the twelve Canada Council Community Musicians working in a program devised in the seemingly more affluent and culturally enlightened 1970s. She was patient, thoroughly professional, and put us through our paces every second Monday night. I was, happily, found to be a soprano again, stationed between two ministers' wives who were seasoned, capable singers.

Finally, I was learning about The Voice, the physical facts of singing, little tricks for breathing properly, and the importance of smiling, thereby raising one's cheekbones to create a resonant inner chamber which releases rounder, more pleasing notes. Pear-shaped vowels, precise tongue-work on consonants, calibrated beginnings and endings, all these things and more I learned. Almost every other Cardinal could read music. I had to rely on my ears to memorize the words, the tune, the rests, the dynamics, everything.

I was often too tired to drag myself to practice or to focus well enough to gather momentum once I was there. Instead of feeling renewed by singing, it was just one more stress-inducing thing to do on my long overachieving list. When the choir was asked to perform at a Health Fair in the region, I blurted out that I couldn't possibly make it because, once again, I had other commitments. The director looked up, peered at me as if to recollect who I was or how well I sang, and then said in her mild-mannered way, *"Well, I suppose it won't make...much difference."*

The minister's wife on my right clutched my hand, giving it a quick squeeze. Chastened, I said that I would do my best to attend, and I did. We sang five songs, struggling to keep smiling instead of collapsing into giggles. It's not every day that a person gets to sing in the acoustically challenged environment of a hockey arena while hundreds of people are trying out treadmills, heart-rate gadgets and healthy hors d'oeuvres.

After I too left that rambunctious town, I eventually landed a caretaking position on North Pender Island, BC, complete with two dogs, a large garden, wood heat and a four-storey cedar and glass mansion. I joined the choir of North and South Pender Islanders, and I was the youngest member by at least two decades.

There was something so wonderful about walking into the little hall and having people smile with genuine affection as they greeted me. I had been a rolling stone for the best part of twelve years, working in Asia, Europe and all around Canada. It was quickly established that I was a full-timer on the island, not a mere weekender or summer cottage subspecies. The only thing better would be owning a place on the island like most of my choir pals, all gleefully retired.

One of our members took on the job of wrangling the thirty to forty of us through our sheet music while another good soul accompanied us on piano. We made our way through great old tunes like "Summertime," "Stormy Weather," "Hit the Road Jack," and of course, the familiar canon of singalong Christmas carols. We dressed up in our individual versions of seasonal finery and sang at the Christmas concert in the school gym, then promptly disbanded for the spring and summer to tend to visitors, gardens, grand-kids and sailing.

The second winter we imported a director from Saltspring Island, an ex-nun who quickly curtailed the quarter-hour visiting session we usually warmed up with. We picked up the pace, learned our music faster and began to occasionally meet in small groups to tackle our parts. I was discovered to be a mezzo-soprano in this choir, and enjoyed singing in my natural range at long last.

I was definitely the oddball in this merry band of seniors, "that writer-gal looking after the modern place up on Schooner," but I blended in vocally and rarely missed practices. Choir was a social occasion, a mini-community, as well as a place for learning and enjoying music. That was the gift I took away with me from that lovely place.

In Nelson, BC, I joined the Images Ad Hoc Singers, an *a capella* feminist group featuring four-part harmonies, feisty, often revisionist lyrics and a two-hour practice every Tuesday evening. We appeared at five or more public events annually, the West Kootenay Women's Festival, and other cultural shindigs, such as Vancouver's Maywerks Festival, the national conference of Women in Trades and Technology, and a peace conference in the acoustically sublime Doukhobor hall in Brilliant.

It was great fun to be entertaining, I discovered, as we cheerily sang about a male contraceptive device or the pitfalls of marriage. We stood in a staunch semicircle, the better to hear ourselves. New songs took months to learn because only a few of the twelve singers could read music with any proficiency. We learned mostly by ear, and we increased practices in small groups as performance dates loomed closer. I learned much about dedication to practice in the seven years I performed with this group. And I learned, again, about the undermining politics of some collective efforts.

Solos were frowned upon by some fiercely vocal members because they called attention away from the group and focused on an individual for a line or even a verse. Subversive resistance was the strategy encountered by any brave soul who stepped forward to lead the collective. Several times during my stint, musically trained and talented women were asked, and even paid, to work with us in order to improve the glacial pace of learning new material or to tackle especially challenging new arrangements.

No one lasted more than a few months.

Several times I would vow to quit when the semantic wrangling over possibly suspect patriarchal lyrics meant that we actually sang for only 32 minutes of a 120-minute practice. But we would usually sing beautifully when we performed, never using sheet music but communicating directly with each other and the audiences. And the audiences loved us and our stage antics, our powerful message-oriented songs and our well-crafted harmonies. I learned to enjoy the applause, to smile and wave and clap along with the audience. We made them laugh, we made them cry, and that's as good as it gets.

SOME DAY I WANT TO LEARN TO READ MUSIC PROPERLY and to take piano lessons, but most of all, I want to play the banjo. I have an unshakeable image in my head of being a sixty-year-old white-haired wild thing in an all-grrrrandma rockabilly band. Meanwhile, I have a living to earn in the bookstore my partner and I run in New Denver, BC, population 650. I have our son to help raise and more books to write. But I keep my ear in, I do, singing in the Valhalla Community Choir, as different and as alike as any other choir in the country, I'm sure.

This is the choir that, in my own middle age, gives me a safe place to sing unafraid, to throw my plumb line down the well to find my voice and to release it, along with joy, forgiveness, sorrow and stress. This choir is composed of more than forty people, aged 14 to 84, with musical "ringers," which is to say exceptionally skilled singers, in every section. Some have near-perfect pitch; most of us have good ears; the rest sing softly or worse, loud and clear. Our director Francie is a beaming dynamo who says she simply loves choosing and then hearing a work of music evolve. I suspect she loves seeing us evolve, too. Under twelve years of her direction, we are learning more and more difficult pieces at a faster and faster rate, many of us learning to read music en route, a thrilling fact. So far, we've sung in Latin, Spanish, French and German.

This is the most diverse group I've ever sung with. For starters, there are lots of men. We are the envy of several regional choirs for the breadth and depth of our male vocal section. Our pianists are both accomplished musicians and talented singers. The director, who works full-time at the local hospital, constantly scouts for interesting arrangements and earns not one *sou* for her efforts. To help all of us learn our parts, she and another choir member have learned to transcribe onto audio tapes each part for each song. Choir members are identified by wearing headphones for months and humming something not quite recognizable. Sheet music plus audio tapes plus weekly two-hour practices plus as many small-group practices as we can manage – all this for several spring concerts and the all-important Christmas concert, preceded by three studio-recording sessions to produce CDs and tapes.

When I walk up to the hall on a rainy October night to sing, after a long day of standing in the bookstore, I often sink gratefully onto the first wooden chair I see, rising only when we sopranos sing our parts. During that two hours, however, something marvellous happens. We get to focus on our vertically-challenged director, standing on her chair at the front of the hall, beaming at us when we've pulled it off, arms waving frantically to bring an errant section up to snuff. Then again, the whites of her bright brown eyes flash, alarmed, when the first sopranos screech, when the mezzo-sopranos lurch off-pitch, the tenors warble off-key, the altos slow to dirge tempo and the bass-baritones break up with laughter in the back row. Sometimes we are overwhelmed by the difficulty of the music we are handed at the start of the season, and sometimes there is eye-rolling at the fondness she has for stretching our musical boundaries past old chestnuts and favorite hymns and easy-listening singalongability.

In this choir are people struggling with failing businesses, miserable marriages, unhappy children, broken-down vehicles, addictions of all kinds, deteriorating bodies and sagging spirits. I swear sometimes I can practically see all these spectres, the vapours of our daily afflictions, wafting above our heads and away into the ether. How can I worry about money or the wretched teacher inflicted upon my child when I am sweetly singing "A Gaelic Blessing"? Of what import are the trials of earthly life when sixteen of us step forward and romp through the "Magnum Mysterium," that lovely Latin call to wonder and awe?

To be sure, there are prima donnas, complainers, the less-than-gifted, those with bad breath and the compulsion to chat. I've learned to appreciate how we have all dragged ourselves out to practice, on icy mountain roads and in pelting rain. Singing brings us joy; it eases our burdens and, for some of us, I have no doubt, it is the highlight of the week.

IN MY THIRD YEAR WITH THE CHOIR, THE DIRECTOR flummoxes me, and certainly others, by announcing that I will take the soprano part in a quartet singing "Es Ist Ein Reis Entsprungen" at our Christmas concert. I am thrilled. I also endure some gimlet-eyed scrutiny from reigning soloists.

Well over three hundred people attend our concert in the Silverton Memorial Hall, arriving early to get good seats even as we are readying ourselves for the candlelight procession to the stage, singing "Dona Nobis Pacem." Once there, we sing "Gloria In Excelsis Deo," a zippy, complex version of "Deck the Halls," the beautiful "Kyrie," and others.

All too soon, our quartet steps forward. We sing in German, a capella, note by note in complete accord with each other, no one grandstanding, no one hanging on for an extra

eighth, just a delightful carol simply offered. The sour, judg-
mental ghosts hovering over me, humming "Loch Lommond"
off-key, are sent packing at long last. I sing like a freed canary.

THE HARDEST TEST FACES US: SUMMONED WITH A
day's notice in midsummer, nearly forty of us gather to
rehearse "Deep River," a song to comfort the bereaved. In one
of this life's random acts of senselessness, an aneurism has
claimed Marian, mother, singer, teacher, artist, clown, age
forty-two. No one could belt out the rousing gospel tunes or
wail the blues like our Marian. But now we must pull ourselves together and sing the sombre song of the final camp-
ground for Marian, who would have sung the lead.

This time more than four hundred people jam the hall and
pay tribute, in speech and song, to a remarkable woman. The
choir sits at the back of the hall, many of us weeping, waiting
to stand up and sing. And as we stand on the stage, I know in
my sad, grieving heart why the slaves sang for hours and
hours, finding harmony with each other, sounding out the
pain of existence, and soaring beyond it, pure and free at last.

We'll walk each other home in little duos, trios and quar-
tets, talking, singing, laughing, not fearing human predators
but alert to the last bears of autumn rooting in compost bins
or straddling the pear and apple trees. I'll stand on my deck
and listen for the final wisps of lyrics spiralling up from the
streets of my village as we sing each other safely home.

DEAF MUSIC

Margaret Hollingsworth

EVERY SATURDAY MORNING MY MOTHER STRAPPED me into the canvas harness that housed my hearing aid. I was eight and didn't need her help, but she wanted to make sure it was secure; after all, sound was a priority in a music lesson. On weekdays I managed the buckles myself. My mother knew I hated the hearing aid, and she tried to bring me around by giving it a name – we called it Muriel. At home I was allowed to abandon it, but when it came to music there were different expectations.

My deafness was diagnosed when I was seven. Prior to this, in my Infants School, they were aware that I had speech problems (I was born with a cleft in my soft palate), but they dismissed them as something I'd eventually grow out of. Teachers paid special attention to me, and I learned to read and write along with the rest. I was loved and protected. The other children accepted me and never questioned my preference for non-verbal communication. Maybe the teachers told the kids to be kind to me; if they did I'm glad I didn't know.

When I moved up to Junior School at seven everything changed. I was supplied with the hearing aid, a rather crude model, that was issued free on the British National Health Service. Everyone thought I would be delighted, but the reverse was true. Sound was a novelty, but nothing I needed. Suddenly I was different. Not special. Different. In the first week that Muriel arrived in my life, I shook uncontrollably; my palms were so sweaty my pencil seemed to be paddling and my writing slipped all over the page. I hated the crude noises that blasted into my ears. The whistling kettle, our neighbour's motorbike, even the wind, became enemies; people's voices were intrusive, unexpected, the sounds I heard often carried no meaning. When more than one person spoke at once, I ducked. The only way I could remain in control was by keeping my finger on the off switch. But there was no way of hiding the clumsy box that was strapped to my chest. It measured about three inches by four and it was almost an inch thick. The twin pink wires leading from the protruding pink receivers in my ears screamed "look at me." If I wore the amplifier under my gym slip, the fabric rubbed against the microphone, giving a raw, scratchy foreground to the jumble of sounds I was supposed to decipher. If I wore the harness over my clothes I was an immediate target of derision, the butt of the class wits, or of other kids who would run up as if to embrace me, then veer away at the last minute and scream into the microphone so that my head leapt with pain. The world of sound was jagged and spiky. Cruel.

I suffered the contraption for a week, and after that I dodged into the local park on my way to school, tore it off and flung it into my school bag. The relief was immediate: my world flattened out and I was at its centre again. I sat at the back of the class, copied from the board and from the exercise book of the girl sitting next to me and kept my eyes firmly fixed on the teacher's face. Muriel's absence went unremarked since I worked at making myself invisible in the class of forty children. I maintained average marks and I cultivated a dreamy, abstracted air to account for my failure to answer questions.

The fact that I had no friends also went unnoticed. It didn't bother me – I was happy in my safe, predictable world, free of taunts. At home I killed Muriel off, which meant that I had to forgo the sound on our rented TV, but this was a small sacrifice. I devoured books, made models, and I had a symbiotic relationship with my ginger cat, Bill, who understood everything I said. My mother never drew attention to my deafness or my cleft palate. We sat together at night in the big armchair in front of the TV, and she encouraged me to put my ear against her breastbone so I could hear the vibrations of her voice; secure in the O of her arms, I joked and gossiped and teased, chattering non-stop. I heard her voice as soft and mellifluous, not hesitant and accented with northern vowel sounds like the voice that Muriel transmitted. This was all the proof I needed that Muriel was a distorter of the truth.

I WAS AN ONLY CHILD (MY FATHER WAS NEVER IN the picture), and though she never put it into words, I knew my mother wanted to believe she had a normal child, and I usually did my best to back her up. When we went shopping, Muriel remained at home. We held hands and communicated by squeezes so no one ever had to hear me speak; we giggled a lot and I acted as if I were following the conversation when she stopped to chat with neighbours. It was a game. When we got home we always cooked a pan of french fries together. On the rare occasions when I went on an errand alone, she gave me a note which I handed to the shopkeeper, head bowed, pretending to be shy.

The music lesson was something new. My grandmother in Sheffield had died and left me her piano. All my parents' relatives lived "up north," and I had never met any of them. We wrote to them regularly, and they sent me gifts at Christmas and birthdays. I don't know if they were aware of my speech and hearing problems. One Christmas my Auntie Mary sent me a music box. I could feel the sound with my fingertips as I watched the ballerina whirl in front of her mirror and I longed to know the tune she danced to. When I set the box down and put my temple to the surface of the table I could almost make out the melody, though the top notes were missing. I wound it up so often it broke. I think this convinced my mother I was musical. The piano had been sitting unused in the front room for a year when she announced that I would be going to Miss Beamish's for a weekly half-hour lesson and I'd better be good at it, because we'd be going without the Sunday roast in order to pay for it.

Miss Beamish lived in a street of Victorian mansions. I refused to let my mother accompany me to my first lesson, and I stood outside the house for ages, wondering whether to go in. Between the sidewalk and the road was a wide flower bed, thick with rhododendron bushes. These provided the ideal cover for unhitching Muriel. She slid into my music case and I trotted up the wide staircase and planted my thumb on the doorbell, hoping it was working.

I don't think I had any expectations except that this would be a one-shot deal. I could certainly never have dreamed up Violet Beamish. She was a garage mechanic by day and a music teacher by night and at weekends. She had thick, pebbled glasses, gray wispy hair cut like a man's and her knuckles were ingrained with black oil. Her voice boomed and she spoke slowly so I felt immediately secure. She lived with her mother in one of the largest houses on the street. The old lady was always lost somewhere on the upper floors, I imagined her like Mrs. Rochester in the novel I was reading.

I followed Miss Beamish into an enormous room which she described as the music room. It was perfectly preserved from the mid-Victorian period, a crowded jungle of heavy furniture and marble tables with huge mirrors and gilt legs. There were mahogany shelves thick with a tantalizing collection of Victorian bric-a-brac. There were glass domes sheltering dried flowers and stuffed birds, Chinese vases full of peacock feathers, statues of Greek gods, an ivory chess set, and a gramophone with a huge bell big enough to house my head.

Reluctantly, I turned my back on this treasure house, and seated myself next to Miss Beamish on a bench at one of the two upright pianos which nestled between stacks of music. She placed my hands on the keys and indicated that I should watch and imitate. Then she hid her hands and I repeated the exercise. After several tries I managed a single octave scale. She seemed pleased. Jamming my knees under the keyboard augmented the sound; it passed through my thighs and up into my tummy. I was excited. This was something I could actually do.

Miss Beamish never asked me to repeat what I said, and never mentioned my deafness (I convinced myself she hadn't noticed). I was treated exactly the same as all her pupils. At the end of each lesson there was always a reward, a slice of toast, browned in front of the two-bar electric heater and slathered with butter. Sometimes she was late for the lesson and I worked my way round the magic room, studying the paintings of women in plumed hats and the foxed photographs of ancient clerics until she arrived straight from work, puffing like a bellows, still clad in her grimy overalls.

I practised on the piano for hours, working at being so proficient that I wouldn't need verbal correction. By the end of the year I had leapt ahead to Intermediate Level. At the start of each lesson Miss Beamish played the piece I was learning twice. I concentrated, watching, listening and physically absorbing the rhythm of the music through the frame of the piano. I put all my senses into top gear, learning to trust them absolutely, and experienced my first taste of complete understanding, complete communion with someone who was not my mother. When I played particularly well, she hugged me and I buried my nose in her skin which smelt of Lily of the

Valley perfume and motor oil. I felt I was betraying the intimacy I had with my mother, but I couldn't help it. I looked forward to my lessons with a passion that made me pray for the week to dissolve and for it to be forever Saturday.

I took my music exams and passed Grade Four and Five with distinction. I was not doing so well at school. My marks had fallen, and even though my lip-reading had improved, I was finding it harder to keep up. Sometimes I stayed away altogether, wandering the streets until home time. Once, the boy in the seat across the aisle flicked a folded note onto my desk. I opened it and read the word MORON printed in bold capitals. That night I locked myself in with the piano and pounded the keys till the pads on my fingertips hurt. I couldn't confide in my mother; I was terrified she would be ashamed of me, love me less, or worse still, leave me. I dared her to talk to my schoolteachers when she fussed over my school reports. The reports repeated the same refrain: Margaret could do better; Margaret must learn to pay attention.

At the beginning of the third year of music lessons, Miss Beamish came across Muriel as she rifled through my music bag for a lost sheet of manuscript paper. I had grown, but the hearing aid still looked mountainous. The two pink receivers dangled on their twin pink wires like fallen climbers as Miss Beamish held up the harness. I refused to look at her face but she grabbed my chin and waited till I had plugged Muriel in and turned up the volume to squealing point. "Do you wear this thing when you're practising?" I shook my head. "Do you realize how much time you have wasted? How far we could have progressed?" I shook my head again.

She put the lid of the piano down. "What is your mother thinking of?" I wanted to explain that my mother didn't know that I never wore my hearing aid, that Muriel distorted the sound, made it tinny, unpalatable, took away the purity I heard inside my head, the true sound, the sound that Beethoven must have heard (I had just discovered that he was deaf). Far from making me love him, I began to resent him bitterly. He was a handicapped cretin, all the world knew that was true, no matter how brilliant his music was. I opened my mouth to explain, but Miss Beamish clamped her hand over my lips. "It's time we stopped playing games, Margaret. Let's face it, you're deaf as that doorpost and I've heard parrots speak more clearly. Teaching you demands so much energy and you refuse to help yourself. You're draining me. It's all effort! You need to be shaken up. Do you want to spend the rest of your life on the sidelines?"

I was mortified – hadn't I proved to her that I wasn't on the sidelines? I was her star pupil. How could she think I was a parrot? I tore the receivers out of my ears, threw Muriel into my case, abandoned my music books and rushed out of her house.

The next week I didn't go to my lesson, and I didn't touch the piano. The following Saturday I told my mother I was needed to help with a nature study project at school. We had no phone, so Miss Beamish didn't contact us. The Sunday roast was reinstated, but by the third week the need for my lesson was so great that it overtook my humiliation. I had no particular plan but I didn't bother to strap on the harness. My mother made no comment as she handed me my music case.

It was snowing, and I liked the feel of my silent footsteps as I made my way to Miss Beamish's house. The silence of snow is different from other silences; there are so many kinds and qualities of silence, the deaf know them intimately.

I rang the front doorbell as usual, but no one came. There was no note to say the bell was out of order, so I pushed on the door and went inside. The wide black-and-white-tiled entry hall was empty. I could see the music room through the double glass doors with their pink bevelled borders. The pictures and the ornaments were still in place, the electric heater was on. A slight smell of motor oil hung on the air. I concentrated my attention on the soles of my feet, trying to detect whether Miss Beamish had taken another pupil in my place but there were no vibrations. I went in. The room was empty. Should I call her? I hesitated to shout her name, "Miss Beamish...." I couldn't get my tongue round a *sh* or an *s* sound, so I often substituted words that didn't contain those letters. If this was too hard I kept quiet.

I sat at the piano nearest the heater. My music was piled at one end, neatly separated from the rest of the scores. I picked up the top book. It was a volume of Chopin; I opened it randomly and started to play. The instrument responded immediately; my fingers were sure and confident, and I could feel the music spraying through my hands into my forearms, my elbows, my neck, my whole body, unreeling, unwinding, carrying me into a place I had missed so badly it made me dizzy. I was playing for Miss Beamish, the music was not forgiveness, not a gift, but an ecstatic "up yours."

Suddenly I sensed that someone was in the room. I looked up, expecting to see her standing in the doorway, her face all wrinkly and smiling, but the person I saw was a diminutive old woman, her thin gray hair plaited on top of her head, her body lost in a large flowered apron. This must be Miss Beamish's mother, Mrs. Rochester from upstairs. I saw her mouth moving, but I couldn't make out any sound, and her lips were tight as wires and impossible to read.

"I don't get you." A rare admission.

She came in and seemed to be repeating what she had just said, enlarging on it, shunting words at me. I watched her mouth and her filmy eyes, trying to concentrate, trying not to panic. No vestige of meaning filtered through.

"Weren't you told? I'm deaf like that door." It was the first time I'd ever admitted it aloud. Deaf was a word that was too close to death.

Her body was taut and erect, her hands clamped to her sides; her expression a blank, there were no clues.

She moved to the piano and picked up the red pen Miss Beamish used for correcting theory. She scrawled across my Chopin étude: Violet is gone.

I stared at her. She made a motion with her hands, bringing them together to make an implosion of air. What did it mean? Still, her face gave nothing away. Pushing her aside, I darted out of the house into the snow which seemed to be falling more erratically. It was suddenly chill. I realized I'd left my music behind, together with my coat and my bag containing Muriel. I couldn't go back. I was responsible for Miss Beamish's disappearance.

My mother showed me the death notice in the local paper. Violet Beamish had been trapped under a van when a jack collapsed. It was an accident.

THE FOLLOWING DAY I WROTE A NOTE TO MY FORM mistress excusing myself from further classes on account of my deafness. I signed it with my mother's name. She hauled me into the staff room and rained questions on me, telling me (I think), that she had been ready to refer me to the local asylum for assessment. (I later found out that a good many deaf children have grown up in mental institutions.) Why, she demanded, had the staff not been informed of my handicap – I could have been put in a special class. I shook my head, and feigned ignorance though I wanted to bash her face in. There was no way to explain how my skin contracted at the words handicap and impediment or any substitute word that sweetened the pill, or how I cringed at unrequested kindness. My mother was the only one who understood.

Soon after, I failed the Eleven Plus exam which was a watershed in every child's life in Britain at that time (a pass opened up the possibility of higher education). I changed schools, and my mother found the money for a commercial hearing aid, much daintier than Muriel. It was easily concealed in my new training bra and I wore it more often, and gradually came to rely on it. Life began to change. The new school arranged for me to see another speech therapist. After weeks of no progress my enunciation improved, and, to my chagrin, my school reports called me plucky.

The next year I played centre in the netball team, and joined the stamp club. I even sheltered a secret ambition to be an actress. I made no protest when my mother sold the piano.

I left school at sixteen and found a job as a filing clerk in a large multinational corporation. I handed most of my weekly pay packet over to my mother, but I still managed to fund the course of intensive speech therapy that was required to exorcise my glottal *S*'s and *Sh*'s. The following year I had an operation: the hearing in one ear was restored, and I threw away my hearing aid for good.

I finally diffused the problem of my residual speech impediment by immigrating to Canada where it went unnoticed since voices are more nasal. I have travelled a long way since Miss Beamish died. My life has opened up immeasurably, but I still find it difficult to listen to Beethoven. In my most intimate moments I have yet to obtain the oneness I felt in those music lessons, and I have never been able to find the quality of inner stillness I knew when I wasn't wearing Muriel. Occasionally, when I come close, I catch a whiff of lily of the valley and motor oil.

PENSIVE NUDE

Kristjana Gunnars

IT HAS BEEN RAINING ON THE WEST COAST OF Canada for about a year. The drops fall heavily onto the verandah railing, forming puddles on the new slate-blue paint. It was a colour called "shale" we mixed at the building store, something that came closest to the grey, overcast hue of the ocean and the mountains behind. The water forms pockets that look black, and the robins stop there to reflect themselves. They stand on the railing peering into the small puddles, just big enough for a comfortable mirror. The robins don't seem to mind the rain. They fly energetically across the grass, just grazing the tops of the blades like B-52 bombers, no matter what is coming down. Sometimes they stand on the lawn with their heads sideways, listening for worms. When they hear a worm, they poke their beaks into the grass and come up with a wiggling creeper. They don't eat it immediately either. They stand there basking in the triumph of the moment, perhaps hoping to be seen, the worm writhing in their beaks.

But I got tired of the rain. At first I thought it was picturesque. So many days of water. It was cozy to sit inside then, the fire going in the old wood-burning stove, listening to the drops on the window and reading a good book. I was reading a collection of essays by Paul Auster, so it was all right to have lots of rain. The only problem was, there was so much to think about that I stopped reading far too often and looked out the window. There is nothing but green outside the window. Thick forests of trees crowding in on the house, which is why I have a lawn there. Des Kennedy, on Denman Island, also has a huge lawn, and most country people are lawn haters. They ask Des why he has so much lawn. After all, that's a city thing. He says if you don't have grass to keep the jungle away, the jungle will not in fact stay away. Your house and property will be eaten up by the bush. That makes sense, because it rains so much. I have a square acre of grass for the same reason, but leaning into it are the wild woods of BC. There are hemlocks and cedars and alders by the millions, firs and blackberry and salaal bushes and ferns and maples. They lean over the grass in a threatening manner. A family of racoons lives on the edge of the lawn. Sometimes they play on the grass, lying upside down with their paws in the air. There's a bear too, on the other side, who creeps out of the jungle at night. A family of robins whose three youngsters have begun to practise flying and worming. They tumble over each other awkwardly.

It wouldn't be a problem to stop and reflect on a book, ordinarily. But with the heat from the flames in the woodstove and the lulling sound of the unceasing rain, I fall asleep. Any time of day, really. I heard about a condition someone had called narcolepsy, where she fell asleep all the time. As soon as she sat down, she was asleep. They asked her how she got cured of it, and she said it helped to get away from her husband. But for me, there wasn't anything to escape from. Perhaps the rain. After all, there has been far too much of it. My neighbours tell me they're getting depressed. They actually miss the snows of the prairies now. Even though they retired from the prairies to so-called beautiful BC, they didn't foresee the rain. I knew about the rain, of course. None of this surprises me. But it's the combination of nothing going on and the deliberate, persistent rain, that makes me feel like I did when

I was a kid and it was Sunday. Nothing to do. Snow falling down. The day was endless.

On reflection, Paul Auster represents such an anachronism, for he's an urbane New Yorker. He was talking about despair and how when a person despairs, the very act of despairing makes a person despair more. That's how you get those downward spirals that end in hunger and then death. There's no way to go but down. Despair becomes a force of a person's own making, and also a dictator whose every command must be obeyed. It's what he calls "a Godless hell." Apparently you lose your identity in this kind of situation. Without an identity, you disintegrate. I was reminded of the Woody Allen movie *Deconstructing Harry,* where one character finds himself out of focus. He's an actor in a movie, and somehow the camera can't get him into focus. They call him over and find that it isn't the camera, it's him. He goes home and his kids say, "Is something the matter, daddy? You look out of focus." That was, of course, a metaphor for the writer who gets trapped in his own little Godless hell. I never actually saw Paul Auster, but I saw his wife. She was in Oslo when I was there. Salman Rushdie was also there, and he stole the show. He always steals the show, and the other writers and visitors somehow go out of focus.

But I saw Auster on television, which is sometimes a substitute. He was a very forthcoming individual. He has a pretty good mind and the right attitude. There are lots of lacunaes in the book-making life, and most people just brush over them. Like the blank page or writer's block, which was Woody Allen's subject. The writer who can't write. Sad story. Godless hell. But Auster has the answer to that, which is, speaking mystically, to embrace the silence and make a poem of it. Go ahead. Walk into it. It's just when you have nothing to say that you should start writing. When you think you have something to say, don't. It's not even interesting. Just at the moment you have nothing to say, write. Reach for the annihilation of the word, and grab it just as you would a fleeting butterfly. Just as it's flying away, see if you can catch its shadow. Because, Auster says, "if words will not give way, they will become a wall." It's possible for a writer to become imprisoned in his own text. A captive of his own verbal construction. The art of it all, the impossible art, is to make those words so light that you can fly out of the labyrinth yourself.

It's a movement towards freedom, towards an understanding that what you say is never exactly what you meant to say, so you'd like the opportunity to try again. Auster talks about this in a more phenomenological manner. Writing is something, he says, that must offer itself "nakedly and unasked for" in the middle of the surrounding silence. Although things are never quite silent. There is the city and the noises of the crowds. The media, the television, the screaming automobiles and subways and airplanes. Or in the country, the screaming birds. We have one that sounds like a ululating female from the Middle East. There she goes again, we say when it starts up. She's mourning or she's excited or she's cheering. It's a piercing sound that emanates from the big maple leaves. Then there's the rain. If all else is silent, there is always the sound of water trickling from the sky. It falls on wooden railings and porches. That's a flat sound. It falls on the aluminum gutter, the drainpipe. That's more resounding. Then there's the plastic porch table, a clicking sound that stops abruptly like a clucking tongue. And the skylight makes a whole other sound, something more furry. One of my relatives who is a composer actually made a composition in which one of the instruments is "the sound of rain." Even if you didn't have rain, which you always do out here, there would be the primordial cosmic sound out of which they say the whole universe is made. The Superstring.

But out of this sound-filled silence, the writer emerges

naked. That means vulnerable. Not too self-assured or smug. Always with an eye open for irony. But it's a tough call and it's not hard to see why a person would balk. Why make yourself so vulnerable? I'm taking nakedness as a metaphor. Maybe it isn't. If not, I'm sure you could go out in the nude here. It's so private. There's a deck in the back which is completely shielded on all sides by the jungle. There's an overhang above, so it's possible to sit there in the rain and not get wet. Sometimes we do that, in the afternoons usually, when we've had enough of the day's worries. We'll take some wine, usually Australian shiraz, and get over the day out there on the lower deck. Sounds like a ship. The lower deck. It can rain all it wants, and we don't get wet because of the protruding roof. We also have a good view of the roses from there, and the hydrangeas. The hydrangeas are blooming madly, but they get beaten down by the rain. The water falls so heavily that the flowers eventually stoop all the way to the ground. They don't straighten up until the rain lets up. And that could be when-ever. Or never. We sit there and feel sorry for the hydrangeas and listen to the ululating female.

I took a long time to read those reflections of Paul Auster's. In fact, I haven't finished them. It's all that rain. And the pensive mood one gets into. For example, he's talking about Franz Kafka and he says that Kafka was always moving because he wanted to stop. The desire to stop kept him going. It's the irony that catches my attention. It's precisely the desire for one thing that keeps us moving in the opposite direction. We are contrary creatures, but not out of perversity. Out of necessity. That's the way everything is constructed. Because you want to eat, you fast. Because you want to stay awake, you sleep. Because you want to read, you write. I like that last one. I've actually heard writers answer "why did you write this book?" with "because I wanted to read a book like that." Presumably, the writer sensed a lack in the world for just such a book and decided to fill the gap. Only the gap never gets filled. Instead, a new gap is created, which brings on a need for another book. The writer's trap is that she writes one book which she discovers is misread, so she has to write another book to rectify the misunderstandings of the first. It's what Auster says about Kafka. On this road, you are never free. You are always a captive of your own originality, your own uniqueness. You also lose your perspective along the way. You manage to convince yourself of your own fabrications. For example, I saw Barbara Gowdy say in an interview that nothing is ugly. If you look at an ugly thing long enough, you see the beauty. If you think something is ugly, it's actually your own problem. I thought, that's a mouthful.

The thing about Kafka, however, is that it's precisely his sense of alienation that enabled him to describe things so intimately. Because he did not feel connected to it, he lingered over it. The irony is that you long to touch precisely that which you cannot, must not, touch. That's what makes people touch things in stores. They go around and place their hands and fingers on items they cannot buy. They must touch that silk suit that costs five thousand dollars or that glazed vase they have no means for or that soapstone sculpture for twenty-five hundred which could never be theirs. Just to run the fingers over the back of that bending sculpture, stone as sleek as if it had been wetted by rains. I heard an antique dealer describe how prospective customers come into the premises and wander in circles around objects. The words he used were "they hover like sharks." And sure enough, when I looked, people were circling around objects, like sharks. And reaching out to touch them. It's a form of self-subversion, where what you do is intended to undermine yourself. To render yourself vulnerable. Something like what Edgar Allan Poe calls "the imp of the perverse."

It's about constructing walls around yourself to provide the illusion of security. Shoring up against disaster. That's why people do everything. That's why they get married, even. On that score, I was listening to a painter from Saskatchewan on the subject of happiness. She said you can't just rely on one person, your companion. If you do, "you're just one person away from disaster," she said. You have to have your own friends, your interests, work, joy. The idea caught my imagination: that you are face to face with "disaster" unless you protect yourself. Existential reality is, in so many words, "disaster." There are people who do face disaster, and survive. They discover it's not, in fact, disaster. That goes back to this Woody Allen movie. The protagonist, the writer, goes to hell to retrieve his girlfriend. He finds people down there are actually very comfortable, wouldn't want to be anywhere else. That's why there are writers. Or so Paul Auster would say. Talking about Georges Bataille, he accedes that literature is disruptive. Writing disrupts the force of mind that makes people try to protect themselves against the unknown, build walls, construct ideologies, go to war, because they think disaster is around the corner.

The essential feature of Auster's argument is that literature, writing, art, is created out of need rather than the will. We don't even like reading books, he says, that we feel the author was not "compelled" to write. We want to sense that desperation, that willingness to face the unknown, that comes with the metaphor of nakedness. The idea is not to "order" the world, but to rediscover it. If you want to organize the world, create order in it, then you must be some kind of ideologue. Instead, it is more interesting to simply experience the world. Not to create that distance between you and whatever it is that makes a person call it "disaster," but to take hold of it. It will be something like that butterfly that continually eludes your grasp. To Auster, writing is a religious act. Because a truly religious act is to present yourself naked before the unknown and face it. What counts is the effort, not the result. What he actually says is this: "art is almost an incidental by-product of the effort to make it." Art, and in this case the act of writing a poem, is a force that is larger than the person herself. The poem is almost an accident along the way. There will be many more such by-products. It's the pearl syndrome over again. The oyster is busy doing something essential, but in the meantime incidentally produces a pearl.

I suppose this is why it makes sense to love pearls. Because they are born of distress and they are beautiful. They resemble solidified drops of rain. I had a recent experience with pearls which caused me some reflection. When my mother-in-law died, I was given her pearl necklace. I would not have this string of pearls if she had not, in fact, died. That's the cold truth. Her dying was not easy, but the pearls are beautiful. I have others. In fact, I have lots of them. Seems like I always get some when a female in the family dies. That's what becomes permanent in all this fluctuating mutability. The gems. The pearls.

Speaking of such things, I noticed that the price of gold was going down. That's because of the world economy, I guess. But most of the gold in the world is actually mined in South Africa. There the miners have to be tested on treadmills in a hundred degrees' heat before they're allowed to take the job. That's because it's so hot down in the mines. They go down to shafts two miles underground. It takes them an hour and a half in the elevator to go down. Three hours a day they spend in the elevator going into the shaft and out again from it. The further down they go, the hotter it gets, until the light is eerie orange. One little spark down there would ignite a firestorm that would rip through the shafts and kill them all. I heard that over seventy percent of all the privately owned gold in the world is in India. Indian women wear it. A wealthy woman will be so decked in gold bracelets, rings, necklaces, nose rings, anklets, that she will sparkle in the evening sun. This is to take the place of banking. When the family runs into hard times, they start selling the gold off again.

Paul Auster said when he was interviewed that he didn't get along with his father. His father was, it turned out, precisely the kind of man Paul didn't like. He was a "slum landlord." He owned large tenement buildings that were rented out to the poor, and he didn't look after the buildings so they became decrepit and substandard. Sometimes the boy Paul would accompany his father on his rounds to collect the rent, and these desperate, extremely poor, people would answer the door and have to dish out the last money they had. The thing that caught Paul Auster's imagination is that when his father died he got some money. It was his father's money that finally enabled him to live the way he wanted to live. As a writer, taking risks and writing what mattered, something that would make the life of the extremely poor, say, more human. The classical ironies of life are his subject.

Ironies such as this one: the duty of the poet, he says, is to be invisible. The poem should be so tangible in itself, that the frame, the image, the sense, of the poet behind it should vanish. The enemy of the poem is the ego. If you insert yourself continuously into your poem, you don't have a poem. You have a platform on which you put yourself. He uses an example from Charles Reznikoff. A very short poem by Reznikoff, called "Moonlit Night." "The trees' shadows lie in black pools in the lawns." That's the whole poem. The moonlight is so stark when you're away from the city, that it literally lights up everything as if it were dusk. It's a milky, ethereal brightness that has a life of its own. A silvery, neon atmosphere. The moonlight produces shadows, only shadows in the night are quite surreal. It's almost outer-planetary. The rain that's been falling continuously all winter creates black pools everywhere. But in the moonlight they take on another degree of blackness.

And then they're not really water, because they're on the lawns and they only look like water.

Nature fools you like that. But then, they say all is illusion anyway. Or rather, the Buddhists say so. All is fluctuating sound waves, really. You think you see something, then you don't. Even on a more phenomenological level, you get fooled. Take the rain. Sometimes you can't see that it's raining. You squint your eyes and try to see if there are raindrops falling down. You look directly at the darkest spot in the forest to see if the translucency of the raindrops stands out against the darkness. You see nothing, and you figure the rain has stopped. Then you go out under the open sky, and of course it's raining madly. It's just that the drops have become so fine, they're almost like mist. We must have many words for rain here on the Pacific West Coast, just like the proverbial many words for snow among the northern peoples. There's rain, drencher, flood, torrent, sprinkle, drizzle, sleet, hail, flurry, deluge, downpour, monsoon, drops, shower, mist, dampness. Sun shower. I like that. Sun shower – that's when you think it's a sunny day and suddenly it rains. Sometimes the drops are quite large, and they plunk down on the hood of your car with weight. You look around for clouds and see none. It's just one of those things. What happens is the rain is falling somewhere else, but the wind carries it in your direction.

We don't have that problem here, though. Not now. It's overcast in a big way. There is mist everywhere, and the mountains in the distance fall away like pastel illustrations in a fairy tale. The sound of the rain is steady and relentless. I have a big upholstered chair right under the skylight, where the sound of falling rain is very loud and it echoes. This tends to put me to sleep. I'm thinking about something Paul Auster said about writing. The aim, he says, of writing is simply clarity. That's all. Clarity. That means becoming invisible so the thing being looked at can be seen. If you move to possess something, it vanishes. He goes so far as to say you can only do this in the city. "Only in the modern city can the one who sees remain unseen, take his stand in space and yet remain transparent." He must mean this in terms of anonymity, the anonymity of the urban setting. But this may be an illusion too. Why would the observer in the country be less transparent, or more intrusive? Does the observer not vanish in the natural forces that coalesce all around her? Do you not become part of nature after a while, if you are quiet enough and let the rain fall on you long enough? If you do not try to possess the cedar trees and maple leaves and dogwood flowers and hummingbirds?

To be human, he says, is to be in exile from eternity. That is the human condition. I suppose the writer, the poet, tries to create the bridge between those two. Between eternity and the human perspective. Because our vision is so limited. The mist covers everything. We cannot see the mountains in the distance on most days. What we do try to possess comes across as futile. Like the fuchsia plants. I bought two hanging baskets of fuchsias, or bleeding hearts as they say. I thought the rain would water them for me, so I left them alone and wondered why they got so yellow in the leaves and why the flowers were hanging so heavily. I discovered the raindrops never penetrated into the soil, because they hit the leaves and fell off them onto the deck. Fooled again.

COUNTING THE Rs IN LONDON

Nancy Mattson

NEVER HUNGRY FOR TRAVEL, I TOOK IT FOR GRANTED I would live in Edmonton all my life. My taproot reached a mile down to the Precambrian basement of Alberta. I didn't want to follow literary exiles to Paris or London, or drive a Land Rover across velds, pampas or outbacks. My journeys were mainly through books or across Canadian prairies. Good enough for my grandparents, wide enough for me.

Alberta gave me all I needed: chinooks and music; northern lights and theatre; jobs in the oil-boom years; a daughter and son grown tall on beefsteak and seven-grain bread; camping trips beside wild rivers; mallards and pickerel brought in by dad, gutted and cooked by mom; their enduring love; friends who could transform fish to ceviche and marinate words in oil and lemon; encouragement to write and publish my poetry.

In 1983 I left 19 years of marriage and moved from the suburbs to Old Strathcona, an authentic Edmonton village. I eventually holidayed in some of the exotic places I never wanted to live in, though I accepted the given wisdom that being a tourist was somehow an inauthentic experience.

Canonbury Square, Islington, N1, October 1990: After three weeks in London I've had about all the authenticity I can take. It's the smells, the crush of people, that get to me the most. I'll take the bus to work in Mayfair today instead of the Tube, where I gag on recycled sardine breath and rotten onion sweat.

Have to wait at least half an hour for my bathwater to warm. The bathroom has a suspicious dead-dog smell that Dettox and Harpic subdue only temporarily. I wonder what it is. All the things I took for granted in Edmonton don't pertain here. I am become a child again. This is how to heat water in the boiler. This is how to construct a kitchen one fork and one spoon at a time, a bathroom one towel at a time. This is how to buy the right kind of light bulb, the one with bayonet prongs.

Hungerford Bridge, October 1990: The noises and crowds have peeled away my skin and I'm a throb of nerves. But walking across this footbridge, I feel a measure of peace for the first time in London. Mercifully, there's no train on the bridge beside me. I can't hear any sirens or lorries or taxis or buses. All the English accents are huddled up in coats and scarves, heads down to avoid the puddles. I pause in the middle of the Thames and gaze for a long time at the floodlit dome of St Paul's.

Canonbury Square, N1, November 1990: Travel opens up the narrow, provincial mind, so goes the myth. But I come from the width and wealth of Alberta, and the truth is that I've gone backward, to that pinched time of early-twenties poverty.

London may be glamorous to the rich or leisured; the borough of Islington may be desirable among the cognoscenti, and Canonbury Square may be a posh address, but Michael and I are struggling here. The address devours three-quarters of my Canadian salary, and he has no work permit yet. We forage in the market for turnips and potatoes, learn to wait till late in the day to buy perishables, when the barrow boys shift their fruits and lettuces at half price. No longer do we throw away leftovers. We've even become scavengers. A child's desk discarded on the street works as a coffee table. If only I'd picked up that portable wringer on the skip on my way in to the newsagent's – someone else nicked it while I counted out the pence. Now I have to keep doing the urban pioneer wash-erwoman thing, squeezing out shirts and towels in the bath-tub.

Travel tangles the mind, more like. I've developed emo-tional, even literal, dyslexia – after two months of buying fags at Mr Zoa's beside the 19 bus stop, I looked again at the sign: Mr Oza. Wires and pipes spill their guts and mine out on the streets; bus and tube routes twist my headmap. One cannot help but be overwhelmed by all this; one cannot as yet shape it. Oh, that sounds ridiculous, but what's correct here? Do I write one or does one write I? Them or us? Pronouns flake off and settle in the cracks between words.

I'm certainly not one of them and don't want to be part of an us. I'm sort of a half of a couple but want to live alone. I'm Canadian, but they think I'm American when I speak. I don't seek acceptance by the English, but find myself annoyed by Canadians I meet through Alberta House who moan about small fridges in the flats their companies or governments pay for, at weekly rents higher than my monthly take-home. I vow to stop comparing – but can't resist multiplying my sterling cheque by 2.35 and thinking what a dollar-rich girl am I. And survival depends on reversing the conversion in the super-market: why, that's a fair pair of chicken legs, only a dollar a thigh.

Michael and I don't fight, just worry together, forget together. We entertain ourselves by walking miles in every direction – there's poll tax, but no pedestrian tax. My co-work-ers (with one poetic and one cynical exception, both of whom I knew in Edmonton) are not people I would seek out for com-pany – they cried when Thatcher fell. I've met a few possible British friends, but so far I'm too scared to follow up on them: British protocol is a maze of subtleties.

York Minster, December 1990: My first escape from London. I was invited to York to read poetry and offer an authentic Canadian viewpoint in a couple of university seminars. The northern landscape enchants me, and northerners are as warm as Londoners are remote.

In York Minster, *The Messiah* in rehearsal. Singers and orchestra wrapped in scarves and coats – just out Christmas shopping, stopped in to practise a little Handel. Cathedrals in winter are cold, but not as cold as the ruins of Fountains Abbey yesterday. Fragments of glory: the pink-purple light, the snow, the eroded columns of honey-coloured stone. It was perfect. Must go back tomorrow to London's pretense of winter, rain-grey and sooted.

No. 38 bus, Zone 1, January 1991: A book review quotes from a British novelist: "White is a lie, you said. A trick of the light. Can't last." Dirt is the lie, my skin shouts. You don't know the Canadian prairie, where white is clean and true and lasts all winter. I feel like a junkyard bitch with grimy, matted fur – but a dog would remember and avoid the one cracked pavement block that's really a trap door hiding a pool of filthy water. Every time I go to work I sink to one ankle in slime.

Canonbury Square, N1, April 1991: I'm worn down by penury, tired of bomb scares, unnerved by cars that lie in ambush on my blind side. I took a risk moving here, but I didn't expect all this. Now the togetherness is gone too. The stresses of our life here have exposed the deep cracks in our relationship that were patchable or ignorable when we lived the easy life in Edmonton.

I wonder how the arm of that stone woman broke off. The tulips are magnificent in this square.

Nottingham Canadian Studies Conference, April 1991: This is just what I need, a jolly group of Canucks and some British academics who see Canada as a place of desire. Had a late-night soiree in my room with congenial souls who sang folk songs from Wales, Scotland, Ireland, other homelands, even England. Their throats were opened by Laphroaig scotch, then Siberian vodka, then French wine left over from the official banquet and rescued from uselessness by the SACS rep – Soviet Association of Canadian Studies!

Yarmouth, Isle of Wight, June 1991: Miracles and signs appear, by definition, unexpectedly. Now I know why I came to England, the little island that Isle of Wighters laughably call the mainland. I escaped to Yarmouth to write poems, think and be alone. Sat on the chalk cliffs above the divided ebb of the Solent. Ate the chalk – a condition called pica, so Rhona says. She must make a habit of eating dictionaries.

He emerged from the sea, I suppose. He was Irish, a man of many lands, including Canada as a child, and France as a Trappist monk in training. Maybe that's where his peace and naturalness came from. When I had nothing of flirtation in me, nothing of expectation after being ignored as a woman for the last year, along came this man. A sign that I must never again accept less than free and total loving.

South Croydon, Surrey, July 1991: Into the arms of my uncle Don, who welcomes me and Michael to his big suburban home. He's actually the widower of my second cousin, but his family are my only blood connections in this country, and he's allowed me to adopt him as a surrogate father. Every couple of months we come here with two carryalls full of dirty laundry. People on the train may think we're headed for a dirty weekend in Brighton, but heaven for me is Don's terraced garden, complete with clothesline and swimming pool. Early Sunday morning, his daughter and I float in the pool, embraced by Our Lady of the Oceans.

Culford Road, Hackney, N1, August 1991: Thank God we've moved. There were RATS under the bathtub in the Canonbury Square flat! That's what the smell was. They made nests of my wandering socks and misplaced knickers. Every morning they were gnawing, inches underneath me as I bathed, only thin enamel between them and my naked bottom.

Salisbury Pub, St Martins Lane, WC2, December 1991: Friends ask me in letters, do I like London? What kind of word is like?

I've just come from the annual Christmas party at the Canada House library – stunning view of Trafalgar Square, white lights on the fifty-foot Norwegian spruce, Kentish angels singing carols beside it. Candlelight transformed the periodical room into a bar. My librarian friends served hot mince pies and mulled wine. I liked the party a lot.

I like this pub too, all Victorian cut glass, mirrors and brass. I've just moved from a stool to a comfy booth and the first half of Castlemaine is gone. I met an acquaintance here, Paul, a couple of weeks ago. We went to Gaby's for Mediterranean snacks, then a Charlie Haden concert at the South Bank Centre. Mellow stuff. Paul wore a Bogart chapeau and red specs – he has the comfortable flair of a theatre man. We met through work when he inquired about making an offi-cial visit to the Banff Centre for the Arts. I like him and think we'll become friends, though Londoners are careful not to commit too early.

A half hour later: My quiet booth was invaded by three men, one very drunk. When he spat crookedly and hit my skirt, the other two apologized. They were barristers, but grad-ually their veneer of class receded to reveal their racist little Englander hides. They presented a case for white British dom-inance in art, literature, manufacturing, invention, even Christianity. Jesus a tin miner in Cornwall? Give me a break.

Do I like it here? Impossible, irrelevant, inevitable ques-tion. London happens to you whether you like it or not.

Culford Road, N1, January 1992: I'm sitting by a three-bar fire, London Electricity's substitute for logs. The warmth is overpriced but essential – the landlady's Laura Ashleys are fluttering in the inch-wide gale between closed windows and rotting frames. A cold butter, damp towel bolt-hole, but at least the curtains are pretty.

We've been fondling brochures on Greek islands, though a trip to Corfu is as likely as a reduction in rent or a marriage proposal from the Irish man I met last summer on the Isle of Wight. Or the man I live with. We've descended into middle-aged agape through habit and necessity – the only ones in London who know each other's families in Alberta and Ontario. A huddle's just a cuddle frozen cold.

Christmas was fine – a two-foot tree which looked ever so real, especially with my paper snowflakes. We roasted half a small turkey in the Baby Betty, that apology for an oven which only the British would need to invent. Last year's neighbour brought over a plum pudding, and Ridley Street Market does a fine range of mashable roots. We shared our meal with Patricia, an American ex-pat who stayed in London to finish a book over the holidays while her partner joined his mam in Cavan. She and Frank live in a mouth-watering flat with gas central heating on Colebrooke Row, near the canal.

Last weekend we trained up to Leeds to see the first British play on the Gulf War. Our host was almost family – I went to grad school with his sister-in-law. Mahmood and I had a meaningful time in the kitchen massaging the trout with olive oil. The next day he drove us to Haworth, where the weather was suitably wuthering – wind moaning through the trees' bones, drizzle soaking the moss on the parsonage gravestones. We Brontéd up the cobblestones and had a pint in Bramwell's local. Picnicked in the car, sardines-in-a-Volkswagen-hammered-by-rain.

Culford Road, N1, February 1992: The landlady dropped a kiss-kick letter through the slot last night. Do we agree that the rent should go up by a third, and would we like to come down for dinner with her and her husband? We'll try to negotiate a smaller increase and, if not, bolt in the dark of March. Just let her try to rent a place with no central heating. That's London; you have a lovely quiet Christmas – wham, the lurgi hits on New Year's Eve and you're in bed for a week. You go to the west of Ireland for a cheap holiday – bam, robbers make off with the only valuables in your flat: computer, camera and jewellery.

The process of shedding possessions is nearly complete. Actually, it's quite liberating. The purity of detachment.

Culford Road, N1, March 1992: In the UK the recession continues to gnaw on those already bitten and chewed. Anyone below the A, B and C classes finds it very tough. English newspapers and demographic researchers actually label people as A1, B2, C3, D4! I don't fit on the scale because of my accent and colonial background. But being marginal appeals to me as much as living in N1 appeals to the discontented of SE14. My postcode is my only sign of social acceptability.

For every toff at Ascot, Lord's and Henley, there's a street-corner vendor of the *Big Issue* or *Socialist Worker.* However shocked I am by the British class system, I'm also learning how complex this society is. Many people at all levels fight against injustices and are committed in their jobs and personal lives to acting decently and fairly towards others – teachers in state schools and further education colleges, nhs doctors, nurses and other healthcare workers.

Culford Road, N1, March 1992: Dear Carol, It will be great to see you at the Belfast conference. What can you bring me? Your good self in hiking boots. Hawkins Cheezies. A new copy of *The Mountain and the Valley,* unless you want to phone my mom and ask her for my old one. She's booksitting for me while I'm away.

I'm glad you suggested some hiking after the conference. I wanna see the bluebells, sing the McGarrigles' *Walking Song* with you.

Here in the land where English was cobbled together by foreign marauders, I've made a few literary pilgrimages.

Wuthering on the heights of Haworth, "where Emily, Anne and Charlotte poured their hearts out." Punting on the Cam, with Lewis Carroll peeking through the willows. Quaffing ale at the George in Southwark, the closest I can get to Chaucer's Tabard. Maybe we can check out the daffs in the Lake District?

Upper Brook Street, W1, April 1992: Rhona has a platinum address in this embassy enclave, but her flat is even tinier than ours. At least I'm alone here for a few days, and Patricia has loaned me a typewriter.

It_makes_you_aware_of_space_not_having_it_I_mean_when _it's_there_space_is_invisible_but_when_you_have_to_sub-stitute_underlines_for_spaces_because_the_space_bar_on_ your_borrowed_typewriter_doesn't_work_you_realize_how_ constricted_you_really_are_

Try.a.full.stop.then.you.lose.the.flow.each.word.an.isolated. sentence.still.sort.of.English.but.not.the.spacious.prairie.sen-tences.of.Canada.my.home.and.fluent.land.

One,is,forced,to,try,everything,here,for,space,but,the,comma, makes,the,thumb,redundant,useless,dumb,opposing,digit, prose,with,a,hammer,

A-hyphen-seems-a-little-better-but-going-to-the-top-row-after-every-word-makes-your-fingers-lose-the-home-line-fin-ger-pecking-mad-

Maybe*I*need*stars*oh*no*they*fill*the*space*so*totally* all*the*stars*come*down*and*suffocate*me*I*need*more* sky*between*me*and*the*stars*howling*babies*scud*mis-siles*terrify*me*for*bloody*sure*it's*fucking*hell*lemme* outta*here*

Gimme/a/slash/baby/slash/my/words/apart/cut/off/my/tongue/
with/a/carving/knife/did/you/ever/see/such/a/sight/in/your/life/

Try'the'single'quote'yes'I'would'say'it'feels'comfy'making'the'
shift'to'single'visible'what'a'relief'

Culford Road, N1, April 1992: I'm taking the devil's typing
machine to a shopkeeper in Turnpike Lane who might be able
to fix the space bar. Then it's Kingsland Road, past the eel pie
and mash shop, averting my eyes from the man who slices live
eels in the window. Down the market I'll jostle with other for-
eigners for tomatoes, a bargain at "6 pan a pan." I'll leave the
mercurochrome-dyed pigs' tails and dried innards for other
people's string bags and shopping carts. I'm not too proud to
have a cart myself, but I use it for transporting dirty linens to
My Appalling Launderette. And it came in useful when we
moved: Okies or tinkers dragging a cart with clothes and bed-
ding piled in, pots and pans tied on, rattling down the dark
streets. A pretty bumpy journey for a forty-something chick
from rat-free Alberta, but I've lost any sense of shame.

Culford Road, N1, May 1992: Not only did Labour lose the
election (glum faces staring into porridge bowls at the Belfast
conference), but one of life's individual planks of bad news has
whacked me between the eyes. Another R word to add to *Rats*
and *Robbery: Redundancy.* The men with the knives in Alberta
Treasury slashed one thousand government jobs and mine was
one. I've gone through the stages of shock, disbelief, anger,
depression and numbness. Now I'm into relief – the strain of
working in such an erratic organization was making me ill. I'm
temping in the City, London's financial Square Mile, while
sending off application letters and CVs. My banker son teases
me on the phone about his hippie mom working in the investment industry.

Rhona gave me her Nouveau Pauvre button to wear and a

bottle of Laphroaig as a substitute for a severance package. We were friends in Edmonton but not intimate; here we cling together on the raft. Canadian sisters.

Culford Road, N1, August 1992: Dear Shirley, When I read the first line of your letter from Strawberry Creek retreat I wailed with nostalgia! It's hot and cramped in this flat, and I have no privacy or energy. By your second paragraph I was laughing manically at the truth of your comment, "Rhona said you'd changed jobs and was trying to explain to me why you wanted to stay on in London, but I'm not sure I really understand." Neither does my mom, nor do I, really. Let me try to count the reasons.

Rejection of defeated daughter role. When I was made redundant, I just couldn't go home to my parents, mom hovering and sighing, *did you find a job yet, oh dear.* No thanks. Much as I love them and miss them, it's not how I want to go back.

A recession in the rain is worth two in the snow. The recession here is terrible, but everyone says it's no better in Canada. My job is temporary, but aren't they all?

*Boracic.** No extra cash to buy a plane ticket and ship stuff back. (*Boracic and lint, rhymes with skint, means skinned, read broke.)

Seductive old bitch. London's delights and oddities do seduce me at times. The friends I've made are warm and supportive. Why leave at the turning point?

Sisu. Sheer, bloody-minded, idiotic stubbornness, inherited from my Finnish ancestors.

Challenge. Testing my mettle in this complex environment, I'm changing in ways I never anticipated, losing my innocence and complacency, gaining a healthy cynicism.

Satisfaction at surviving. I can be stripped of nearly everything I used to consider essential and still enjoy neighbours' gardens, second-hand clothes and novels, the magic of St. Paul's. What a sickening Pollyanna I really am – ignore my previous claims of toughness.

Career overboard. I've discovered I'm not a career person after all. Sod prestige and position and all that. I have nothing but contempt for pig-troughers and power-game players. If I must work at something, better a temp job in the City for filthy lucre than the ulcer-making projects foisted on me by permanent employment.

Pleasures of anonymity. I always loved the familiarity of Edmonton, but I could never go anywhere and cry in my beer without seeing someone I knew.

Fatalism. Nothing left to lose.

Basement Flat, 14 Colebrooke Row, N1, 22 November 1992: Lord and Lady Booby are pleased to inform you of a change of residence. Our new domicile being centrally heated and located, and eminently desirable, it would be our great pleasure to welcome you to our abode. Overseas guests may wish to be accommodated upon a double settee in the reception room. Amenities include eternal hot water which, at the mere turning of a sparkling spigot, falls upon the heads of the unattired fortunate.

Colebrooke Row, N1, January 1993: When Patricia and Frank left for America, we got to move into their heavenly flat. The rent is high, but we both have permanent jobs now. Mine is still computerized basket-weaving, but my colleagues respect me, and there are even cash bonuses. Michael's teaching English as a foreign language in an inner city college – hard work, but rewarding.

Two months later, he drops the bomb: there's someone else. The fourth R of London. *Rejection.* I'm shaken and hurt, but not surprised. For nine years, we rode the Relationship Rollercoaster. It's hard to break off – all our private jokes and codes, good talks, comfortable silences, shared chores. Harder still to know why I stayed. Perhaps for the independence: he refused to own me. Perhaps I needed his cynicism as much as he needed my optimism; perhaps his unpredictability offset my stability. We had the same involvement in ideas, but too often the intellectualizing was a substitute for passion. And the practice of independence a substitute for cherishing.

Canalside, Vincent Terrace, N1, March 1993: The *Guardian* beside me on the bench, bluebells behind me. No walkers, only two solitary fishermen on the opposite bank. I stifle the impulse to reflect on what has happened this week. Instead, just sit and watch the water, the reflections of narrow boats, brick walls, bare trees. This is the mild unseason between brown and green. If I watch long enough, mortar remelts between liquid bricks, square drain holes soften into kissing mouths, the hard edge of the towpath bends into grimaces, smiles. Ripples are not waterflow *(this is no river)* but wind-breath. I refuse to remember griefs, identify longings, ask how long I sit here. Just hold on to emptiness, unreason, unambition. The fishermen cast and wait. Reel in, cast again. Catch nothing.

If I could cry at this *(futility)*, or any other thing *(loss)*, it would be a gift. I welcome the dry ache. Sorrow, not evasion. Walk back to the flat, listen to Casals play Bach.

Colebrooke Row, N1, May 1993: Michael stayed with me for four months after we agreed to part, at first too broke and then too listless to find another place. A strange and subdued time, living separately in the same flat, mumbling in monosyllables; sometimes still talking. We vowed to be honorable, in recognition of the best of our life together. Mostly we've achieved that. I haven't cried, though I've hollered some. I don't believe I'm jealous, but I'm not sure if that's an intellectual position I adopt, or if jealousy is a feeling I don't even recognize, or one I suppress because it's unbecoming. I still do his laundry, and we maintain a joint bank account. Friends are horrified. These practical arrangements seem unimportant and, indeed, were never things we argued about.

I love living on my own at last and will stay here for quite some time, if possible.

The Old Queen's Head, Essex Road, N1, May 1993: Dear Leonard, I want to thank you for last night at Royal Albert Hall. I went on my own, and you picked me out from the crowd. Danced me to the end of love, my partner in black and grey, taking the lead with slow and dignified movements, because there ain't no cure for love. You said, "I want to unify all your deep concerns." I believe you do. "Not that I know what they are." It would take hours to tell you, over a bottle or two of red wine. "Not that I *want* to know what they are." Inward sheep-giggle from middle-aged Canadian woman.

Thank you for offering me the crumbs of love, the ones you left behind. My path through the woods, into the clearing of irony and self-mockery.

When the crowd started yelling requests, you sang *Loch Lomond* and *Rule Britannia* instead. I sang every word of *The Maple Leaf Forever* with you, as I did in the 1950s, a good little Canadian schoolgirl who dutifully swallowed the history fed to her. We had our own private chuckle, the only ones there who knew all the words.

I was touched by your words about your daughter: "She's named Lorca after this great poet. I was so proud of her when she turned eighteen and put a ring through her nose. She was so beautiful when she dyed her hair blue. That's just a father's pride speaking, but I can't help it. You know how it is." Yes, I do. The mirrored sphere in the ceiling threw coloured lights all over the Great Wide Royal Circular Albert Hall, wrapping all of us in three-four swirls. Take this waltz, this waltz, this waltz....

A little friendly criticism: you played too many encores. It was rather unseemly, but then I understood: "Thanks for lingering on with us. Everybody thinks we're in a rush on a tour like this, but we actually don't have anywhere to go." You could have come to my flat. We could have talked about our daughters.

Royal Opera House, WC2, November 1993: I arrived at Floral Street first, stood near the Amphitheatre entrance as instructed and held my £20 note primly in my hand like all the rest who wanted tickets to the last, sold-out performance of *Die Meistersinger.* The official queue for standbys was out front, we were just a straggly lot with our backs to the wall.

Finally along comes Philip, my ever-lovin' musical guide to Wagner, fresh from a session with a clarinettist. We develop this strategy to split up and work both ends of Floral. It doesn't work. He comes back a few minutes later with Strategy B: removes his jacket and – take a breath – his Shetland jumper. In his dazzling white shirt he stands right out in the street in that sort of London you-don't-know-how-it's-happened-because-you-can't-see-any-raindrops-but-somehow-your-clothes-are-all-damp rain. I pull my eyes away from his shirt and buckle down to raising my eyebrows meaningfully at strangers and thrusting my £20 note just a little bolder. No joy.

Five minutes before the four o'clock curtain, the great white music lover comes grinning smugly down the street. He's bagged two tickets, one for £7, one for £62. Gallant as ever, he offers me the expensive one first, and I race up the Grand Staircase with my rucksack flapping as an usher tries to stop me, says I have to check it, but it's got all my credit cards in it and money and my whole life and my birdwatching glasses and it's four o'clock so he lets me go, trusting I'm not a Canadian member of the IRA and anyway you can hardly tackle a woman in a denim skirt and jacket as she's running up the Grand Staircase under the crystal chandelier at the Royal Opera House.

I swoon through the first two acts in the lower circle. For the third and longest act we trade seats and I'm in the upper slips, the worst seat in the house, but hey it's inside, innit? The quintet begins, first one voice, then the others join in one by one, the blood drains from my head and I can't breathe and why doesn't it all end right now and how will Wagner ever build a musical bridge from paradise to the next scene?

From here on in, if anyone asks me why I came to London, the answer's on my lips: so I could faint in the slips during the quintet in *Die Meistersinger* while my white-shirted knight sat on the other side of the chasm watching act three through my birdwatching glasses.

Colebrooke Row, N1, June 1994: Coming up to four years here, I'll find it hard to leave. At first it was the friends I've made – the tribe of poets from the Troubadour coffeehouse, the other assorted artists of life. Now the countryside is getting under my skin. In March my blue suede hiking boots and a couple of blokes took me to the Pembrokeshire coast in Wales – sheer cliffs, 180° coves that made walking on cliff edges seem like manoeuvring a circular escalator drunk in high heels.

But the landscape that slew me was North Cornwall in May. I spent a week there, with Tuula from Toronto, in a seventeenth-century thatched cottage. Two-foot-thick cob walls kept it cool by day, the fireplace warmed us in the evenings, the slate floors caressed our bare feet. We lived a life virtually unchanged from three hundred years ago, though we didn't have to fetch wood and carry water – as we both did on our grandmothers' farms in Finland and Saskatchewan. No radio, telephone, TV or car. We walked six or seven miles a day, cooked simple meals, talked, read, wrote. Mothered and sistered and grandmothered each other.

Within three miles of our cottage our hikes took us to vertiginous cliffs, coves with slate-razor rocks and granite boulders inspired by Henry Moore, Mother Goose fields of sheep and cows, forests with bluebell floors and wild garlic accents, streambanks edged with orchids. We were miniature Alices in lanes between giant hedgerows bursting with spring flowers and birds, stripy snails, whist butterflies.

In Duckpool Cove the tops of boulders glistened with seaweed – webs of green-black hair, cellophane lace, antimacassars. (I can hear my prairie forebears muttering, stones are just stones, and too damn many of them sprout in the fields each spring.) The cottage library had a natural history book – was the seaweed serrated wrack or channelled wrack, flat wrack or bladder wrack? I never did decide.

The older I get, the less I want cities, the more I want any wild and lonely spots I can find on this island. Rare as shy fritillaries, they take my breath away.

I'm beginning to claim this landscape by leaving parts of myself in it. I've searched the Norfolk dunes at dawn for an earring dropped in moonlight, my gift for the rabbits to nibble. I've planted a medal of the Virgin Mary under a new totem pole in Bushy Park. I've left walking sticks for other hikers to find in Wales and the Lake District. Some people gather souvenirs, I donate them.

Colebrooke Row, N1, August 1994: I'm content to be in midlife, between cultures, alone with fragments of old selves and reinventions. I've slept with some men, sharing tenderness and respect, though not love. I've fallen in chaste and redemptive love with others I didn't sleep with. Born-again virgin.

This past long weekend I spoke to no one for sixty-six hours. Trappist-in-training. The flat was tidied, a poem written, letters answered. Patient Griselda. Some reading was done: Karl Marx abandoned, Ivan Klima edged out by Charlotte Brontë. Hampstead Heath was explored, and a long unknown street trodden to see where it led. I have no one to caress my face. Crone-in-progress.

Colebrooke Row, N1, February 1995: While I am away my daughter watches over my parents, who age in my absence. Finally she calls me to say what my brother, mother and son have been sparing me: Dad has mild to moderate dementia. I have seen the best of him; they monitor his mental decline. I am inept at the end of the telephone line. But the idea that my presence in Edmonton for two weeks, flying in like Lady Bountiful, would have any lasting effect on dad or mom is sheer megalomania. (Let me be honest, the last statement is rationalization. The truth is, my passport stamp has expired. I can leave England but can't return.)

Meanwhile I'm robbed again. I thought this flat was safe behind grilles, but even triple glazing can be broken and padlocks sheared off. After the police and the landlords leave, I tape a plastic bag over the broken window, sit among the debris and watch a TV documentary on Jacqueline du Pré. Wine and the cello – a temporary escape. Fatalism indeed.

Colebrooke Row, N1, July 1995: My journals have disintegrated into scribbles of pain about my father's dementia, the dilemma of whether I should go back to Canada for good – as if good and bad were distinct poles, each with an obvious essence. My daughter Leah is getting married in August, and I long to be with her. But after the ceremony she'd go off on her honeymoon and there I'd be, jobless in Alberta.

I finally told Leah the truth about my passport and was amazed at her response. She was generous and mature, or perhaps as selfish as me: she didn't want a depressed and unemployed mother on her conscience, so I'd better stay until I was really ready to come back. She'd miss me at her wedding, but we were strong enough to disregard the expectations of others.

In June, Myrna came from Edmonton and stayed with me. We went to Bath and talked for eight miles along the canal to Bradford on Avon, where we climbed the terraced hills to a tiny Saxon church. I sang "Amazing Grace" to test the acoustics, she sang a hymn in Ukrainian.

By the end of June, Leah had almost convinced me I should stay for one more year, use the time wisely, save money for my return, work on another book. She promised that she and her husband would visit me. It made some kind of desperate sense, but I was still shaky. Prodigal mother.

I'd bought an antique writing slope for them as a wedding gift. Something beautiful yet practical – like my daughter. Something quintessentially English. When I asked Myrna to take it to Edmonton for me, I knew the choice was made.

I enrolled in a poetry retreat for the last week of August. My consolation prize.

Hockliffe, Bedfordshire, October 1995: Dear Myrna, I'm sitting in the upstairs study of an ordinary house in Hockliffe, an hour north of London. It's not a charming village with half-timbered cottages, a local butcher, baker and teahouse, a duck pond across from the cricket ground. It's at the crossroads of two highways, and from its three shops one has the choice of buying stamps/newspapers/fags, a Harley Davidson motorcycle or a saddle and riding tack. Sheep graze in the field beyond the garden.

What's going on here? Has the old doll met a man who could entice her to the Bedfordshire prairies? Is she in love or something? Yup, and yup again. I'm smack in the middle of a wondrous and totally requited middle-aged love! Six weeks ago at Lumb Bank, the writers' retreat in West Yorkshire, I met Mike.

Snap, and my life has changed utterly, delightfully. He's a reader in mathematics, a poet, psychologically healthy, energetic and funny. Like me, he has a grown daughter and married son. Unlike me, he's a grandparent. His wife died three months after their granddaughter was born. His elegy for her is moving and profound.

You and I have often talked and written about men, love, the erotic, the painful, the disappointing. Once you wrote about being cherished; I'm beginning to know what that's like. It was a hothouse environment, isolated from our day-to-day lives. Yorkshire was in the middle of a drought, and water was rationed. On the last night we dipped into romance and haven't looked back, except to marvel. He mostly stays with me in London during the week; I come to Hockliffe on weekends.

We've done some things besides gaze into each other's eyes and smile goofily. A gripping *Coriolanus* at the Barbican; Bert Jansch on guitar at the 12-Bar Club; the African Proms at Royal Albert Hall with Rhona, Al and Jane. One friend called me a dear and lucky woman. Another said my voice sounds younger and chucklier. Another that no one deserves it more – but I can't accept that. All I can say is that Mike and I are either middle-aged crazy, or wise enough to recognize and welcome grace when it appears unbidden.

Once in Edmonton I had a little friend of four who was learning to write. Every time she achieved an R she celebrated with a somersault. Like her, I am become a child again, learning a whole new set of R words. Some I thought could only be found if I returned to Alberta. Others I believed could never exist anywhere in the world, only in the dictionary. I'm starting with *renewal*, celebrating a day at a time.

A GUEST OF KAREN BLIXEN

Betty Jane Wylie

"THERE YOU ARE," I SAID, "THERE YOU ARE."
I wasn't aware I had said it out loud until I read it the
next day in the Danish newspaper, *Politiken*. I had
been so intent on answering the reporter's questions that I had
scarcely noticed where we were going, until we stopped at a
clearing in the shade of an enormous beech tree where lie the
remains of Baroness Karen Blixen, the author Isak Dinesen.
There she was, with her last dog Pasop, and there I was at her
home in Rungstedlund, the forty-acre estate where she was
born and where, after her return from Africa, she wrote the
books that keep her memory alive today and send people like
me to Denmark in pursuit of her.

The Baroness Karen Blixen was sixty-four in 1948 and a
legend in her own time when she met the thirty-two-year-old
struggling poet, Thorkild Bjornvig. They formed a pact of
friendship overwhelming in its intensity. Over a period of several years, the young poet would spend three to five months
living at Rungstedlund (in the west wing, where I was bil-
leted), his mind challenged and his art nurtured by his dazzling mentor. In the end, he feared the loss of his autonomy
and withdrew from the magic circle.

Blixen had charged Bjornvig not to write about her until
after her death but then to be sure to do so. In 1974 he published the pact, "My Friendship with Isak Dinesen." It was

published in English in 1983 (translated by Ingvar Schousboe and William Jay Smith). It wasn't until I went to Kenya that I got hooked on Blixen. I acquired the dramatic rights to the book and began to work on a stage play about the poignant relationship between the young poet and his enchantress. Responding to a draft I sent him, Thorkild invited me to come and talk to him in Denmark.

Although I had met him at Harbourfront (in Toronto) when he had come to read there, and had corresponded with him, I knew only a young, paper Thorkild. He had a suggestion: to visit Rungstedlund and work there with him.

"As a member of the Danish Academy of Literature," he wrote me, "I can invite you to stay there; you can go and see the parc (sic), and together in the green room we could, perhaps in the invisible presence of the Baroness, discuss the play and find out."

Thus it was that for five days one May that I was the sole occupant of Karen Blixen's home. Not the sole occupant of the building; on the other side of the green room wall is an apartment willed for life to Caroline Carlsen, Blixen's last housekeeper. Mrs. Carlsen used a secret door when she came to talk to Thorkild or me, stepping carefully over the threshold so as not to jar the ash from the cheroot in her mouth, removing the cheroot only when necessary to cough violently. She didn't knock because, she said, according to the Baroness, "You don't knock at the door in the house you live in."

Rungsted is a suburb about twenty kilometres from Copenhagen on the Strandvej, halfway to Elsinore. In Blixen's day, and before, there was a narrow road between the house and the beach and the author used to take a morning swim early and late in the season and her life. Now the four-lane Strandvej runs beside a forest of masts in the marina, and it's worth your life to cross it in the rush hour. You can still see the sea from Blixen's upstairs bedroom window, but it's much more pleasant, and quieter, to look from the windows of the green room at the back, out across the lawn to the pond with its ducks (and eight new ducklings when I was there) and the little white bridge that leads over to the woods with its tame foxes (Mrs. Carlsen feeds them) and that grave at the foot of Ewald's Hill.

I had written Ewald's Hill into a scene in my play; my characters climbed it, panting, and looked down on the sea. In actuality, you follow a winding path up a small knoll, overhung with towering trees that obscure the view of the sea. There is a stone bench to rest on and a small needle monument marking Ewald's connection with the hill. (I rewrote the scene.)

The Danish lyric poet Johannes Ewald lived as a lodger at the Rungsted Inn from 1773 to 1776. According to the plaque in the front hall of the house, the building was licensed as an inn:

UNDER CHRISTIAN II (about 1520)
KING KARL XII OF SWEDEN STAYED HERE AFTER LANDING
IN HUMLEBEK ABOUT 1700
WILHELM DINESEN BOUGHT IT AND LIVED HERE
FROM 1879 TILL HIS DEATH IN 1895
KAREN BLIXEN WAS BORN HERE
AND THE FAMILY AND SHE LIVED HERE
TILL 1958
THE RUNGSTEDLUND ESTATE WAS NAMED
A BIRD SANCTUARY *(fuglereservat)*
AFTER KAREN BLIXEN'S DEATH
THE BUILDING BECAME A HOME
FOR THE DANISH ACADEMY

Blixen didn't die until 1962, but she leased her home from the Foundation from 1958 until her death. In 1960 she became a charter member of The Danish Academy and monies were finally found to renovate the rambling, uncomfortable, cold, charming house. All these arrangements had something to do with tax shelters, according to Blixen's good friend and adviser, Knud Vig-Jensen, founder and director of the modern art gallery, Louisiana. There never was enough money to do all the public things Blixen had hoped for until after *Out of Africa* was filmed. (The birds came and stayed without any financial outlay.) Proceeds from *Africa* and *Babette's Feast* paid for renovations to the former stables: a museum, lecture-cum-concert hall, and a cafeteria, all of which opened to the public in May, 1991.

The Rungstedlund Foundation, with income derived from Isak Dinesen's literary estate, oversees the property and leases the main building at Rungstedlund to the Danish Academy, according to the author's will. The fourteen members, senior literary figures in Denmark, hold their monthly meetings in the house, and have guest rooms at their disposal. The Academy pays the Foundation for the use of the place and in turn gets a grant from the Danish government to go about its cultural business. That particular May it seems that I was part of its cultural business, thanks to Thorkild Bjornvig. He was seventy-five when I met him, a distinguished, white-haired GOP (Grand Old Poet) and senior member of the Academy, who apparently had no difficulty persuading his fellows of my qualifications.

"You're staying where??" the Canadian ambassador to Denmark said to me in disbelief, on the phone the day after I had settled in. The ambassador at that time turned out to be a former classmate of mine from the University of Manitoba. Like many readers of Dinesen's haunting stories, Madame Ambassador had longed to see Blixen's home, so I invited her for tea and she in turn took me to Dyrehaven, the deer park near Klampenborg where Blixen used to love to walk to see the hawthorn trees in bloom. I was too late for the blossoms, but the ambassador and I had a delightful reunion and dinner.

I woke up every morning brimming with glee, bathed in the incredible white light of the Danish spring, scarcely able to believe where I was, lying on linen and lace-covered pillows under a delicious duvet in the west bedroom at Rungstedlund. I padded out to the kitchen to make tea and brought it back to bed to drink while I plotted my work for the day with Thorkild, who arrived about 9 a.m. We would sit and drink coffee in the green room at the table where he had spent so many hours with his friend and mentor, he in his chair and I in hers, talking and talking about the Baroness.

Lunch was a Danish smorgasbord at the same table (they always ate there, too, except when the Baroness had guests for dinner, then it was served formally in the dining room). We ate dark rye or pumpernickel bread, cheeses, smoked salmon, cold cuts, egg salad, cucumber salad, with schnapps for Thorkild. We usually went out for dinner in the neighbourhood, but one evening we stayed home and I cooked. Morten Keller brought me fresh salmon and I poached it in white wine, made hollandaise sauce and served it with fresh asparagus and tiny new potatoes. It had to be good; the Baroness would have wanted it so.

As Mrs. Carlsen writes in her memoir of her employer, "A good dinner at Rungstedlund consisted of genuine ingredients tasting of what they were and not of anything else...."

The kitchen had obviously been remodelled, with a new gas stove, lots of cupboards and counter space, an automatic coffee maker, and a MagiMix (the European version of a Cuisinart). Caroline Carlsen describes the kitchen in her book, how it used to be: "...old-fashioned, [with] a vast kitchen range, a scoured white table with a curtain, and an enormous ice-cold pantry. When the house was restored, the range went. In a way I was sorry to have to part with it, for I always loved the open fire. It had a special charm when we came down in the morning, got the fire up, made coffee and sat round the warm range."

I mentioned Morten Keller, who brought me my groceries and kept the house filled with flowers. Morten is Blixen's grand-nephew, grandson of her brother Thomas Dinesen. He cares for the house and grounds, living there with his beautiful Spanish wife Marta and their two sons. They're in the gardener's cottage, handsomely renovated (by the films); they worried about the day when the museum would open and the parking problems begin.

It seems that everyone who ever had anything to do with Blixen wrote about her. I have already quoted Caroline Carlsen, Blixen's housekeeper, who arrived with her small son Nils on June 1, 1949, to put the house to rights. "It was an awkward old house," she says in her book. "There was no bathroom until the house was rebuilt in 1960. We had two water closets, and the Baroness used a small bathtub of the kind you fill with water from a jug. Every morning and evening for many years, we took hot water up to her in what we called *opsigelseskanden* (the "notice jug"). The Baroness used to say: "Well, if I had to carry water up in that jug, I would immediately give notice to quit!"

What Caroline doesn't tell is that the way to Blixen's bedroom led from the "water closet" at the top of the back stairs through an open, uninsulated loft under the roof. Thorkild told me it had drifts of snow across it in the winter. A graceful curving staircase from the front hall to that bedroom wasn't built until the renovations in 1960.

There is a beautiful Norwegian cast-iron stove in every room. Until 1960, these stoves were the only source of heat in the house. Caroline writes: "When it was really cold in winter, the Baroness would move into the west wing, where we now have a guest apartment, and if we had visitors, we had to make a fire two days in advance... Jamb stoves (so-called) are a sort of continuous-burning stove: you cover the embers in the evening and uncover them in the morning. Every morning we would revive the embers by means of a pair of bellows; it is not difficult if only you know how to. Sometimes the Baroness would light the fire, and no mistake if you looked at the floor around the stove."

Yet the house was maintained in beauty and style. Morten Keller still spreads the long white-lace curtains like a bride's train across the floor at the foot of their windows in the drawing and dining rooms. Those curtains were a sign of summer, replacing the heavy drapes drawn against the drafts of winter. The house was full of flowers when I arrived, as the Baroness wished, great vases in every room filled with rich sprays of pungent lilacs, fragrant freesias, and other seasonal flowers from the gardens.

Clara (Svendsen) Selborn, Blixen's secretary and executor of her literary estate, in her book *The Life and Destiny of Isak Dinesen,* describes how every night before she went to bed, the Baroness would open the door to the yard and look out, and then go to Ewald's room, and close the door. Finally, Clara asked her employer what these actions meant. Blixen answered that she looked towards Africa, and then went to the room to look at the map of the Ngong Hills. I saw that map, framed, hanging on the back of the desk, which is set at right angles to the wall and window. But, Selborn points out in her book, "there was a photograph of Denys on the windowsill by her desk," implying that was the real reason for the visit.

I sat at that desk, too, with its sloping surface and worn leather insert. I picked up that picture and studied the confident, handsome face of the man who, Blixen wrote her brother Thomas, was her "living ideal."

Thomas Dinesen, of course, also wrote a book. His grandson Morten lent me a copy of it in English translation, and I read it in the green room one morning while waiting for

Thorkild to arrive. "I want to be where there is life," Blixen told her brother, and, "I cannot live without fun in life."

Blixen's idea of fun seems surprisingly playful to those who are familiar with her strange, resonant stories. Caroline Carlsen reports that a game played in the house was "simply to steal about the house with a cup of water in one's hand...the idea was to throw the water into the face of (an) innocent victim." She says she managed one day to avoid being the victim by tickling Clara Svendsen or the housemaid or Nils, Caroline's son, whenever they tried to get near a water tap to fill their cups. They complained to the Baroness, who spoke to Caroline:

"What's all this, Mrs. Carlsen? I hear you can't leave Clara and Else and Nils alone just because they are ticklish." And at the same time she emptied a big cup of water over my head...I know people of today would call this kind of behaviour tomfoolery, but that's how we played at Rungstedlund."

Thorkild's pride still rankles at the memory of a time he describes in his book when Blixen threaded freesias in his thick, curly, black hair and forbade him to remove them. He had to pick up a friend and bring her back for lunch but he got lost and had to stop three times, "stick my daffy flower-embellished head out the window and ask for directions." Both the friend and her mother took his appearance in their stride, gave him sherry and a tour of their mansion before he took the woman back to Rungstedlund. (I wrote his flowery head into a later draft of my play.) When he told her how much he admired her for ignoring the freesias, she laughed, saying she knew immediately that it was "one of Tanne's gags." Old friends and relatives called the writer Tanne, the name she called herself as a little girl before she could pronounce Karen. Her lover, Denys Finch-Hatton, changed it to Tania.

One night at dusk, without turning on the lights, I wandered into the green room, wound up Denys's gramophone, the one he gave Tania in Africa, and put on a thick, old, but still unscratched record (the Adagio of Tchaikovsky's First String Quartet) and walked through the house, letting the sound carry me back into Blixen's past, and Bjornvig's.

"Just listen to the music," she said to Thorkild then. "Think of nothing else...later in life, you will always remember these evenings and this green room where you first heard it."

Me too.

NOT MY HOME

Daniel Coleman

This world is not my home, I'm just a-passin' through
My treasures are laid up somewhere beyond the blue
The angels beckon me from heaven's open door
And I can't feel at home in this world anymore.

OUR VOICES, THIN AND HIGH, BRIGHT AS BIRDS, rose in the late afternoon air in the chapel at Bingham Academy, a boarding school for missionaries' children in Addis Ababa, Ethiopia.

I remember the songs and the ten-cent pieces. We were handed a copper coin on the way in to Loyal Ambassadors for Christ, the Sunday afternoon chapel service, and were expected to put it in the offering when it was taken up later in the program. The drop-and-roll of ten-cent pieces from the grade one bench peppered the songs and choral readings of LAC. If you rubbed the coin hard with your thumb, you could make a shiny new profile of Emperor Haile Selassie emerge from the dirty copper before you put it in the collection plate. If you sucked on the coin for a minute first, the grime loosened more easily, and you could make Miss Macdonald turn green if you let her see you do it.

> *Miss Macdonald had a class, eyi-eyi-yo*
> *And in that class she had some kids, eyi-eyi-yo*
> *With a nose-picker here and a bed-wetter there*
> *Here a picker, there a wetter*
> *Everywhere a picker-wetter*
> *Miss Macdonald had a class, eyi-eyi-yo!*

This song could get you thrown out of LAC, but if you whispered "eyi-eyi-yo" quietly, you could ripple the grade one bench with giggles.

"This world is not my home," warbled Timmy Murray beside me on the bench. As he sang, he rubbed spit across the Emperor's receding copper hairline. The old Negro spiritual was one of our favourites. What did we know about African slaves in the American South? What did we know of the clapping and swaying gospel choirs in African America? Next to nothing. As far as we were concerned, this was our hymn, a hymn that explained to us where we were, and why we were here.

Just like Abraham in the Bible, our parents had heard the call of God to leave kith and kin and go to a land God would show them. My mother was nineteen when she left Canada for Ethiopia, my father in his early twenties. They gave up the care of their own parents for the care of God.

The story was simple. Once you had heard God's call and been Saved, you realized this world was not your home and you were just a-passin' through on your way to heaven. Your real home was never here, always Somewhere Else. This realization changed your whole life. You gave up the ways of the world and committed yourself to the ways of God. You became charged with the responsibility to Witness to others, to help them realize the spiritual choices they needed to make.

"I am the door into God's sheepfold," Jesus had said. And we caroled:

> *One door and only one and yet the sides are two*
> *Inside and outside. On which side are you?*
> *One door and only one and yet the sides are two*
> *I'm on the right side, on which side are you?*

Witnessing was tricky. You had to screw up your courage to confront people with choices they didn't want to face.

Luckily, you could use approved ways of Witnessing which formalized these confrontations so they didn't feel so aggressive. The best of these was the evangelistic Crusade. What did we know of medieval knights hacking with the broadswords of Saxony and Gaul into infidel skulls? What did we know of the Templars in chain mail who blistered under the Mediterranean sun in search of slivers of the cross and whiskers from the apostles' beards? Next to nothing. For Crusade was our special word, one that helped us downplay the personally confrontational nature of Witnessing.

Our parents had organized weekend Crusades at their down-country mission stations. We knew the requirements: first, a guest speaker; second, simultaneous translation from the foreign speaker's tongue to Oromiffia or Amharic; third, a *dass* of eucalyptus poles and branches for shade; and finally, a pasture area for the people's hobbled horses and mules. When these arrangements had been made, you were ready for action. The actual services had several other essential components: preaching through translators; singing in the five-note Ethiopian scale; taking up an offering; and praying out loud.

And so, armed with conviction and a clear procedure, Dougy Stinson and I hosted Crusades in the boys' dorm. We called our listeners from board games and Marvel Comics and Dinky Toys and GI-Joes; we called them in their blue jeans and bathrobes and T-shirts and overalls. After our audience had comported themselves under the *dass* of bedsheets stretched between bunkbeds, we began the solemnities. We mimicked Ethiopian singing in a mournful five-note hymn:

There were ninety and nine that safely lay
In the shelter of the fold
But one lost lamb was far away
Far out on the hills and cold
Away on the mountains, wild and deep

Away from the Shepherd's love and care
Away from the Shepherd's love and care.

A wastepaper can passed from hand to hand and imaginary bills of great denomination were placed ostentatiously in the collection. Then, with a dignity beyond my years, I stepped behind the pulpit of dresser drawers and began to speak in a tongue never heard before. Dougy translated into an impassioned dialect of Amhar-English. My sermon leaned heavily on the words *ha-ti'at* and *Yesus Cristos*. The boys responded with appropriate exclamations of *Amen* and *Exabi'er Yemesgegn*. For the benefit of the city-bred boys who didn't know Amharic, Dougy would translate the thanks-be-to-Gods and original sins for the poor lost anglophone lambs.

Many boys were struck by conviction and Saved at our Crusades. Then we commissioned them through gospel words in song:

I will make you fishers of men
Fishers of men, fishers of men
I will make you fishers of men
If you follow Me.

The songs we sang taught us to understand all kinds of figurative language. We performed actions that went along with "Fishers of Men," and, though we tried to cast our imaginary lines farther and reel them in faster than each other, we knew the song was not about real fishing. It was about Witnessing, about hooking people and bringing them to Jesus. Now that Dougy and I had fished the boys from their sins, they in turn would fish others.

Finally, the closing prayer. This element required the translator to borrow from the liturgical model of Mrs-Johnson-before-bedtime. Every evening after story time, our dorm parents would lead the grade one to four boys in a nighttime prayer. During her husband's comforting, monotonous prayer, Mrs. Johnson snapped her fingers sharply at anyone fooling around. Her vigilance reminded us of the watch we needed to keep over our fidgeting wayward selves, as we'd been taught in LAC song:

> *Oh be careful little hands what you do*
> *Oh be careful little hands what you do*
> *For the Father up-a-bove is looking-down-in-love*
> *So be careful little hands what you do.*

With Mrs. Johnson's fierce-fingered model before us, I flattened my pulpit voice in profound prayer, while Dougy Stinson snapped away at the briefest flicker of a new convert's eyelid. And so, many were Saved in the grade one to four boys' dorm. And eventually our captive audience was free to return to their Dinky Toys and library books. Dougy Stinson and I, meanwhile, had discharged our obligation to Witness.

We had shown ourselves worthy inheritors of our parents' missionary calling. We knew from our parents' conversations that you couldn't be a missionary if you believed all doors led into God's sheepfold. You needed to be sure of the One True Door, and you needed to be clear about which side you were on. So, when we were old enough, we knew we would go to Bible School to learn what we believed. After three or four years of learning, we would emerge, filled up with beliefs and ready to carry them to the ends of the earth. This was the story we inherited from our parents. We chorused:

> *Far, far away, in heathen darkness dwelling*
> *Millions of souls forever may be lost*
> *Who, who will go, salvation's story telling*
> *Looking to Jesus, counting not the cost?*

We knew the answer. Our parents would go – our parents *had gone* from their Canadian or Australian or American homes to Ethiopia, salvation's-story telling. They told the story in hospitals, mission schools, leprosariums, and orphanages. They preached it under thatched roofs in the countryside and tin roofs in the cities. They preached it in *dasses* and in the open air. And we were the children of their adventure.

Even before I was old enough to read the words in the hymnal, I mimicked the vowels and consonant-clusters while the older kids sang the LAC theme song every Sunday afternoon. The kids old enough to read sang,

> *I am a stranger here within a foreign land*
> *My home is far away upon a golden strand*
> *Ambassador to be of realms beyond the sea*
> *I'm here on business for my King,*

while I sang something like this:

> *I am a strain-er here withinna foar-in laan*
> *I ho is far away ah-pawna old-en straan*
> *Am ass a door teebee of relmsby on da sea*
> *I'm here on biss-niss for I'm King.*

Eventually, we sang the hymn enough times for me to pick out the words. But knowing the words left me undecided about their figurative meanings. I knew the "golden strand" meant Somewhere Else like heaven, but I also thought it might mean Somewhere Else like Canada, which was the mythic home my parents talked about. Canada was a rich place with lots of gold. I had been there when I was a preschooler, and I could remember Grandpa Adamson's black Chevrolet whispering down a highway smooth as glass.

Our chapel hymns celebrated the impossibility of home

and the permanence of pilgrimage. We were not like the thorny *garar,* or acacia trees, rooted deep in the red Ethiopian clay. We were like the *bahar-zaff,* or eucalyptus trees, imported from Australia. Their Amharic name literally meant "overseas trees." You could transplant these Australian gum trees and then chop them down every other year, and they still sent out pungent green shoots, even on this other side of the world. We were here on business, rather like the children whose parents worked in the diplomatic corps. These embassy kids would attend Bingham for a year or two and then their parents would be transferred, and we never saw them again. We stayed longer, but on a limited contract defined by the length of a visa.

I knew, too, we were singing about God the King, not a real king like Emperor Haile Selassie I, Lion of Judah and King of Kings. Yet this knowledge didn't stop me wondering if Ethiopia was a foreign land. But how could it be a foreign land when it was the only land I knew with any certainty? I knew I was a foreigner in the Ethiopians' land. It was not my land, but I knew no other. So which land was the one "Far, far away, in heathen darkness dwelling"? Maybe it depended on where you were when you sang the song.

And how were we students to understand ourselves? Sent away to boarding school at the age of six, I saw my mother and father for a weekend once every month or six weeks. Some children, whose parents could only get to Addis by plane, had to wait for Christmas, Easter, and summer holidays to be with their families. There were kids who felt abandoned by their parents at Bingham, and I certainly hated to go back after weekends home. But I think I speak honestly when I say that, although I missed my parents, I loved school. The dorm was twenty friends your age at a permanent pyjama party. And these friends became as much like family members as my older brother and sister, who had gone to Bingham before me and were there to help me adjust to life away from home.

Bingham offered plenty of diversions – besides periodic Crusades in the boys' dorm. The library had rows and rows of books whose spines were washed every afternoon with warm sunshine from the big west windows. Upstairs, a whole room full of *National Geographic* magazines offered pictures of sharks and naked people and volcanoes. The wide, green soccer pitch urged us to whinny and gallop like the Black Stallion and his wild mares. In the school's six acres of *bahar-zaff* woods, we built forts and dug caves into the red hillsides.

The dorm too, offered comforts. Mrs. Johnson had told us we should think of it as home-away-from-home. And she tried hard to make it so. There was solace during story time, just before lights out when she gathered pyjama-ed and bathrobed boys on her livingroom carpet and read the Laura Ingalls Wilder "Little House" books aloud. While Laura's Pa bowed his fiddle, we sang:

> *Oh give me a home*
> *Where the buffalo roam*
> *Where the deer and the antelope play*
> *Where seldom is heard a discouraging word*
> *For what can the antelope say?*

When we chortled our replacement of the song's last line, Mrs. Johnson frowned and said, "Some boys are just a bit giddy." But she didn't click her fingers. Clicking was reserved for prayer.

Wilder's stories of homemaking in a land we could only imagine riveted our ears to Mrs. Johnson's voice. We listened in rapt attention to careful directions on how to make calico curtains or sugar donuts. What did we know about the best way to saw ice blocks from a frozen lake? What did we know of keeping sleigh horses' noses defrosted on frigid Dakota nights? Next to nothing. But these stories were our stories, acquainting us with the world far, far away which our parents called "home."

After story hour we went to the bathroom to brush teeth and wash up. Every event had its own entertainments. In the bathroom you could practice seeing how far you could stand from the sink and still hit the bowl when you spit out your rinse water. You could play the same game when you peed at the urinal. Then, you could slick back your hair with a wet comb and pretend to be Mr. Schneider. Or, you could hide away partial tubes of Colgate toothpaste and enjoy the peppermint taste at your leisure the next day in your fort of *baharzaff* branches. In the fort, you could get dizzy on the menthol smell of green eucalyptus, a scent as pungent as the English-made bottles of Vicks Mrs. Mead, the school nurse, kept on a shelf in the infirmary. There was always something interesting to do at Bingham – so many things to do that, sometimes, visits from Mom and Dad seemed like an intrusion.

But a weekend visit home to Obi would quickly dismantle my indifference. I would develop sudden headaches when we had to drive back to Addis and school. I could even turn on a mild temperature when Mother tested me with the thermometer. Such scenes watered my parents' eyes when they waved goodbye and drove out the school gates. They hated to live apart from their children, but what else could they do and still follow the call God had placed on their lives? They had given up the care of their own parents for the care of God, and now they had to give the care of their children up to God, too. Bingham was the best solution, my parents reasoned, not only because it gave us a good education but also because it was run by their mission. My mother served several terms on the school board and so would have had a say in what went on. Our parents loved my siblings and me and wanted to be with us. But God's work came first.

Seek ye first the Kingdom of God
And His righteousness
And all these things
Shall be added unto you
Allelu, alleluia.

We sang the words, and I knew what they meant. God came first, family second. We children were loved, but we stood in line behind God. The song, however, was subtler than this obvious meaning. It celebrated a contradiction. If you put God first, the song said, then everything else you desired would be added as well. The tricky part was that you had to keep the order straight. You couldn't just pretend to put God first merely to get all the things you really wanted. That would be cheating. You had to put God first, period. We knew the story of how God told Abraham to take his son, Isaac, on to a mountaintop and offer him as a sacrifice. It was a test. Not until Abraham actually raised the knife glinting into the sunlight could God be sure that Abraham loved him first. And when God was sure, he rewarded Abraham with flocks and herds and a whole nation of descendants through his son Isaac, who, of course, was spared the knife.

So the hymn taught us a paradox of love: when God's work came first, family would come first, too – in a different way. God would make sure. I understood, just like the embassy kids, who didn't stay in the dorm because their parents lived and worked in Addis. Even though they lived at home, they knew their mother's or father's day at the office had to come first. So they didn't complain about being raised by nannies and housemaids and chauffeurs. They had to negotiate their parents' commitments just like we did.

We did not know childhood could be any different, for the missionary story was the air we breathed. We needed that air to sing our hymns. And these hymns carried compensations for us children, too. If heaven was our real home and we were merely passin' through this earth, so too our real father was God. If our earthly parents had to be absent, our heavenly Father was just a prayer away. And this father was a King, Creator of the Universe, Potentate of Time. We were soldiers in his army.

The hymn "Onward Christian Soldiers" was our grade one class's LAC favourite. The martial rhythm inspired parades down the dormitory hall, regiments of roommates who shouldered brooms and floor mops and shouted the words:

Onward Christian soldiers, marching as to war
With the cross of Jesus going on before
Christ the royal commander leads us as we go
Forward into battle, see the banners blow
Onward Christian soldiers marching as to war
With the cross of Jesus going on before.

Marching was the closest we ever got to dancing. It made our hearts race. Our arms and legs entered the music in time with our roommates' arms and legs, and the music welled up in our bodies till it burst out our lips with all the force of our lungs. We drummed on plastic pails and wastepaper cans until Mrs. Mead banged on the ceiling of the infirmary one storey below. We heard none of her protests. Parade! Parade! We were soldiers on parade!

We were as full of glory and purpose as the parades I had seen at Obi mission station where Mom and Dad taught school. The orderly lines and the straight-straight backs had made the Oromo students more than children. They had looked ready and strong, as though they had made a firm resolve and were on their way to secure it. The tri-coloured flag of Ethiopia – green for growth, yellow for gold, and red for blood – rippled powerfully from the top of a long *bahar-*

zaff pole. The Emperor's insignia of the Lion of Judah, with his standard clutched proudly in one paw and jutting over his powerful shoulder, shimmered and danced in the middle band of yellow-gold.

> *Etyopia, hoy!*
> *Dess ye-bellish*
> *Be-Amlakish hile be-Negusish*
> *Tebaberowal inah arbignochish....*

The national anthem soared from the marching lips, a proud prayer of accomplishment and promise. I knew some of the Amharic words. I knew the first three lines meant "O Ethiopia / Sing out your joy/ In the power of your God and King," but I didn't know till I was an adult what *Tebaberowal* (united together) and *arbignochish* (your patriot-ancestors) meant. What did I know of the Oromo resentments against the Amhara landowners who came at harvest time from Addis Ababa to collect their half of the tenants' crops? What did I know of the secret indignation building toward the overthrow of Haile Selassie in 1974? Nothing at all. His Majesty's noble hairline was permanently etched on the copper coins. His reign was as necessary as money. He was *garar,* as permanent as Ethiopia itself. The song made a family of all Ethiopians forever. To my preschool eyes, the Oromo marchers were uniformly Ethiopian. I couldn't join the parade because I was Canadian. They had brown skin; I had pink. Zenebech and Fantaye's school would teach them Amharic; my school would teach me English. My young heart had thrilled with the grandeur of the parade as well as the sight of Ato Fergassa, one of the Oromo schoolteachers, thrashing with a green *baharzaff* switch the bare legs of a student whose feet could not find the beat of the march.

The songs at Bingham confirmed what I had already

known. Our marches were different from theirs. *"Etyopia, Hoy!"* was a song to which I could never belong. Our hymns, like theirs, urged us to be happy under the power of God and King, but our God and our King were different from theirs. Our God was real and our King, figurative. Their King was real (I had seen him walk down a red carpet) but their God, questionable. They couldn't have the same God we did because we sang "One Door and Only One." And so we couldn't be united together, nor did we share the same patriot-ancestors. We were not *garar;* we were *bahar-zaff.* We were not endemic, but an improving strain. So I couldn't be part of the Obi parade; it was out of the question. And every Sunday in LAC, with an awareness that grew by increments, I stood with the others at the grade-one bench and sang:

> *I am a stain-er here withinna foar-in laan*
> *My home is far away ah-pawna gold-en straan*
> *Am ass a door teebee of relmsby on da sea*
> *I here on biss-niss for I'm King.*

OF REMNANTS AND RICHES

Pauline Holdstock

I AM STANDING AT A MARKET STALL IN THE *Mercato Nuovo,* the tourist market in the centre of Florence, a vibrant razzle of silk in front of me, silk of every imaginable colour (an artist's palette!) reaching from the gritty pavement to the canvas awning overhead and extending the entire width of the stall. My head is crammed with research. It's why I'm here. For the last year at home on Vancouver Island, surrounded by heavy Douglas firs and mists creeping in from the Pacific, I've inhabited the bright gold and lapis of fifteenth-century Italy. Through books of every kind, including out-of-print books acquired through the Internet, I've lived in a virtual Florence and been a receptacle for information on every aspect of the Renaissance city, from the structure of its patrician society to the practice of stuffing food (almonds, figs, small birds, pies) inside other food (bigger pies, bigger birds, peacocks) to escape the sumptuary laws forbidding – well – sumptuousness.

At home I enjoyed a virtual banquet of my own, feasting my eyes on superb reproductions of all the major art works of the city: Cimabue, Giotto, Botticelli, della Robbia, Donatello – some of them already by 1500 long held in the highest esteem, all of them with names themselves practically good enough to eat. I lived in another world, memorizing street plans circa 1490 and poring over architectural drawings and recipes for gesso. Through the printed word, I heard the voices of Lorenzo de' Medici singing carnival songs and Leonardo da Vinci giving instruction in the proper manner of dissecting a human cadaver. I was swept away by the outrageous sexual exploits of the goldsmith, sculptor, and braggart, Cellini, and soothed, in calm counterpoint, by the temperate voice of Lucca Landucci, modest apothecary who most conveniently for me recorded in his diary an unruffled account of the daily comings and goings of fifteenth-century Florence.

And all of this information poured into me as if I were a vessel created for its sole purpose, a blank disk waiting to be filled; only now, suddenly, standing in front of this silk stall, I'm picking up another stream. I'm conscious now of the whole long history of this city's magnificent cloth manufacture, the great bolts of luxurious wools and glorious satins and silks, reduced to these rows and rows of head scarves and ties, these Gucci knock-offs. Like a haywire short-wave radio, I'm picking up a scramble of German-French-English-American from the tourist babble around me, from the flyer advertising *Radio Maria* FM88.6 and the peeling poster advertising *One Love Hi-pawa Concert Starfuckers Rock n' Roll*. This second stream mixes with the first so that I feel like a flask in which a marvellous new solution is being mixed.

There's no stopping it. I recall the smell of stale beer and the urine stains on the five-hundred-year-old steps of the *Ospedale degli Innocenti* where the foundlings of the city were once laid at the tender (one hopes) mercy of the Guild of Silk Merchants; I recall the insistent beep of a hand-held computer game in the courtyard of the Brancacci Chapel. The words of the plaintive Englishwoman in the money exchange, *I don't know what today is,* suddenly take on a new significance. Everywhere I turn, the same alchemy is at work and the two streams are so mingled, so compounded that I can no longer say if what I see are sad tatters or splendid remnants.

For one of these shuddering time-jolts, come with me to the Palazzo Strozzi, fifteenth-century family home of the fabulously rich Filippo Strozzi. "Palace," with its connotations of gracious living is not the word for this rectangular pile of rough-cut stone built to brood over its wealth. It's a massive manifestation of power and domination, a fortress. Its front door is thick enough to deflect a cruise missile. Its windows open from behind rigid iron bars. As a symbol, it's the Renaissance equivalent of the banking tower. But gleaming glass towers lack its square-shouldered solidity and are unlikely – as befits erections based on speculation – to be around in five-hundred-years' time. The Strozzi Palace seems to me to be based on muscle and sweat and gold, the prize of the bully who has won his ground.

It may be my imagination, but the sun seems to cloud over every time I come here. I come to work in the *Gabignetto Vieussex,* a tiny library with access from the central courtyard. It's the home of an institution engaged in significant cultural projects but it has an impoverished air about it – grey walls, metal-topped tables in hospital puce – as if it would die for a shot of that Strozzi wealth. I feel like a poor relation too shabby to be allowed in one of the elegant salons. The walls of this little room are three and a half, perhaps four feet thick, cut away at an angle at the high windows to admit the light. It could be a dungeon. If you stay long in this room, you begin to feel as dusty and faded, as parched, as the books.

But we do not have to stay. What I want to show you is outside in the square, you can hear its tinny music. There is no one about, but there, turning in the centre, in the long shadow of the palazzo, is a glittering, ornamented carousel. And if you stand a moment and allow the surprise to settle, if you listen for a moment to the music that no amount of tinselly sparkle can keep from sounding forlorn, you will begin to think positively medieval thoughts: about the ambitions and achievements of bankers; about the faux glitter of this world. For all the imposing grandeur of their palace, Palla Strozzi and his son Filippo are still as dead as the deserted square; if they were as obsessed with fortune as the building suggests, it is quite fitting that no children play here and only May breezes ride the roundabout.

NOWHERE IS THIS VIOLENT COLLISION OF IMPRESsions, this speed-of-light rewind into *then* and fast-forward back again, more forcefully experienced than in the heart of the city itself. To come upon the Duomo, the glorious monumental confection that is the cathedral of Santa Maria del Fiore, suddenly – for there is no other way in this maze of narrow streets – is to be dazzled by the brilliance of its conjuring trick in a city of yellow stone. Nothing prepares you for the shock of your first glimpse, just as nothing, no visual image, prepares you for the blue of the Caribbean, or, here on the West Coast, your first killer whale, your first hummingbird. You knew it was there all along, certainly; Brunelleschi's massive brick cupola has been appearing over terra cotta rooftops and disappearing behind yellow walls all the way, like the great shoulder of a shy, crouching giant. But now, standing in the square, you can only be dazzled by its outrageous, improbable and improbably lovely cladding of shining white and pink and green marble. It is a conjuring trick in stone, and you feel yourself at once as naive and as dumbstruck as any fifteenth-century traveller. A white-uniformed mounted policeman rides by and lets his coolly appraising gaze rest for a moment on the freshest and loveliest in the shambly crowd of tourists, and he is suddenly a proud *condottieri,* she a hapless maiden. But he rides on, and we are fast-forwarding again to the present while she gets on with the serious business of sharing out gum to her friends.

The noise and the press of people here on the cathedral steps cannot be so very different from the atmosphere that would have prevailed on any one of the many holy days at this church built to accommodate thirty thousand faithful at a time. It is a human swarm. There is a certain olfactory swirl created by so many bodies standing in the sun: leather, vinyl, sweat, mint, shampoo (smells that may be less noxious but not less toxic), sunscreen, garlic, tobacco smoke, breath, and yes, in the face of all scientific advances, wind.

And everyone here in the Piazza wants to buy or to sell something at the great honey pot of the Duomo. The engravings and aquatints of later centuries have been replaced by colour prints and postcards of world-famous masterpieces. Challenged only by Rafael's much-abused cherubs, Michelangelo's David is top of the billboards. He is everywhere: whole Davids, parts of David, David's head, David's hand, and especially David's genitals, sometimes computer-enhanced and once wearing Groucho glasses and moustache. The buzz is all around the souvenir stalls, just as it must have been around the vendors of relics and religious indulgences. Of course! It's so obvious. Tourists. Pilgrims. It just happens that in Italy our circuits are identical. No wonder we keep colliding. Look at us lining up at the doors to the cathedral museum, guidebooks like missals in hand, ready to be blessed by the experience of beholding genius. And there it is again, that collision: a newspaper headline announces that the Vatican has just issued an update on its inventory of indulgences, including one that might be earned from giving up smoking. Once you put on these lenses that look both ways in time, you can see forever. Sometimes they will deceive you. If you attend a mass here, you will assume you are on the receiving end of a world-class recording broadcast on a state-of-the-art sound system – until you realize you are hearing the human voice exulting against the arching stones exactly as it would have been heard five hundred years ago. Enough. It tires the brain and leaves it like an overloaded circuit board zapping and crazily sparking. We'll go, since he is everywhere beckoning, to see David.

ON THE WAY TO THE *Galleria dell'Accademia* THERE IS A gauntlet of pavement artists and poster sellers. Otherwise there is a pleasing lack of commerce. The *Accademia* exudes serious devotion to aesthetics. It is spacious and spare. The sense of anticipation in the foyer, before entering the David space, is palpable; this is high-tension art. We enter at one end of a long gallery, the colour of thin cream. At wide intervals down its length, two on each side, are the Prisoners, *I Schiavi*. These are four of the six slaves begun by Michelangelo for the tomb of Pope Julius II and never completed. Their silent presence is tremendous, almost in the original sense of the word: to excite trembling. I for one become instantly an unbeliever. Absurdly, in defiance of all documentation to the contrary, I can believe only one explanation for these human figures in superhuman scale struggling eternally to free themselves from the stone: Michelangelo *meant* to leave them trapped. The symbolism of the work and its clear reference to the human condition is overwhelming, almost crushing. I find it suddenly necessary to sit down, to stay with them a while and listen to the reverberations of time trapped within the marble, the spirit within the flesh. Light pours into this quiet room from the long windows high on the opposite wall. And as I sit within my own experience, within the gallery, the windows, obeying some invisible electronic sensor, detect a threat to this climate-controlled environment and slide closed and the long white curtains glide silently together to shut out the late sun. The slaves imprisoned in stone, we in our technology.

The experience is powerful. I pay homage to David in his semicircular space at the far end of the gallery, alone and splendid – but I shall remember the slaves.

WE NEED AIR. IT'S TIME TO GET OUT OF THE CITY with its maze of narrow streets. There is a bus that climbs the steep hill to Fiesole. It winds its way between the high stone walls of villas, brushing the thick foliage that overarches the road, and passing every so often an iron gate that teases with a glimpse of a view back towards the rooftops of the city. The bus is crowded. Standing room only. We all dip and bob inside trying to catch one more preview of this new perspective of Florence. Almost at the summit, the bus disgorges us in the main square of this small town built on the site of an ancient Etruscan fortress and commanding a truly wraparound view of the valley of the Arno and the lovely undulating Tuscan landscape. Up here you can breathe, you can see. You can almost drink the limpid beauty of the blue-green hills rolling away to the edge of sight. They entice you to walk out from the pretty square with its pollarded plane trees and its ancient town hall, its raised loggia hung with baskets of flowers; to separate yourself from the flock, become a wayward sheep instead for a while and take one of the narrow streets that does not lead to a monastery or an amphitheatre; to breathe the air and imagine yourself into the landscape.

But already there is a distraction. There is a crowd over there by the ancient medieval cathedral of San Romolo. It's a wedding, and the guests are arriving. The place to be is with the other tourists on a cobbled road that runs at a steep angle up from the tiny piazza in front of the cathedral and affords a perfect view of the Romanesque entrance. Everyone hopes for a glimpse of white, an ethereal airiness of veil, a drift of immaculate satin. But here first is the overture, a visual fanfare in the form of sleek limousines that slew to a standstill on the stones of the forecourt and release their elegant occupants, the wedding guests. And, oh, what guests! They know their part, are Oscar winners all, pausing to lay long pearl-tipped fingers on the crown of a shiny black straw, bending to adjust the blue ribbon on the daughter's frock, checking the seam of the stocking (yes the seam, yes silk, in this age of Lycra) with a backward, over-the-shoulder glance that shows to perfection the arch of the eyebrow, the flutter of the eyelid. It's all a wonderful tableau – the wind whipping the edge of a narrow navy linen coat, the quadruple kisses of greeting, on each cheek and then each cheek again, the clipped trees in their great terracotta pots flanking the doorway, lemons glowing from their dark leaves. And here at last is our reward for our part as extras in this crowd scene – the bride untangling her dazzling self from the creamy leather interior of the car. Ahh! We make all the right noises as she emerges, and as she turns to bestow a smile on us there it is again, that collision in time. In five hundred years we have not changed at all but are as simple as any lumpen cloth worker or cloddy vagabond feeling pleased and possibly blessed by this smile from a bride.

Florence has not changed and nor have we. The city itself has made that clear. The same sympathies and affections, the same appetites and the same vanities persist across cultures. The extravagant fashions in the Via Tornabuoni echo the opulent gowns of Ghirlandaio's women; the self-help books telling us how to live well are not so far removed from Savanarola's posthumous sixteenth-century best-seller, *The Art of Dying*; the clients at Eduardo Scissorhands, having bottles of colour emptied on their heads are not so different from the discontented Florentine ladies who treated their hair with a brew of orange peel, sulphur, and eggshells and went up to the rooftop terraces of their houses to bleach it in the sun.

More than any other feature of the city down there in its beautiful valley, the fresco paintings make the parallels clear. Look at us with our long love affair with film, which shows no sign of abating, and look again at all those frescoes. How they must have amazed and delighted with their new trick of perspective! Men and women so lifelike "they lack only the power of speech," as Vasari put it, catching his breath in amazement. They were video; they fed the endless craving for story. Some, the great narrative cycles, are the forefathers of the comic book; some are loving biographies, others blatant mythologizing; still others, cathartic and powerful, are magnificently composed cinematic shots in a great drama that ends at the Last Judgment. Like film, they have the power to conjure the hellish vision from a box of colours – or to seduce with a dream of possibilities. Like film, they show the preoccupations, the obsessions, the fears and dreams of their age. And then there is sex and violence, the ecstatic Saint Stephens bristling with arrows – but if we go there we shall never get back.

Northrop Frye observed that great literature is always great literature in any age; it does not get any "better" as it develops over the centuries. So too with humans: there really is no such thing as progress. But this is not a lament; it is a jubilant discovery. It is peculiarly comforting to know that moon walks and global corporations and cyberspace have changed nothing. We have the same ability to hurt and destroy; dying in one of our abominable wars is as pointless and painful as dying in a Ghibbeline squabble. But the converse is almost too good to be true: we have the same burning loves as Petrarch, the same passion as Michelangelo and when we look at della Robbia's foundlings, the *gettatelli*, asking for protection, or at a small anonymous Madonna and Child, the child clutching, probably squeezing, a small bird, we know we have the same tenderness.

The bride has gone into the church. The bridegroom, looking as dashing and slightly alarmed as we knew he would, has followed. Across the main square, there is a narrow lane that will lead us out of the town and away from the crowd. An even narrower walled lane leads off to the right and curves around the face of the hill, opening on one side to a landscape of incomparable beauty and harmony. We stand at a stone wall above the garden of a house hidden behind a huge pine to the left. In front, its narrow garden falls away in a tumble of shiny spring grass tangled with wild flowers. There are two giant azaleas exuberant with blossom, a smothering of wisteria over an old wall, a small stand of foxgloves, some lilies growing up recklessly at the bole of a peach tree. From this shambly Eden wafts a perfume fresher than lilac, less spicy than wall-flower. A perfumer would die for the code of this scent. Beyond the garden, the land slopes away to a valley running across our line of sight, its far side rising again in a symphony of greens and greys and white as the olive groves and vineyards and chestnut trees embroider this incredible tapestry. All, all exactly as in any Book of Hours. Nothing changed, nothing. It is a harmony that caresses the eye and nourishes the spirit. The hill with its greens and silvers, its little blocks of ochre and its spears of darkest cypress rises up to a ridge where there is a village and a large villa and behind this another distant hill, and behind that another, on into the misty green-blue and palest blue-green – nature making her own most eloquent plea for respect in our abusive relationship with her. Easy here to believe in the possibility of heaven, the certainty of love.

Tomorrow I shall leave Florence. I shall walk to the station past stalls displaying soccer scarves like the banners of ancient guilds. And from the train window I shall see an old couple of sixty years or so sitting on the stone bench in the station concourse. He will be short and broad with a Roman face straight out of Asterix. She will be lumpily shaped and have poor hair and a weak chin like a character from an old TV show. Oh, but she will love him. She will have her head on his shoulder; he will have his arm round her, she hers round him, and now and then they will kiss, and no they will not be drunk and it will all be so intimate that I shall not want to watch any longer. I shall try instead to record the beauty of this landscape, and I shall take out my journal and give them back their privacy.

STONE JOURNEY

Eileen Delehanty Pearkes

*You may melt your metals and cast them into the
most beautiful moulds you can; they will never
excite me like the forms which this molten earth
flows out into.* – H.D. Thoreau

I FOUND A SMALL, ALMOST SQUARE PIECE OF ARGILLITE
the other day. The rock is waxy-smooth, like a hunk of
hard cheese, and holds the olive green of a summer thun-
derstorm on its muted surface. Plucking my treasure from a
beach of coarse, unpolished granite and limestone pebbles, I
lifted it toward the weakening October sun. Rays of autumn
light tilted across the surface of the stone in lustrous curves. A
silhouette against the shimmering sun, this hard piece of the
earth had a story to tell.

I live in a narrow valley in southeastern British Columbia,
a deep cleaving of alpine peaks just west of the great Rocky
Mountains. Almost everyone I know here takes an interest in
rocks, whether to scale them, mine them for minerals, roll
them out of the way or simply collect them. I moved here six
years ago. Gradually, I have become more like everyone.

In these Columbia Mountains, some people say we have
only half a sky, the other half engulfed by the rippling, cobalt
layers of granite peaks too numerous to all have a name.
Geology refers to this terrain as "youthful," the glaciers having
passed through as recently as 9,500 years ago. The powerful,
adolescent surge of mountains crowding for space all around
testifies to the genesis of landscape, to the rugged and unfor-

giving nature of geological movement, to the intense energy of a newly formed place. Near the base of these slanted mountains, cliffs of igneous rock interpose their weight, casting inert shadows onto the swelling waters of Kootenay Lake.

Rock defines this landscape. It is everywhere that water isn't. Even where granite and schist cannot be seen in an extrusive bulge, substance lies thinly disguised beneath the soil of forested terrain. Mineral deposits dot the region's geological survey maps like birdseed spilled from a feeder. A brief walk into the woods almost always yields a lichen-crusted pile of boulders on a steep slope, the memory of a once terrifying avalanche. No day in the garden would be complete without a shovel hitting a rock: usually granite, sometimes too large to dig around, often dense beyond lifting.

Geologists would say that there is nothing special about the Kootenay region, that rock defines all landscape to some extent, and they are right. But in this place of towering granite and loosely strewn boulders, I have felt most palpably the connection between rock and the terrain, between rock and human existence. Rock is simply unavoidable in these tight, rippling valleys, and its configurations impose limitations that are insurmountable, even to the most clever of human beings. The ineluctable heft of this element mocks my own brief and ephemeral visit, reminds me that I have much listening to do.

Stones are the most concrete of natural elements, yet their origins and meanings remain highly abstract. Even the message of a small pebble stretches so far back in time as to test our ability to hear it. Geology books talk of millions and billions of years, not decades. The transformations of rock cannot be absorbed the way we perceive the life cycle of a tree or the movement of the tides, by our own witness. This natural history has to be taken more on faith, and that is the challenge. Stone, the foundation of landscape, has its own narrative. It aches to define us, to remind us of our place in history.

Without any scientific background to speak of or any illustrated books to identify what I find, I am what most serious, educated petrologists would call an amateur rockhound. Our varnished dining room sideboard holds haphazard bowls full of rough limestone, granite, and mica-laden "jewel stones" – my children's favourites for the way they glisten silver and bronze in the hot summer sun. In the kitchen, on the windowsill above the sink, I keep a few round rocks whose names I do not know yet, but I treasure them for their soft, creamy colours: the palest of butter yellow, apple-blossom pink, luminous white. They are moons for me – placid, spherical and permanently risen. I watch them while I spend many hours peeling potatoes or doing dishes as my mother once did. I watch them while I wish, as my mother once did, for a nicer view out the window.

Tucked in beside my moons rest some hard-edged hunks of grey marble. The marble, threaded with smoky wisps of white or black, is so unlike the statue or floor tiles I've always associated with that type of stone. My pieces are unrefined and have mutability embedded in their dusty veins. Marble forms from a bed of crushed seashell, compressed by the quiet weight of time to become limestone. Having been cooked in one of the earth's deeply buried kilns, the limestone transforms into an element much harder, more permanent, more able to hold a polish. But originally, this marble was a gathering of sea creatures, whose long passage has taken a brief detour to my windowsill.

Often I come across a single rock with layered texture, specks of mineral, or veins of surprise and pop it into my pocket to wonder about. Before I learned about metamorphosis, deeply buried fires and explosive pressure, layered rock used to impress me as nothing more than a visual marvel. I now study two bands of colour within one rock and try to imagine the moment millions of years ago when those halves were pushed together, just as my mother once pinched pastry at the edge of a pie. I run my fingers along the join line of the rock but find no groove, no place where pounding could loosen the bond. These rocks are like children, each one formed and pressed by forces outside one's reach. My children, my mother's children, her mother's children – the permanent, unbreakable union of a chance encounter, wearing the join line, making two into one.

We often spend weekends in the summer and fall exploring the shores of Kootenay Lake by boat. Given the steep, impassable terrain that falls precipitously to the edge of the lake, many of the nicest beaches have no roads nearby and can only be reached by water. The Sinixt and Ktunaxa First Nations – who camped on these beaches uninterrupted for thousands of years – used the lake and rivers of the region as liquid highways. With their elegant, superbly designed canoes, they reached many of the best summer fishing and hunting spots. Our aluminum outboard motorboat is a poor substitute, but I am grateful for it all the same. It takes us to many beaches that feel less touched by development, to more isolated places along the rocky fringes of this lake where the weight of spirit can be felt.

The shores of Kootenay lake are heavily pebbled, mostly with glacial deposits of granitics: dense, unbreakable rocks that have taken a ride on moving sheets of ice to emerge round and plump, seemingly undisturbed by the passage, resolute about their place of rest. Occasionally, we find a limestone beach, and these are my favourite. Finer-textured, less dense and smoother than granite, limestone pebbles clink together when I scoop some up. They smell strangely clean. Yet when I run my hands through a pile, they feel dusty with a powder many centuries in the making.

These granitic and limestone pebbles form a cast of many thousands on the lake's beaches. Stone players left behind from another age, they invite interest merely by their multitude. When dry, these rocks appear a ubiquitous grey, white, beige or dark blue, like rolled-up socks in a drawer. But when the gentle, freshwater waves bathe their surfaces, they sparkle like opaque crystals. Their colours deepen to complex charcoal, platinum, salmon pink and cerulean tinged with forest green. They catch the eye, and then curiosity about their journey begins.

I started collecting rocks several summers ago in the same way a child gathers autumn leaves from the ground – simply for appearance. I spent a good deal of time looking at wet limestone and granite, finding the colours so much more prominent, the beauty more obvious to understand as an attraction. I could wade for hours along the shallow edge of the lake, hounding the pebbles that shimmered beneath the magnifying, sun-bright water while my feet grew numb in the chilly water.

But the longer I have collected, the more I have looked above the surface of the water, further beneath the surface of the rock. I can now pick up a dry, ordinary hunk and hold it still for my imagination to listen to its passage. I am learning that beyond the crust of every stone, even those without obvious features of value or striking appearance, rests an enduring history. Embedded in the rock is a trek across time and place, a movement along sheets of ice or veins of magma, a series of transitions that belie the inert qualities of stone, that dwarf our own movements across the curving earth.

On one summer boat-camping trip, a few months before I found the argillite, I sat sifting carefully while the children played until my hand held only small, creamy-white, oval pebbles of limestone. Each of them sparkled with fine shavings of quartz crystals like the tiny sequins sewn to the tulle on my mother's wedding dress. Of course I brought that handful of white stones home with me. Now they sit in a white bowl, where I marvel at their purity, their faint iridescence, their strange innocence. Sometimes I pick one of them up and caress the powdery surface, coating my fingertips with the talc of my mother's dreams.

Unlike many rockhounds who collect for scientific specimens, for mineral deposits, for a representative assortment from this montane region, I have gradually learned to gather stones for feelings, for inexplicable attractions and inarticulate appeal, for the qualities that cannot be labelled. Casting my eyes downward – on lake beaches, abandoned railway beds and river fringes – I allow myself to pick up a certain piece because it asks me to.

That is what happened when I saw the argillite during a last boat excursion before winter, on an October day which seemed promising and fair but held only false warmth sent from a tired sun. We intended to make the most of the sun's waning comfort, and set out for a day trip to one of our favourite summer beaches. There, in a sea of dusty blue and grey limestone where we stopped to eat our lunch, lay a glassy green stone of entirely distinct texture, a stone calling out to me to pick it up. Only when I held it close did I realize that it was Kootenay Argillite.

Geologists call my little stone salisified argillite, a name originating from argillos, the Greek word for clay. Books describe argillite as being relatively hard, but smooth-textured like shale. Argillite's microscopic quartz crystals are hidden within the density of an ancient clay. These buried crystals catch the light not in sharp points but with a gentle lustre. My flat, green shard of stone does not have a discernible grain like a hunk of granite. Here is an infinitesimal melding of particles too small to separate with one's eyes. Here is a spirit too dense and compressed to sparkle.

Salisified argillite formed in the Kootenay region many millions of years ago when the fine clay of a silt-laden ocean floor was heated and pressed by fires deep within the earth. Eventually, when the ocean retreated, those new slabs of rock shrugged up to became part of the Selkirk Mountains now thousands of feet above sea level, peaks casting dense autumn shadows along the west side of Kootenay Lake, opposite the beach where we had stopped. As Selkirk glaciers washed back and forth in tidal sheets of ice, chunks of argillite eventually worked themselves loose from the alpine ridges. Like growing children, the chunks tumbled away from their source down to the lakeshore, where they came to rest along the outwash of the Kaslo River.

Local archaeologists have a different name for salisified argillite, one that reflects the importance of place in human history: "Kootenay Argillite." They theorize that the Sinixt and Ktunaxa First People exploring Kootenay Lake by canoe during the summer months discovered the unusual stone while they fished for trout near the outwash. The hunters realized thousands of years ago that these hard chunks of mudstone could be smacked against an even harder piece of granite, loosening clean shards of the metamorphosed ocean floor to form finely worked arrowheads or knife blades.

Having no material more permanent than rock at their disposal, this region's neolithic First People used ingenuity to adapt many forms of stone for their needs. The Kootenay argillite, wilful enough to penetrate the tough hide of a caribou, but not too obstinate to be shaped into a weapon point, appealed to them for obvious reasons. I wonder what they thought about when they searched for the right piece of argillite. Did they feel the weight of spirit that I feel when I pick up a dense, sun-warmed stone and hold it in my palm?

Archaeological work of the last 50 years – both accidental discoveries on summer beaches and systematic, government-funded digs – has pieced together the human stage of argillite's journey. Along a tranquil curve at the north end of Kootenay

Lake, near Johnson's Landing and several miles north of the argillite deposits at the Kaslo River outwash, aboriginals found the extended hours of sunlight, viewpoint cliffs and habitat for deer that made an ideal summer hunting camp. Framed by towering mountains on all sides, they smacked hunks of argillite against granite boulders, loosening clean flakes, littering the beach with tool-making debris that tells the story of their craft. As the stone was shaped, a raven would croak on the mountain's forested shoulders, smoke from fires would curl into a haze over the placid lake, clouds would sometimes wrap a wispy cape around the alpine tiaras of the Selkirk Mountains.

But the small piece of stone that I discovered was on a beach far south of Johnson's Landing and the Kaslo river outwash – more than forty miles down the lake, in fact. Knowing the scientific origins of Kootenay Argillite and the archaeological theories of its use, I was surprised when the smooth scrap asked me to collect it from an obscure shoreline tucked in against the steep side of a rising mountain on the Lake's far and opposite shore. I may never understand exactly how this piece of argillite – so unlike any other stone around it, so far from its specific geological source – reached the beach where I plucked it up.

Anthropologists and archaeologists know that the Sinixt and Ktunaxa were, in summer, people who roamed many of the region's waterways in search of game and fish. In an effort to maximize use of the region's food sources, these people were not inclined to make a permanent camp anywhere along the lakeshore. They preferred to capitalize on the shifting sun exposure throughout the warmer months, as well as the movements of mammals, and passage of fish along the currents of this inland, sweet-watered ocean. When the autumn shadows deepened, they returned to more protected places to live out the winter, sheltered from the raw winds that scrape along the water out of the north.

Right after I found the argillite, I cradled it for a moment in the warm curve of my hand, then called my children over. As they stared into my palm, I gave the stone a story, brought up from the past like a sleeve on a sweater pulled inside out. *This stone came from the west above the lake, high in the Selkirk Mountains,* I explained, pointing with my other hand over their shoulders to the jagged, jewel-crusted skyline. *The First People who came here long before us used this stone for toolmaking. It was special to them because it is hard, but not too hard to be shaped.* The children marvelled for a moment, then raced back down the rocky beach with sticks flying, in search of the wild beasts they had been stalking earlier.

I couldn't fault them for their fleeting interest in my ordinary treasure and its abstract story. These boys were living their own story, more vivid to them at that moment than mine. Fair enough. I sat, turning the waxy slice of stone over and over, looking out across the water where canoes once stroked, wondering about origins.

When I hold my piece of Kootenay Argillite, defining its cool, water-worn texture between thumb and forefinger, I marvel at the mysterious capacity this tiny piece of the earth has – travelling from the floor of an ancient ocean to my fleshy palm, preserving a story about a landscape, moving with durability across time. I wish the stone could take me with it, wherever it is going.

LIGHT ON THE LAND

Rita Moir & Shirley Scott-Bruised Head

YOU KNOW HOW IT IS WHEN YOUR OLD DOG struggles to get up. You say, when the day comes when he can't...and then you name the benchmark. When he can't run and enjoy himself. When he can't get up the stairs without help.

When he shits in the house.

But of course, with your help, he does get up, he does run, he does shine in the sun, the obsidian planes, the feathers of his big setter body lifting in the breeze. My big black dog Connor. He is 16 and has been with me longer than any man. We live alone together in the mountains with our cat Dylan.

I dream of him during all of this, when we are preparing ourselves. For years I've had animal dreams; nudging, budging, bashing at me – buffalo and elk swirling around the back of my old prairie shack – laughing at me, barging and roaring off chortling. Sometimes in dreams, Connor chases them back, his old body struggling over momentous obstacles, the Frank Slide, large prairie. Sometimes he swims across wild rivers to find me and help me. It is odd to sit here on the couch with him by me, planning what I will take with me to Southern Alberta after I have taken him to Nelson to put him to sleep. He wants me by him always now on the couch at night, him with his head by my leg, me with a book in my hand. He doesn't like guests much. He falls a lot. We have gone the route of anti-inflammatory drugs and aspirin and getting his weight down. It's just time, that's all, and we only need to resolve when and where. I know I won't come home after we've been to the vet. I know I'll drive to Southern Alberta where I can be alone, where I've carved an emotional niche for myself for this moment. Where I can be alone at the Buffalo Jump, with sky and land big enough to absorb my loss with wind and silence.

I stroke his head and plan to take his picture with me, to take a wet washcloth in the car because already my eyes are so swollen and chapped from crying that only cold water soothes them. I am thankful my practical Calvinistic side is helping me now, making the lists that will see me through, giving me strength and backbone. It is not often the Calvinism and the poetry work together, more often than not they war in me. But right now, like in any good family, they make a truce in hard times, bring out the best in each other.

My friend Paddy goes with me. Connor is beautiful, walking in the sun. The people at the vet's couldn't be better. I ask them to explain everything. Will he jerk, will he cry out? We lay him on his old sleeping bag, and I hold him. They put in the needle, and he dies. Quick, dignified, and a friend was right; I'm glad I've taken this final responsibility. The vet people say, "Take your time," and leave Paddy and me with Connor. I lie on the floor with him, curled around his big body as we slept together so many years. He's peed all over the bag, and we clean him up. I lie back down with him and the vet people come in and out of the room, going about their routine. "Take your time," they say again, and soon, I am propped up on my elbow petting my dead dog, and chatting with them. I ask about cremation, and the vet brings me in some ashes of another dog to show me what they're like, and tells a long dumb story about scattering ashes to the wind and getting a big hunk in his eye. No one says, "Hurry up," or "That's enough now," or "There're other people waiting."

I wanted to drive that night to Southern Alberta, but it's too far and I've cried so hard it's dangerous. It's wet, dark and November 20. I aim for Fort Macleod, think I'll make Fernie but only make Cranbrook. I call all my family, in Nova Scotia, Minnesota, Manitoba. They all know Connor well. I listen endlessly to the bagpipes of MacPherson's Lament.

Before I left BC, I'd called two people in Fort Macleod, told them haltingly what was happening and why I would be coming. Irene at the Fort Motel, where I've stayed before, booked my room. Shirley Bruised Head I'd met a few times at Head-Smashed-In Buffalo Jump Interpretive Centre, when she'd helped me on some botanical identification and read a manuscript I'd written. She's a writer as well as the Education Officer at the Interpretive Centre, and we've started to visit a bit, too. She said when I arrive, we should have coffee.

When she called   she was feeling pretty bad about having to put her dog down –   to hear her suffer across miles of telephone cable is frustrating,   not the way it should be.   The need to help is strong but listen is all I can do.   She said she would be coming down this way once Connor was gone.   The sadness is overwhelming.   I know the feeling of having people around to help you get through the pain   I remember the good people who came to me   and I understand only too well the emotion.

Irene meets me at the motel door with a hug and key to my room, number 15 with a kitchenette. I like this motel because of all the bright oranges in the rooms. They warmed me once on a cold bleak day, and I haven't forgotten. But room 15 is all beiges and bland – fully equipped but on the shady side of the motel and offering me no hope or colour. I unload the car, put up the picture of Connor, the books I've brought, everything. And each time I walk into the room, I think, "Well, it will do."

And then I think "It isn't good enough right now." I want something that will make me smile this week, the colour orange, sunlight, something when I walk in this door. Irene gives me the key to room 20, where there is sun but no kitchenette. Above the bed is a large framed photo of the coulees bathed in storm light, a big spreading tree on the lip of the coulee. On the desk, an embossed map of the world. Orange towels. A bright multicoloured bedspread. I smile and think, "Fuck the kitchenette" and drag everything over from the other room.

I invite her to the house to spend the afternoon.   I don't invite too many people to my home   but I feel for her: to lose a loved one and to reach out to another takes a great deal of courage. I think about the coulees,   those healing places filled with shrubs of saskatoon   chokecherry   currant   gooseberries   wild mint sage,   those quiet peaceful places filled with sunshine.   The coulee directly east of the house   runs north and south   and across it is a spring;   the spring seeps water down steep sides   year round. To the north of the spring two huge sandstone blocks shine whitely in the sun.   Items found here   trade beads   dishes   the kids know to leave them alone.   Last traces of once-lived lives their journey home assured with prayers and the burning of sweetgrass and sage.

I get my morning at the Buffalo Jump. Alone. It's Saturday, and Shirley invites me to come to her house afterwards. I'm glad it's off season, and I can mostly find moments alone here. The place gets me, like big chords from church organs get me, like bagpipes that drain me and fill me up again. In the hallway, in a dark corner by some stairs, I bury my head in the mane of a big stuffed buffalo, say "Hello Baby," then go out into the wind. Before me are vast blocks of solid colour, wheat-straw blonde forever, blue sky forever. My breathing grows deep, and I know I am a prairie person who has always surrounded myself with solid colours instead of patterns. Solid black dog. Gray cat. Red Table. Blue Floor.

It's a funny thing, this grief. I thought this would be the big moment, out here on the lookout, this place where death and life met, where I could let go, join my howling to the wind's. But instead, I am happy to be alone, look through the viewfinder, identify the mountains. It's how I thought the hardest moment would be his dying, but it wasn't.

Before I leave the Interpretive Centre, I stand by a big rock display, and I like the words that light up on it, "Summer is home days when we move down on the prairies." Ronald Four Horns, who works here, comes over and asks if I have an old man and says how I should come out of the mountains this summer, come down to the prairies and dance at the powwow, and then he asks again if I have an old man. I say a bit jokingly and probably crying too that the only old man I had I put to sleep two days ago and that he wasn't my old man, but better than most. And then Ronald said I'd like Shirley's place because there were lots of dogs there to greet me.

Shirley has given me directions to her house on the Peigan Reserve. The kind of directions an old prairie girl like me likes a lot: "Go down the dirt road and turn at the tree," she says.

Hers is a bare house, lone above the ravines. Seven dogs, at least, greet me. Some are excited and wiggling. Some hang back. Some bark and bluff. Two watch me closely. I greet them all the way they want to be greeted.

The babies   two and a half   one and a half   and an eight-month-old girl are fussing today.   The other two   their parents are whining about not having enough time to themselves   ask me to babysit.   The smell of diapers   toys scattered around   bits of food trail through the house   babies crying   dogs barking magpies stealing dog food   cats jumping up   hanging off the

screens   meowing.   My life is so much fun.   I agree to let the
parents out for the night   but they have to help me clean the
house.   The babies are put to bed;   they sleep right away,   a
small blessing.   Pick up toys   vacuum   sweep the kitchen floor
wash dishes   answer phone   a quick cleaning   a putting away
of daily lives.   Dusting can wait another day.   The babies awake
too soon   scatter toys   tear up magazines.   Why do they misbe-
have just when you need them at their best?   These little people
hold me together   the parents disappear downstairs   I don't mind
but they seem to forget or ignore the fact that I am expecting a
guest.   Showers   setting out of clothing   makeup   gel sound
of hairdryer   twins taking turns speaking to friends on the phone.
These days children are so self-centred.   I make coffee and try to
make the house welcome.   Sometimes the house feels cold   like
the people who live here are merely in transit   maybe because
we are in transit.   This is   just a place to come and stay for the
night –   five years and the boxes are still packed in the basement.

Inside Shirley's place, the TV is on. Figure skating. I was
watching it earlier, too, and sink right into a chair. Hey kids,
she calls out to the back rooms, Lu Chen's on. I smile to
myself. What did I think, Indians don't watch figure skating?

We watch the skaters while the kids get ready to go, and
the coffee perks. The shades are drawn against the hot afternoon sun. There's no snow yet, even in November. The big
grass fires will come later.

She arrives with doughnut holes and cinnamon rolls.   I intro-
duce her to Sonny   his wife B.J.   Riel   Tee   and Sunny-Dawn
my adopted twins Rolanda and Victoria   B.J. and Sonny leave.
A car pulls up and Rolanda and Victoria run out the door calling
out their see you laters.

When they're gone, I ask the kids' names again. Sunny-

Dawn, Tee and Riel. Shirley tells me that the family is somehow related to Gabriel Dumont, and there's usually a baby named Riel in each generation. I look at Riel again thinking, how neat, one of those sweet rewards of living – to connect to the past by the explanation of a child's name. I tell Shirley how back home the Doukhobors will have a commemoration, and someone will read greetings from Russia, from a Tolstoy, generations down from the Leo Tolstoy who helped them come to Canada, and there it is, a connection maintained and nourished through a name.

As I set out coffee cups   she plays with the three babies   on the floor in the middle of the living room.   Sun shines through the window   sparkling off dust motes in the air   impressions of little fingers on glass.

As Shirley walks to the kitchen to pour coffee, I call after her, "Hey Shirley, you cut your hair," and she says, "Yes, it's a Blackfoot custom to cut your hair when you lose someone."

I don't know her family or friends but think perhaps an aunt has died. And then Shirley turns to me and tells me her daughter, Leslie-Dawn was killed in a car crash two months ago. She'd just started college. It was a Saturday morning in September. September 27. Clear open roads. Sunny. The man in the other car lived. Leslie-Dawn died.

I'm not sure what my first response is. I think it is to realize I actually phoned this woman to say my dog was dying and she said, "Come for coffee." She didn't say, "My daughter's dead." She said, "Come for coffee."

And so our time together begins, Shirley's and mine. It could become one of those "I have a headache," "So what, I have a brain tumor," moments, a contest in the grief parade. Like how could my grief even register, and I would understand that. But it doesn't happen that way.

Instead, we sit at her kitchen table, and she shows me pictures of Leslie-Dawn, the basketball player, with her friends and family, Leslie in her dress for the grad, speaks of how she refused to find a dress, to wear any dress, until the last minute they went to Lethbridge together and blew a month of her mother's wages on the best, the most beautiful.

We talk about Leslie, and we talk about Connor. I tell her I am having him cremated so one day I can scatter his ashes from every high point we've ever walked together. Scatter him to the river valleys and oceans on one last trip together.

When she comes to the table we sit and talk about Connor and the feelings of pain and loss.   It's hard to lose a pet;   we talk of this dog   a companion and friend of 16 years.   Hell   this dog was a part of her life longer than my first marriage and the failed second attempt.   The dog becomes a living being as we sit and talk   his personality comes through.   He knew everyone in the neighborhood she says.   She lives next door to a community centre.   I get to know Connor through Rita and picture this big black friendly dog greeting everyone on his daily trips around the town. The sense of loss and the rationalization and coming to terms with death is something we must go through.   Rita and I sit and talk   try to work through her pain.   It's odd this pain creates a feeling of oneness that can never come in any other way.

Sometime in the afternoon I go to the car and get my pictures of Connor, of our trips to Nova Scotia, stories of our life together, the dreams I had about him before he died. Shirley doesn't brush them aside. She listens, like I listen. During the afternoon the phone rings, diapers need changing, more coffee gets made. She tells me how everything reverted to the easiest form after her daughter died. The grandson's toilet training forgotten for a while, the bottle given again. She tells me about the phone call from the police

after the accident, her son's dreams before, men on horse-
back against the buttes, the men are crying.

We go through the photo album and come across a picture of
Maurice Leslie's cat.   Maurice was a large tawny-coloured tabby
cat.   He was like us   distant   arrogant   living in his own world
not bothering with anyone or anything.   Leslie fed him through a
cold snap   when she was young   hid him under my bed   would
sneak food to him.   Her brothers and I pretended that we didn't
know.   When the neighbors moved they gave Maurice to Leslie.
The landlord pretended that he didn't see the cat living in our ani-
mal-free apartment.   The only time Maurice became a cat   I tell
Rita   was when we brought home fried chicken.   He would rub
himself against our legs and purr and talk and beg.   Leslie would
give him a chicken leg and laugh.   She used to say   I can just see
Maurice   sitting in an easy chair   choking back a beer   chowing
down on fried chicken and watching TV.   The image and voice stay
with me and I smile.   The tears and pain when we found him dead
the insistence on an autopsy to find the cause of death   the tears
as we buried him.   Tears in the following weeks as I held her in my
arms to comfort her.   Rita makes a comment which gives the
impression that my loss is worse than hers.   In some ways   yes
in others   no.   Loss is loss.   No matter who it is or what it is the
pain travels through a person's being like no pain that is ever felt in
life.   In some way   talking about Leslie and Connor eased the pain
for a while   a lessening and a short reprieve from this day-to-day
existence.
Existence   moving through the days   can't remember what
happened yesterday.   The only constant   my boy   my grandson
Riel   a shadow   a little person   part of the little people   pulling
me together reminding me that he is here.   His needs have to be
filled right away   not this afternoon   not tomorrow   not next
week but right now   He's small but he already has large shoulders
He's my constant companion   travelling with me day and night.

We talk a long time, Shirley and I, and we decide to bundle up the kids and go for a walk to the Old Man River down below her house.

The afternoon goes on   the warmth from the late autumn sun begins to fade   the coulee would be nice.   Coats and hats for the babies it's chilly this late fall day.   As we leave the dogs follow excited   finally someone going for a walk   they must get pretty lonely too   the dogs were always with her when she ran spring summer   winter   fall   they always followed along watching over her.   I keep seeing her   running across the land   an image imprinted on my mind   Leslie-Dawn running along the road to the house   appears on the road   Clover behind her   Sugar next Mister   Lucky   Jade and the three cats   Fat Cat limping along on three legs   he waits at the point of the road where the wild roses grow   Mordecai tail standing straight up and then Sam the little gray female cat   all following behind in a straight line.   I called to the kids   look at this   as I stood looking out the kitchen window   dishes forgotten as I watch her run.

It's so familiar to me, this river valley, from two decades ago when I lived not far from here, out west of Lethbridge. It's the same river, the coulees, the same light and the old bleached cottonwood to perch on. The dogs run wild through the river flats and brambles, their bodies young and supple. He used to run like that. They're chasing lions, the kids say, and they carry sticks to fight off the lions, get tumbled instead by madly scrambling dogs. The other sound, when there is quiet, is coyotes yipping and singing. Sometimes the boys take my hand, and it is sweet and lovely to be accepted and welcomed by a child.

Sunny-Dawn   in her pink snowsuit   looks like a fat pink bunny   Riel wants to be picked up   he holds my jacket crying

*he's jealous because I carry Sunny-Dawn   Clover walks beside us
and tries to comfort Riel but he pushes her away   Tee as usual
finds a stick   which he picks up and swings through the air like a
sword   Rita picks up Riel when we get to the bottom of the hill
he quits crying.*

A long-legged blonde dog joins the others. Lucky, a Peigan
Purebred, Shirley says, and I tell her about all the black dogs
in my valley. Variegated Slocan Valley Black Dog, a neighbour
calls them.

As each dog races by, she tells me its story, whether the dog
is her own or a visitor. Two do not run and play. They walk in
turns or in perfect unison behind her. Clover and Sugar, red
heelers, Leslie's dogs.

*Clover runs ahead and Sugar takes her place   these two dogs
have always done this   each of them protecting us as we walk
along   when they first came to us   as pups   I was very ill   I
couldn't walk very far and Leslie insisted I walk with her and the
pups   as they grew I began to feel better became stronger until I
could walk a great distance without help   these dogs and Leslie-
Dawn made me well again   they were always with us   now they
walk with me   Riel is happy now   as we walk along the broad
flat area below the hill   Tee finds the bullberry bushes where we
usually pick berries   He's disappointed because the berries are
dry now and few remain on the branches   we continue walking
along   Tee exchanges his stick for a better one found on the path
I remember   Tee and Riel walking through the early October snow
laughing   the ache engulfs my soul   the sun shone briefly that
day and then large snowflakes slowly drifted down   I picked a
small ice cream pail of bullberries as the snow came down then
we headed to the coulee   we made our way up the side of the
coulee   east of the house   slipped and slid   sweat ran down
my face and into my eyes   I couldn't catch my breath   I pulled*

at small shrubs   pushed the boys ahead   and we inched our way
to the top   the boys were laughing and crying their voices like
magpies teasing dogs or hawks in early summer riding updrafts
along the coulee side   their sharp cries piercing stillness   in
beauty floating effortlessly across the sky   it's hard to believe that
less than a month ago   snow covered these hills and coulees and
this flat area   the Old Agency   I tell Rita as we walk along   the
people used to come here for rations   flour   sugar   meat   things
to keep from starving   an old school stood somewhere in this area
we walk across the flat and make it to the trees   and walk along
until we get to an open place   Tee finds a better stick   hunt lions
he says   and takes a mighty swing   You're going to hunt lions
better take the dogs with you   he reaches for Mister who walks
beside him

The late fall sun shines down on the trees   soft light reflects
off dry leaves   we walk under a canopy of cottonwood trees almost bare of leaves   a path made through the trees earlier in the
year   imprinted backhoe tracks still visible in the soft soil   off to
the left is the sweat lodge hidden behind a dense growth of willow
I don't mention it   we walk along   a prayer running through my
mind   comforted by the nearness of the lodge   we turn on the
path to the right and walk along to an open flat area   as we walk
I look at the cottonwoods surrounding us   I can see the house on
the hill   bathed in soft brown light   the hills and coulees reflect
this light   softening the contours of the land   colour of buckskin
soft as doeskin   the land looks warm, the way I remember it
the way it was when I was a child   The soft crackling of the grass
and leaves as we travel through the trees   the coolness in the air
a hint of the coming winter   we stop near the picnic place   my
arms ache from the weight of the fat little girl   Rita wants a picture of us   Sunny-Dawn is placed on the limb of the cottonwood
tree that shades our picnics   she's asleep has been since we stepped
out of the house   when she goes out the first thing she does is fall
asleep   I place Riel and Tee on either side of her and stand behind

*the limb   the dogs bark and head off into the trees   probably
scared up a deer   Rita takes a photo of us   Riel and Tee love to
get their pictures taken and pose beautifully for the camera   we
pick up the children and cross the washout   soft sand makes walking difficult   the crunch of gravel and then under the cottonwoods
again   Lucky arrives and walks beside me.*

Lucky leaps into the river, fords it through crusts of ice.
Thuds like giant rocks being thrown in are beaver tails slap-
ping a warning. The light is pink on the river, gold on the
coulees, like the picture of the Burmis tree above my bed at the
motel.

*Willows appear as we near the river   this pile of gravel and
the fallen trees are from the '95 flood   I tell Rita as we make our
way through the willows   I'm tired   Sunny-Dawn feels like a
hundred-pound load   I don't say very much   just walk along
enduring the pain   the riverbank appears sand   and rocks   and
then the river   it is here that we burned her things   work started
on a Tuesday morning and ended on a Saturday afternoon   we
knew she had a lot of things   we just didn't know how much   I
and my son Ian carried them from the car to the riverbank   the
wind began to blow   it blew so hard that I told him   let's just sur-
round them with dried wood when the wind quits we'll come back
we picked up dried logs and placed them up against the mound of
belongings like a tipi covering   we filled the spaces with smaller
pieces of driftwood until everything was covered and secure   Ian
left for Lethbridge that evening worried that the mound would not
be safe   he would phone each day   ask if we had finished the
work   each day the wind howled and screamed   on Thursday
Sonny and I went to check on the mound to make sure that it was
okay   a small skinny brown dog was curled up next to the mound
she came and greeted us   Jeez   even here she gets a dog Sonny
said   with a soft laugh we checked and placed more wood around*

the sides   the dog watched us from the willows   the wind was
still too high and we decided to wait another day   the dog disappeared   Saturday morning arrived   cold   we drove to the river
Riel   Sonny   and me   we brought more items that we had found
we started the fire and flames shot to the sky   the little brown dog
came over and watched with us as the flames devoured the wood
and the items in the mound   we got more wood and the flames
continued to rise   all that day we gathered wood   silent   and
placed it on the fire   in late afternoon there was nothing left just
ash   as we turned to leave the little brown dog followed us   we
took her home and named her Driftpile

   To the edge   the cold silver sky reflects the cold water of the
Old Man River   a bank of dark cloud makes the opening in the
sky brighter and sharper   the dogs run to the river   Sugar runs
in   stops   and comes back   too cold I guess   Lucky swims across
and shakes himself free of water   it's quite chilly now and the kids'
noses begin to run   time to get them back to the house   clear
sharp silver colours the sky   contrasts with the shadow of trees
in the river valley   the valley appears dark   as we walk back my
tiredness begins to tell and I wish I had taken the offer to   drive to
the river in Rita's car   in a way this walk   two months after Leslie
died   is like a reaffirmation of life   the world as we know it   the
soft coloured hills and coulees   the going to sleep of the cottonwood and willow   the sharp crackle of dried leaves underfoot carries the message that life is a part of death   I haven't felt anything
my life goes on each day   waking and sleeping and waking again
when we get to the bottom of the hill just below the house I accept
Rita's offer to get her car   the children are tired and cranky and
want to be carried   that last hill before the house defeats me   Rita
goes ahead and I walk with the children and the dogs to a place
where we can sit and rest dusk falls

   Shirley's been carrying Sunny-Dawn, who is bundled and
sleeping. The boys have taken my hand. But now the kids are

worn out, hungry and cold and it's a long way back up the coulee. I scramble uphill for my car.

Night arrives on dusty wings   dust from passing vehicles clouds the air   I hope Rita knows how to drive in these conditions who would have thought a traffic jam way out here on the prairies the road up the long hill is tricky   the ninety degree turn at the bottom is dangerous at night   I breathe a sigh of relief as I see her car come down the hill   the children are happy   the dogs are happy   but the dogs will have to make their way home   they'll probably run up the short coulee and be home before we get to the turnoff at the bottom of the hill

In a city I'd get lost. But not here. These are my kinds of roads. I plough through the dust, a rural woman who knows her way.

Home again   we bring the children in   darkness is complete Rita can see the yardlights of homes across the river shining like stars against the blackness of the night   during the day it is easy to believe that not too many people live in the area but at night yardlights tell the truth

At Shirley's house, we say goodbye, then she says, "Wait I have something for you," and gives me a clay buffalo, almost two-dimensional, glazed with blues and greens. A surrealistic buffalo, she says.

I hope she makes it to her hotel all right   driving at night in this area can be dangerous   sometimes deer and other wildlife decide to go for a walk at night   the strangest is the buffalo   as you are driving along you just can't believe that a buffalo would be walking along the road   eyes tell you it is   but the brain refuses to believe   when she leaves I put the children to bed   it's

odd I wanted to take her to the coulee to the east of the house
maybe the time for healing is not right   the sleep of exhaustion
takes over

At the motel, I set the surrealistic buffalo on the map of the world, by my picture of Connor. During this time Connor doesn't come back in dreams. Nor any animals, as if they all walked off together, them helping Connor, and said, figure it out for yourself for awhile. Fair enough, I thought. I guess it's part of the deal.

There are moments I feel whole here, not fragmented, obsessed and bedraggled as I am at home. There are time I look up from my work, up from the map of the world and the picture of my dog and the buffalo, and see myself in the mirror. And I feel not completed, but at least content.

A few days later, Shirley takes me to Leslie's grave. She points out white crosses atop hillsides, where long ago bodies would be laid out for the elements and the animals to finish. Being with Shirley is like being with my friend Edwina in Nova Scotia, their stories pouring out, their strength and humour and integrity. And also, perhaps, some quality that can only belong to a mother who has buried her child.

That night, or another, I lie in bed and can't sleep. I sing "Hear that lonesome whippoorwill...." I'm singing it to Connor. I curl myself around a pillow as if it were him and weep and sing. I give myself a stern lecture, turn on the light and read *The Snapper* by Roddy Doyle. Irish and crisp and funny and tender, too. In the night I weep again for my dog. The train's going by, high long moaning and I realize that women in my family have gone to prairie shacks with the wind and the sound of the train to mourn their dead, and this is exactly what I have done. I have come here to the wind, and the trains calling in the night to mourn my dead. He is my only, my only born, my first loss, my boy. In the early morning

I walk out on the prairie to take a picture of the pinkest moment of morning. It lasts no more time than his dying. I write a postcard to a friend, who'd once asked the origin of Connor's name. I say he was named after Conor Larkin, the big black-haired Irishman in Trinity. Before, when he asked, I was crying and couldn't say it well. Now I am crying and can say it better.

At the gas station on the way out of town, very early on Sunday, a fellow from the *Lethbridge Herald* delivery van walks over to my car. "Are you headed west?" Yes. "Would you be willing to take these papers over to Brocket – they're extras. To the Napii Service Station." Sure, I say, taking some delight in this trusting and casual encounter. "And oh," he says, "keep one for yourself."

Time flows along with the rising and setting of the sun   work family   work work and more work fills the void and darkness fades into exhaustion   a letter arrives from Rita it reminds me of cottonwood and willow   she writes of a custom practised by the Hospice groups in Canada   each year at Christmas a tree is set up in one of the malls   families bring cards with the names of those who have died written on them   these cards are placed in the tree in remembrance   she writes that she has placed Leslie's name on a card and placed it in the tree right next to Connor's she asks if this is all right with me   I picture a tree with sparkling twinkling lights and a card with Leslie's name written on it tucked away in the mountains   I can almost see Leslie and Connor running across the mountain tops   sheer exhilaration showing in their forms   yes   it is all right.

A HONEYCOMB OF MEMORY

Louise Bernice Halfe

I WATCHED TWO INUIT WOMEN RECENTLY, FACES AN inch apart. In their grunts, groans and rippling, meowing, and cawing I heard the song of the brook searching. I saw a crane gracefully stand on one foot meditating. A frog croaked. Nearby a praying mantis sucked dew from a fresh born leaf. A beaver screamed, its paw caught in the iron jaws of a trap. Thunder shuddered. A pair of lovers parted under a tree. Lightning smiled through one lover's heart, his mouth releasing stars. The women coached the falling dew that rolled from her lover's face. Their voices beat the drum of death. Nearby a deer rubbed her nose into her mate, pranced into an open field and in silence fell as an arrow found its mark. Her robe was sliced with fluttering hands. Her bones become the flute, scraper, skinning knife and needle. Her flesh sinew thread, rawhide bowls and folding boxes, drums and medicine bags. Her skin became a lodge of stick and hide. Her hair a fresh mattress. Close by, men dressed in deep fur sat drumming. The enthralled listened.

This mating is a community dance between the women oralists and a story which rolls off the birchbark scroll of the tongue. Its story has been woven and lifted from the forest floor where the bed of knowledge is caught in the fibre of wood, water, wind, rock and all the creatures of the earth. The story's Voice is found in song, and in the whisperings and rumbling of its animals.

As the earth developed each new face, it covered the passing of her people. Centuries later, archeologists took off her many skins until her bones revealed the stories of our ancient existence. Like the song of these women, stories are passed mouth to mouth, stored into the heart of memory, and joined with the findings of these archeologists. Our history lives and speaks through her many forms.

Like the chanting exchange of these two Inuit women, a Vision is created through the mirror and membrane of language. We can be enticed, caught in the web of mystery, horror, magic, wonder, confusion and lust as stories unfold in our imagination. This waterfall sings the passion of darkness and the flame of sun where all truths reside.

AN OLD WOMAN SITS ON A FEATHERED BUCKSKIN blanket, fingers bending and weaving red willows. She dips in a pottery cup for the red-stained root, her voice rising and falling as smoke rolls up the arms of the tepee. The fire crackles. As have so many stories before, this one also begins, "*Kiyas esah*" and "A long, long time ago our people were filled with mystery and unexplainable powers." Eager to absorb her every word, a child listens, skewered, as the story gnaws into her ears and eyes and chews into her heart. She has waited for this night. Waited for the river to wear her gown of laced ice suet, waited for snow to bathe her snowshoes and trace rabbit trails. Waited for these stories.

"*Kiyas esah*" she repeats. "A man and a woman left the main camp with their two young boys. They travelled for a long, long time. Sometimes thick in the forest, their thighs sucked deep by muskeg, mosquitoes fell in hordes and the young boys' cries raged like rivers. In the pines they gathered blueberries and cranberries, and what the chickadees and sparrows left of dried saskatoons, chokecherries and rosehips.

Eventually they came upon a clearing surrounded by aspen, birch and dried flowers. They were certain they'd have honey when the earth completed its turn. Not far away a brook sang. Before the sun rose the man left with his bow and arrows to stalk the woods for the offered game. Each evening when he returned supper was late. He noticed that his boys hadn't gathered enough wood and his wife hadn't tanned many hides."

She takes a swig of tea and pokes the embers. She sits silently studying her basket. The child's mind dances as each moccasined word slips into her ears. She sits, tongue possessed. She concentrates on the snow sprinkling in, waiting for the awakening splutter. She learns she cannot catch a ghost and make it dance. She cannot hold a spirit and give it form. Presently the old one crumbles a tobacco leaf, lifts it to the sky and feeds the fire. She continues, her voice guttural, the beasts quiet, the wind silent, the fire's flame creeping, fixing the air with small stares.

"The father asked the boys what their mother did all day. The boys wrestled with their tongues and when the eldest spoke, a swarm of bats fluttered, 'After she feeds us and instructs us never ever to follow her, she gives us our chores.' His mouth pursed, pointed to a light trail leading into the wild. For days the father followed his wife's every movement. He shadowed her among the trees. One day he filled his bundle with his usual tools. A bit of tobacco, stone ax, sharpened arrows and a freshly made bow and sinew string. He took his sons aside and gave them a bone drill, a sharp stone, a flint, a beaver tooth and stone chisel. He filled their heads with plans should he not return. He watched his wife move among the trees as a deer. She sniffed, ensured her moccasins were gentle where dew rolled off the grass. The grasses, wise in their knowing, called the wind to bend their backs. She untied her raven braids till strands kissed her cheeks. He followed, each move watched. She sat on a log, sang a Creation song, fist drumming. A large snake slithered out, followed by many small ones. Each squirmed at the delight of seeing her, feeling her warm hands on their cool long bodies. The man's bellow filled the air. He became a snarling wolf and with arms out-stretched the ax parted the heads off each snake."

The girl's tightened stomach becomes a storm of worms. She scratches her hair, brings each strand to her eye, the mother's voice a drumming stick against her ear. The woman stops as the girl struggles to untangle the net. Again the old one drinks tea, gulping slow, and passes the raspberry water. She pushes a braid of sweet grass to a glowing ember and the wind settles in her chest.

"The woman wept as she fought against the slashing. Her head severed and body in two, the husband threw her into the sky. There in the night you'll see her crawl as if she's dressed in golden fire, purple suns and river beds. But her head remained. It leapt and fixed its jaws around the man's throat. When the thrashing was still she ate. The head then rolled where the grass had bent. In the distance the boys watched the sky. When they saw it turn a bleeding red, they packed their bundles and ran."

The mother tucks the girl into the buffalo blanket and brushes her cheeks with stained hands. She leaves to fetch wood for the dying fire. The young one strains to see beyond the tepee poles. If she can catch a glimpse of the floating body where the heavens exploded, perhaps she can eat one passing star and make a womb's nest of living snakes. Perhaps the two spirits would live and love again. Instead she has to wait, till the earth turns its nightly page.

My mother held a whirlpool of stories. Through the winter I would beg for one unravelling after another. From her fingers the spirits ate and danced. When we moved into the log cabin she brought all of them and I stored them in my memory. I left for residential school and my memory slept. I forgot

further as I was forced to deal with the alcoholism and violence that spoke through my father's fist. My mother's voice
went into hiding. The ages crept into my flesh and I wandered
without a cultural bundle. My medicine bag filled with smoky
vision and sleeping memory. My palms absent maps, biting
spirits tore out my tongue. My feet travelled the same path my
parents took. Heart filled with decay and my own head rolling
I searched among the ruins of our log cabin, the graveyard
where my grandparents lay, through the debris of drumming,
singing, dancing powwow grounds, and still the echo of the
dead roamed beyond my reach. I married a foreigner, two
babies clung to my breast. Slowly my mother's words unrolled
my tongue. *Kiyas esah*....

At dawn the young girl slipped on her snowshoes and made
her way into the willows where her snares hung. Deep in
thought she asked the chickadees, the snow and sky, if she filled
her being with their breath would she be butchered too? Would
she too search for her body? Would she chase what her loins
delivered? Would she be spurred? Forehead creased she bent,
kissed the stiff rabbits and threw them over her shoulders. In
the tepee's warmth she peeled their fur as the sun pressed into
the earth. Seeing their bellies full, her mother lifted a tobacco
leaf, lips moving she filled her pipe and settled in the cushion of
her family's patient wait. The little girl sat with a pole between
her legs as she quietly wrapped the raw rabbit hide round and
round. Her mother began.

"*Kiyas esah, e-matawisit Iyiniwak*. A long, long, time ago
mystery and magic lived inside and among the people." As the
old woman puffed, smoke snaked from her nostrils, eyes
crossed she watched. She continued. "The head wept and
sang, rolled and squeezed through trodden trails. At her home
she was greeted by hungry flames. The fire's tongue licked the
tepee's skeleton, slurped the dried grass and raced toward her.
Off in the distance the boys heard their mother's terrible cry.

They ran, their hearts raced ahead, wind cut their throats, bones bent and stretched. Their mother's breath at their heels."

The little girl's fingers flew around the pole, rabbit fur flying, her eyes darted to her fingers, to her mother. Where was she to sleep tonight? The old woman's voice became a forest of rain, leaves rustled against the ragged wind.

"'*Astum peke we*. Come home. I love you, my babies. My babies,' she begged. But their father's wrath coiled inside their guts. With icy fingers the eldest son threw his father's bone drill. The thorns and rosehip brush awoke and crowned the rolling head. Cheeks torn and gouged, blood sprang from her wounds." The old one took a twig and relit her burned-out pipe. "This blood's become a vein of rivers where her jaws crunch the earth. Much like the patterns we create on birchbark with our eye teeth," she informed her little girl. She could see the story's movements clench her daughter's inward eye.

The stories came as my children grew. With them I entered the Ceremonial Lodge.

Sweat trickled down my body, rain from my face, the old one gave me a name. With my name came the honouring of all my dreams. My Visions took legs and began to walk. I sat in numerous circles of young and old where they wept and wove their tattered tales. These became the sinew to our Memory. We honoured their return. Our wounds we fed to the Spirits, and they come to us through Voice, the feather quill, these paper leaves.

When the child's face settled, the woman began. "A beaver swam up the river blood, chewed through the thick bark and released the head. She continued her exhausted roll. She called and called. Still the boys ran. Again she begged her sons, through severed breath she sang, 'Oh love, oh love...come home to your mother's hearth.' Again the eldest boy threw a sharp stone, his father's parting gift. Large stone hills with pointed edges rose. Crevices and valleys so deep that she would surely fall to her death. Like a frustrated wolf she bayed. The head rolled back and forth. Foam around her mouth."

The young child remembered her mother's arrow; its release arched the sky whenever a crying wolf came too close to camp. With one ear to the story, the other listened to the nocturnal creatures of the snowy night. "A fox came by. His heart filled by the rolling head's sorrowful wail, he led her through a pass. She rolled and rolled, hurrying only as a head would hurry. 'Oh come sweet precious, my boys, my boys' the head sang like the surf. It ebbed and flowed. Still the boys ran, the eldest dug in his bundle and threw one more gift. The flint hit the dirt and pebbled rocks. Here the fire woke. Unable to stop her frantic chase she burned her face. Her blistered skin became the singing sands along the beaches of where we swim." The mother slid her hand down the softness of her daughter's face. "Oh the chase so long, so long" the old woman chanted. With a drum stick she patted the earth. She lifted her face toward the long arms of the tepee, snowflakes settled like gems. She gleamed like a translucent water bag where puckered skin appeared to burst as she mourned her song. "My babies. My babies. My tired babies. Come home. Come home. Come home to your mother's heart." The song stopped and the old woman resumed. "The boys bled too. Their moccasins eaten by their travel, bellies empty, eyes swollen, they limped as they ran. Once again the eldest threw and out of the beaver tooth sharp chewed popular stumps appeared. Trees lay everywhere. And if it were you and me," the mother said to her girl, "we wouldn't have any difficulty lifting our feet high and stepping over these dead tree people. But no, the head, she had to roll under and around where she could. Hours and hours later she escaped. Once again aware that he had only the chisel left, the eldest boy threw and it fell as before between the head and the boys. A great lake formed. Thick as red-blood honey. The waves roared, cackled and snapped. The boys knew that this was their last hope. They walked the shore, afraid the head would figure out a way to reach them. They gave themselves to the night. A large water bird spread its wings and offered to give the head a lift, but only if the head kept still for the bird's back had suffered some lonesome bones. Any movement caused the bird great pain." The old woman's voice droned. Though the young girl's eyes burned, she strained to listen. She straightened and lay her pole aside. In the next week her rabbit skins would be ready to be woven into quilts.

Through dreams, ceremony and the recollection of memory, my community continues to battle the rift between our Native tongue and the foreigner's language. The renaissance and resurgence has fueled a contemporary voice. A voice which creates and captures my community's history, its pain and its revival. There are times when community would rather express itself in the safety of the drum, song and dance, its skeletal wounds often too penetrating.

Story is where the soul resides and reverberates. It must find its expression. In words the spirit sings out its magic and power. Culture teaches the storyteller to handle words with kindness, respect, and care. As a writer who speaks the language, I often have to guide my listeners to the deeper context of words. All too often, we speak superficially, not hearing where the words take us. For example, in Cree to identify intestinal organs one would relate to them as "bodies that reside underneath." Hence all organs have and hold a living persona. Each has speech, thought and action and each cradles responsibility.

The old woman tired, pushed the words as if they'd become themselves the heavy head. "The head clung to the slick feathers. Unable to maintain its grip it crushed against the bird's backbone. The bird screeched and floundered. In the middle of the lake the head fell, deep into the black depth."

The girl's head nodded, her body sank into the waiting welcome of the buffalo robe. She did not hear her mother's final words, "In sleep this is where we go." The embers' fires blinked and became the starlight in the tepee's cave.

Oral tradition prevails amidst the onslaught of computers, televisions, radio, bingo and casino halls and the blurred slurs of damaged spirits. It prevails deep in our memory. It carries the passage of a child into this world, all the manners and ethics of our socialization, laws that govern our societies, medicines that heal us, ceremonies that keep us alive, the mysterious magic of our ancestors. Pictures painted with tongue and hand are etched in the dens of our brains, hoarded in the lodges of our hearts. They take form through dress making, pottery making, rock paintings, song, dance, theatre and writing and are passed onto each generation.

Armed with a spade, shovel, picks as thin as needles, soft bristle brushes, sieves, archeologists haunt the land hunting bones, minuscule treasures of pottery, and human waste. They trace the path of rocks, the face of medicine wheels. With inspection of rock paintings and listening to oral stories, they draw pictures of the past, recreate and resurrect history. With feather pens, the contemporary story gatherers of both cultures, red and white, send lines into the depths of the well of memory. They draw the head to life again. They assist in giving creation, voice.

a

QUESTION
of IDENTITY

BENNY HITS THE BIG FOUR-OH
(Or, Aren't You Rather Young to be Writing Your Memoirs?)

Ven Begamudré

TO START WITH

No matter where they hid the mangoes in that huge Benares house, Babu, crawling, could sniff the golden pulp out from the ripening skin.

PART ONE: BABU MEANS BOY IN HIS MOTHER TONGUE

One – In the spring of his first birthday, he falls so ill that his mother takes him back to his home town of Bangalore, and he lives. That same fall, on their way to graduate schools in America, his parents leave him with his grandmother on an island called Mauritius.

Two – He will remember nothing of his time here unless he later dreams of it. A red toy car, a beach, a dugout canoe. His mother returns to reclaim him even as he turns three, and he learns to call her Amma.

Three – Back in Bangalore now, they live in the "outhouse" of a larger house, and for his first Festival of Lights, she gives him sparklers to twirl. She calls their servant the Black Ayah. One night the lights go out and Amma says, "Don't be afraid. Lightning cannot find us in the dark."

Four – In summer his father comes home to visit, but Babu

does not know what to say. Nor does his father, Appa, so he leaves. Amma moves to a house she calls the coloured house because, once a week, she replaces the bare light bulbs with coloured ones. Their new servant, Mary, is a Christian like the nuns in his school. He learns to sing "Lavender Blue."

Five – The nuns of Cluny Convent teach him to read and write, one hovering over him like a white bird while he links *a* with *b* with *c*. He plays with his many cousins. Amma takes him to Tirumala and offers his hair to his namesake, Lord Venkateswara. Still, a rash on Babu's legs flares so redly that he cannot walk. Mary carries him from class to class, his bandaged legs useless and stiff. He will remember this as the best year of his life.

PART TWO: VB OR TISH, WHICH IS WHICH?

Six – In August, Amma flies Babu to his father in Ottawa and leaves for Toronto. Appa has left America without finishing his degree. They are both good at leaving. Babu, called VB now, is enrolled in yet another posh school, Ashbury College in Rockcliffe Park. He waits for Appa to fetch him in the dark, long after most day boys have left. He begins to learn French. He begins forgetting his life back home since he wants to be a real Canadian, *tu comprends?*

Seven – On his seventh birthday he stays home sick with a nurse hired by Appa. That summer they move from the apartment on Montreal Road to an apartment on Selkirk Avenue but still in the French-speaking part of town. Amma returns from Toronto, then leaves for India. Years later, one of his aunts will admit there was talk of an abortion. It's a shame, if true, since he would have liked a sibling. Then Appa might have made less free with his hand, though perhaps not with his tongue, sharpened by loss. Downstairs, with his new babysitter, VB feels safe. Her name is Granny Going.

Eight – Appa moves to Kingston on the shores of Lake Ontario, to work at RMC, the Royal Military College. VB, called Tish now (supposedly short for Venkatesh), attends Duncan McArthur, his first public school. He joins cub scouts. He rarely sings. His teacher, Mrs. McCracken, screams at the class. She is not at all like his last teacher, Mrs. Dalton, who tried with little success to teach him piano. Still, he feels safer with women and girls than with men and boys. When Amma returns from India, he invites boys home for cookies and milk so he can show her off. He keeps the girls a secret even from her.

Nine – Amma leaves for Toronto again, so he gladly returns to Ashbury, this time as a boarder. Even if it means not playing with girls. His teacher, Miss Black, reads to the class: *Wind in the Willows, Beautiful Joe*. When the masters' backs are turned, a fat Greek from Montreal beats up on the Pakis, the Niggers, the Micks. VB takes refuge in the infirmary with coughs and colds and *The Boys' Own Annual*. That Christmas, Amma comes home to visit but leaves, without warning, for the very last time. He knows it was all his fault. Still, he's glad to get back to the cricket and school ties, the shoeshine every night before showers. His best friend at Ashbury, Mark Akbar, takes him home on weekends to his two parents, a sister, and a dog. Mark Akbar is a Jew.

Ten – And it's back to Kingston, as Tish again, for Grade Six. He shares a desk with Cindy Wall, who reminds him of Mary Poppins. He's been in Canada four years now, but everyone still looks like someone else. Their teacher is a scowly man, Mr. McDonald, who does not like Smart Alecks. At home, Appa treats Tish like a dunce. But there are boys and girls, cub scouts again, stamp collecting, and books. There are always books. The month before his eleventh birthday, he has two operations – one for a burst appendix, one for a mastoid in his ear – and he comes out fat. But there are movies on TV and at theatres called Highland and Biltmore. There are comics like *Superman* and *Classics Illustrated*. And there's a secret agent on new flannel pyjamas: Bond, James Bond.

Eleven – In August Appa returns to Bethlehem, Pennsyl-
vania, to finish his Ph.D. If Tish had stayed in Kingston, he
could have learned the trumpet, so Mr. Gross teaches him the
baritone, and Tish joins the band. The shop teacher, who
cusses and jokes, looks like Red Skelton. The geography
teacher screams at the class. Tish discovers real books now:
*The Three Musketeers, Around the World in Eighty Days, Twenty
Thousand Leagues Under the Sea.* All those numbers. The
books keep him safe from real life: Appa's hand and his
tongue, sleeping on the floor, all those clever Yanks who call,
"Tissue, we need you, achoo!" And there are families who take
pity on him. The couple in the Bach Choir who invite for-
eigners to dinner at Thanksgiving. The family that takes him
to the Moravian Church for a candlelight service on Christmas
Eve. And every night in December there's the Star of
Bethlehem lighting fathers home. Also, if a boy is good, trips
to New York.

Twelve – And it's back to Kingston for Grade Eight in Calvin
Park Public School. The guidance counsellor keeps an eye on
Tish, though he doesn't know why. Not even after the divorce
comes through. He has a million stamps now: a world album,
an American album, and a cousin's entire collection of old
Indian stamps. There's also Kim, who sits in front of him with
her long, brown, dreamy hair. And more books, biographies
now, of Albert Einstein or Harry Houdini. An English teacher
named Mr. Hinch. And a real, adult card at the public library
with all its novels about 007: Bond, James Bond. But there are
injuries on playing fields and gotch-pulling in the locker room.
Tish pretends he's Harry Houdini and always escapes. That way
he never gets his gotch pulled up from behind 'till his balls get
forced up his ass. He had usually escaped at Ashbury, too, from
getting blackballed with shoe polish. The other boarders had
decided his balls were black enough.

Thirteen – Then it's across the road to high school at LCVI, Loyalist Collegiate and Vocational Institute. Girls take typing and accounting. Boys take drafting and electricity. He would rather learn to type. Still, there are visits to Amma in Toronto at Thanksgiving, Christmas and Easter. And losing weight, thanks to a gym teacher named Digiacomo. He has long hair and rides a bike and makes Tish run the hurdles. Over and over 'till he leaves every one of them standing. He does not like team sports although, as Amma keeps reminding him, Appa was a fine athlete. Once. Then there's the new girl, Karen, who has short, dark hair and wears hot pants. But the closest he gets to her is in the library while trading stamps. She has duplicates from Tanzania, where her parents worked. And he finally remembers something without dreaming it first: on their way back to Bangalore from Mauritius, he and Amma spotted flamingoes in Nairobi National Park.

Fourteen – Grade Ten now. Tish is growing up. Last year it was *Gone With the Wind*; this year it's *War and Peace*. Appa keeps his hands to himself, though his tongue is just as sharp. Besides, there's a distraction: Tish's grandmother has come to live with them for a year. She has not aged well. She reminds Appa he has no wife, and Tish stays out of their way. There are movies and games and model ships; there are stamps and books and art; and now, since Appa is still at RMC, there is air cadets. Fifty-eight Kingston Squadron, the Royal Canadian Air Cadets. Parade once a week means drill and field trips and the history of Canadian flight. Tish has become such a good Canadian, he's willing to take up arms. Why, if Pierre Trudeau had phoned during the FLQ Crisis and said, "Tissue, we need you, achoo!" this fine young man would have saluted and cried, *"Oui, mon premier ministre!"* And just hear him conjugate: *"Je suis canadien. Nous sommes canadiens. Nous sommes fiers d'etre canadiens."* *Alors,* it's a pity he's still not white.

THE BORN-HERE IMMIGRANT

Kate Braid

The story is our escort; without it we are blind.
- Chinua Achebe, Anthills of the Savannah

I WAS BORN IN CANADA, BUT LATELY I FEEL LIKE AN immigrant. It's not that I don't know or love this country: I've lived for extended periods in Calgary, Montreal, Sackville, NB and in Vancouver. But lately I have become aware of a growing sense of dislocation. What is going on?

MY MOTHER'S MOTHER WAS AN IMMIGRANT FROM IRELAND. Her father was born in Ontario, a third-generation Canadian. My father was an English pilot, one of those imported during the war to teach flying for the Commonwealth Air Training Project in Alberta. Shortly after he met my mother at a dance, they married and, after a toss of the Commonwealth dice that might have taken them (and me *in utero*) to Rhodesia, they settled in Canada. And so I became Canadian rather than Rhodesian: an accidental Canadian, like all the others who have now been here just long enough to forget our not-so-distant pasts and begin to complain about "all those immigrants." Of course, the vast exception to all this are the native peoples, whose claim to tenure is deeper by several thousands of years.

When I spoke of the feeling of being a born-here immigrant recently at a local college, I was surprised by the number of students who raised their hands to say, "Me too," especially kids from the Prairies. "I feel like I'm just skating over the top of the landscape," one said. Given that so many of us – children of immigrants – were at least born here, why do we, why do I, hold this feeling of disconnection, as if there is nothing to anchor me? The issue of belonging seems even more pressing with the possible loss of Quebec and what that means to a place that's been called Canada for less than 140 years. The urgency of the question also increases with increasing pressure for the "globalization" of culture, which means for most of the world the wholesale importing of American culture: movies, books, TV, magazines, values. But mostly for me feeling unrooted has been a vague discomfort, no big deal, something I wasn't really conscious of.

AND THEN THE SALT FELL INTO THIS BREW LAST SUMMER when I went to Europe and saw old buildings; not "old" as we say it in Vancouver meaning fifty years. I mean old as in five hundred years, the age of my cousin's house – nothing exceptional, he thought. In southern England I visited five-thousand-year-old standing stones erected before there were wheels to move them or metal tools to work them. I could barely stand to touch them, awed by such age, the physical signs of such communal effort, five thousand years before. Something deep within me shifted; it was my ancestors who were born, lived, lifted these same stones all those hundreds of years ago. My hands and feet tingled when I touched them.

And then to Hungary where history bellies out of every stone and every step is part of a long, deep tradition. I loved the ancient, beautiful buildings with their detail that no North American would dream of building in our preoccupation with space and speed. I was fascinated by round corners and cornices, by castles and Roman ruins and by Hungarian museums erected over stone rubble so that you literally walked down into – through – history. Everywhere in Europe I felt unfamiliar (after all, I hadn't been here before – had I?), yet at the same time a strangely familiar sense of relief. This is where I am from, I thought. When people talk of roots, this is what they mean; this odd feeling in my feet as if the stones are alive – the feeling of physical connection – connection through the body – to the land. Here, where I had not been born, where I had never lived, was where I could say, "I belong. This is me." As one friend says, "I was aboriginal there."

But I don't want to live in Europe. I remember one night in Germany with my partner and I both feeling the need for breathing space, when locals all recommended we drive up a nearby "mountain." We drove up the local hill and, sure enough, there were quite a few trees and not many other cars or people. It was suppertime and most of the locals, we later learned, were at home. But as we came down again, the valley spread below us was filled with clusters of light; there were houses, villages everywhere, and this was called "forest"; this was the wilderness of Europe. I had a moment of claustrophobia – and homesickness.

I knew then there is no doubt why I choose to live here, in Canada – young and architecturally ugly and dull as it is. My family are here, of course, and my friends and all things familiar, but mostly I stay for the land, for Prairie and rainforest and cedar trees and the fact that I can truly, routinely, "get away" from people – their lights, their sounds, their smells – as I could not, ever, in Europe. It's a contradiction: I stay for the land, yet the land doesn't feel like mine. In fact, shortly after I returned I saw a native man in a TV ad standing on a Saskatchewan hill and I felt a pang of pure envy. There is no question this is his land; his ancestors have been here forever. But if it's his ground, then who am I? Having decided that this is where I shall live, how am I – born Canadian – to love a land that is so new, so foreign to me, to my ancestors, to my blood?

HERE IN WHAT THE UNITED NATIONS CALLS THE BEST place in the world to live (as long as you're not poor), I begin by asking, "Where is here? What is here?" and to my relief, there are people making a consistent effort to address these questions; they are the cultural workers and since I am a writer and know mostly writers, I shall speak of them in particular, though I know there are also dancers, visual artists, musicians, filmmakers, radio broadcasters and others, doing the same thing.

READING DIONNE BRAND'S *Land to Light On* MADE THE pieces fall together, made me realize how entirely I'm an immigrant. Brand was born in Trinidad, came to Canada as a teenager and now lives in Toronto. She explores in many genres what it means to be an immigrant, black and lesbian – an outsider in almost every way to mainstream Canadian society. Her most recent poetry book, *Land to Light On* (which won the Governor General's Award) opens with, "Out here I am like someone without a sheet / without a branch but not even safe as the sea, / without the relief of the sky or good graces of a door."[1] As I read, I shared this sense of no place to hide, no stone, no petroglyph on which to find indelibly fixed the mark that says, "You. We recognize you from your ancestors. Put your feet here where they belong, anchored to rock." No, there is none of that for us immigrants.

AT THE SAME TIME, I WAS READING ROBERT KROETSCH'S long poem about growing up on the prairies, "The Seed Catalogue," and his essays, *The Lovely Treachery of Words,* that ask the question: "Exactly where are we, anyway? What is this place where all of us (except native peoples) are such newcomers? What is 'home' for a Canadian?" Kroetsch was born and raised on an Alberta farm and spent many of his adult years teaching in the US while writing about being a Canadian. (Maybe it's only exile that can tell us who we are. Why do people go away to write about their home place from a distance?)

When I ask my local library how many of us are first- and second-generation Canadian, even the omnipotent librarian cannot help me. Statistics Canada asks only ethnic origin so, for example, we know that 13 per cent of us identify as being of European origin, almost seven per cent as of Asian descent, and so on, but no one asks "How long have you been here?" In a country of immigrants, shouldn't this be an important question?

Sometimes, with relief, I follow the lead of the comedians: *Saturday Night Live, Bob and Doug Mackenzie, Codco, This Hour Has Twenty-Two Minutes, Double Exposure, The Dead Dog Café...*the list goes on. Most of us may be new here, but humour is a connection. When it's scary, when you're lost, what better (Canadians seem to say) than to laugh? I wonder if the first white settlers laughed very much? Judging from my dour immigrant grandmother, I doubt it, though word has slipped out that there's a deep tradition of humour in First Nations communities. Maybe laughter is in the land itself, and we've caught it. (Does that mean we can stay?) Maybe laughter is the next phase of settling in; in such an impossibly vast and inhospitable space it may be the only thing that can save us. As the feminists say, "She who laughs, lasts." Like the traditional Swiss who yodelled over mountains, or the Basques who also have a distinct call over long distance, perhaps laughter is the Canadian way of talking to each other across a vast land mass and the hillocks and mountains of difference.

Robert Kroetsch asks, "How do you establish any sort of *close* relationship in a landscape – in a physical situation – whose primary characteristic is *distance?*" And answers, "The telling of story – more literally, the literal closedness of a book – might be made to...contain space."[2]

Yes, this makes sense to me; to figure out who we are by telling each other our stories, especially the stories about where we are. Writers (bards) have always done it: W.O. Mitchell's *Who Has Seen the Wind,* Sinclair Ross's *As For Me and My House,* Ernest Buckler's *The Mountain and the Valley,* Margaret Atwood's *Surfacing* and *Alias Grace,* Ethel Wilson's *The Double Hook.* And Emily Carr. And poems. Lately a strong tradition of the Canadian long poem has emerged, as if this land is too large to hold a short one. So there's Ondaatje's *Billy the Kid* and Fred Wah's *Father Mother Haibun,* Phyllis Webb's *Naked Poems,* Patrick Lane's *Winter*...and many, many more.

WE ARE TELLING EACH OTHER STORIES, AND STORY creates a mythology that can explain us to ourselves. All my life, my father, an English immigrant, has complained of how wishy-washy Canadians are and how admirable are the Americans. "For example," he says, "look how proud they are of their heroes!" and rhymes off a list that includes George Washington, Davy Crockett, John Glenn. I always thought he was hero-worshipping Americans. Only recently I realized he was saying, "I want that, too." "Where," my father has been asking, "are the Canadian stories?" In England, when it came time to study Canada, his teacher ran a hand over the large pink block that was the Dominion of Canada. "Wheat," he said. "Now, let's get on to some rousing English history."

In French, the word "histoire," history, means story. The motto of the province of Quebec is all about story: "Je me souviens." I remember. My story is my history. Canada as a nation has very little history, but if ever there was a time to proclaim it, it is now. Telling stories, I become increasingly convinced, is key to the sense of community which we have lost, or never really had, and are now desperately searching for. Peter Gzowski knew this; I think it's why people cried when

Morningside ended on CBC radio. In "the old country," story was the job of the old people, but we have put them aside, in "homes," and can no longer hear them. In Canada, I can hardly find elders at all: Marian Woodman, the Jungian analyist; June Callwood, writer and activist; Margaret Laurence and Robertson Davies, also writers, now dead. So who is there to tell our stories?

Ah, those Americans and their pervasive culture would be all too happy to help. The American poet Robert Frost tells the story of how once upon a time all the Greeks were busy telling each other what the All was. All was the three elements, said one: air, earth and water. No, All was substance, said another. All was change, said a third. Finally they agreed that the best definition of All was Pythagoras' comparison of the universe with number: number of metres, grams, hours, and later population, dollars. And so we have Science and its offspring, Economics. If Pythagoras read the *Globe and Mail* or better yet the *National Post* today, he would think his philosophy triumphant; the whole story of this society, these newspapers say, is number. But I say the metaphor of number does not and can not address everything: it does not address the psychological or certain aspects of the physical, nor can it address spirit. Intangibles cannot be measured. For that, we need another measure.

IN *Land to Light On,* BRAND SAYS, "I WAS EMBARRASSED, standing like a fool, / the pine burdened in snow, the air fresh, fresh / and foreign and the sky so black and wide I did not / know which way to turn except to try again, to find / some word that could be heard by the something / waiting. My mouth could not find a language."[3]

And I think yes, it's about language. When there's something new, we must articulate it, get our tongues around it, make it real, make it last by telling it in a story. But the stories are fragile, grasped at between television commercials and American sit-coms. "Tell me about when you were young," I beg my aging parents. I bought a beautiful book of handmade paper and write their words down, by hand, etching their story – our story – onto this oh-so-fragile medium. "Turn the TV down," I beg some more.

Kroetsch says we must "salvage ourselves, not by severance," not by counting or measuring, "but by the lovely treachery of words."[4] By telling each other the stories that feed our individual and collective spirit. And maybe that's it: we have so few collective stories that the individual ones seem more vital. There is a rash of interest in "telling your own story" courses in creative writing departments these days. In an age that prides itself on the bottom line and all of us becoming rich entrepreneurs – in this society that worships number – our art schools and creative writing and music programs are full. This is inexplicable to the entrepreneurs. In a recent study, the University of Toronto program that had the best job prospects was Dance. In journals, in diaries, on the backs of matchbooks and in dance classes, people are desperate to tell their stories.

THERE IS MUCH TALK IN CERTAIN CIRCLES ABOUT the amount of money "wasted" on the arts, about wasteful efforts to protect Canadian culture at the free-trade table, and about whether we can continue to afford such "luxuries" as protecting our own culture. Everyone's story is important, and it is the artists (of all kinds) who have the time – who make the time – to go down to the roots ("radicals"), who listen and more importantly, who report back.

AS A POET, IT SEEMS TO ME WE ARE A CULTURE THAT has lost or rejected or has never grasped, a sense of symbol and metaphor. In North America, everything is what it is; a gun is a gun, not an aggressive penis; clearcut is clearcut, not the rape of the land and the destruction of our environment; the earth is dirt, not the source of all life. Metaphor extended to story is fable and myth, and we are lacking that, too. We know we are missing something, are ravenous for it, and we assume (since there are no stories, no symbols, precious little myth or imagination) that it must be an object, a thing. So we buy something. If "things" don't fill the hole, we have another drink. Another doughnut. Another lover. Diversion. Don't think. Don't feel.

Psychologist and storyteller Marion Woodman says spirit without body is ghost, but body without spirit is corpse. We are a nation of walking corpses, dead (numb) from the neck down. We don't know what we want, what would satisfy us in our heart place.

Without story, we share a pitifully small collective memory. In a recent article in *Brick* magazine, Simon McBurney says that these collective memories "are like vertical lines piercing history."[5] Vertical lines as opposed to the horizontal ones of everyday life. The vertical lines of collective memory can be gathered together in moments of doubt, used to steer a clear course.

But what kind of collective story might ours be? We have come together so recently and there has been no time. Kroetsch says that in Canada "there can be no joined story, only abrupt guesswork, juxtaposition, flashes of insight. A perpetual delay as we recognize the primacy of the forthcoming and as yet unmade discovery."[6] Ours are "poems in which archaeology supplants history."[7] Lacking a common history, we lay our stories higgledy-piggledy on top of one another: English and French over native, Irish and Italian over that, Chinese and Russian and Ukrainian, South and Central American – our history is a watery one of wave after wave of immigrants seeking peace and quiet and space.

AND OF COURSE, THERE IS THE NORTH. DIONNE BRAND says, "Maybe this wide country just stretches your life to a thinness / just trying to take it in, trying to calculate in it what you must / do...land fills your throat, you are so busy / with collecting the north.[8] What is more Canadian? In the end, the north is what anchors me, where I have always ended up when I was most desperate: Povungnituk, Baffin Island, Dease Lake. Going to extremes, I would go north. *Who the hell am I now?* I would ask, and head north because surely in all that vast space and silence there was room to listen to the voices, the small stories in my own head.

SO WE COBBLE TOGETHER A HISTORY — AND PERHAPS because we don't know what else to do, we make a mark. This seems to be an immigrant, not a native desire. While we immigrants cut the land and fenced it, built wood and later concrete towers and shelters that were cold and damp that would last "forever," native people prided themselves on how invisible they were upon the land. They called it "respect." Is this because the land is so deeply within their being that it is silly to mark one's place? Is it because their right is so unalienable, so unimaginably deep? No wonder we whites must carry weapons: the plough and the post-hole digger and the cement mixer. These are our elders. They shall rumble and rip and belch black smoky stories. Perhaps they are all we've got. This is the contradiction I live: as a carpenter I take part in the cutting of trees and the "paving of paradise" that Joni Mitchell laments. As a human being, I worry about the destruction of forests and the huge footstep we North Americans carve in the skin of the earth. Perhaps this is why I stopped working as a carpenter and became a writer, telling stories instead.

DIONNE BRAND SAYS IT RIGHT OUT: "WHAT I / REALLY want to say is, I don't want no fucking country, here / or there and all the way back, I don't like it, none of it, / easy as that. I'm giving up on land to light on, and why not, / I can't perfect my own shadow, my violent sorrow, my / individual wrists."[9]

And in the end, I can't agree. It is the land, even though it doesn't (yet?) seem "land to light on," that is my foundation, my literal underpinning, the ground I stand on. I begin to lay my stories, à la Robert Kroetsch, over this land in heaps hoping that as (if) we all do this, we shall create *someplace* to light on, a place to rest, maybe even take root. With these overlapping, zigzag stories we are building a country backwards, archeology reversed: piling our stories up, not, as in most other countries, digging down.

But we are still very young, still building a history from the ground up, standing on a bed of ancient tree branches, of vast landscape, creating a foundation, one stone – one precious story – on top of another. What a fabulous, invaluable nation such a creation might be. Let us hope we can do it well enough, and in time, so that more of us will feel – not immigrant – but home.

---

[1]Dionne Brand, I i, *Land to Light On* (Toronto: McClelland & Stewart, 1997), p.3.

[2]Kroetsch, "The Fear of Women in Prairie Fiction,:" in *The Lovely Treachery of Words,* p.73.

[3]Ibid., I iii, p.5.

[4]Ibid, p.160.
[5]Simon McBurney, "Touching History: Private Ryan and the filming of war" in *Brick a literary journal,* number 62, spring 1999, p.25.

[6]Kroetsch, "For Play and Entrance: The Contemporary canadian Long Poem," in *The Lovely Treaaachery of Words,* p.119.

[7]Ibid.

[8]Dionne Brand, *Land to Light On* (Toronto: McClelland & Stewart, 1997), p.43

[9]Brand, p.48.

A QUESTION OF IDENTITY

Nigel Darbasie

I T WAS THE CANADA DAY WEEKEND IN 1989, AND
I had been invited to join a panel on a local radio station
to discuss the "immigrant experience." This set off a flurry
of work. I reviewed material on Canada's immigration policy,
multiculturalism, census data on visible minorities, noting at
the time that at six per cent of the population, the country was
in no danger of being overrun. I wanted to be as ready as I
could, sensing where the discussion was likely to lead.
Furthermore, such an invitation was not an everyday occur-
rence.

In the course of my preparations, I came across an immigration agent's report, dated October 26th, 1910, concerning
the movement of blacks into the newly opened Canadian
West. The writer was C.W. Speers and his candour was striking.

"The peculiar prejudice of our Canadian and Anglo-Saxon
people...may be explained by the fact that, while they are willing to exercise all charity and reasonable equality, they consider themselves superior to the black race and want this to be
retained as a white man's country. I do not presume to be able
to explain this prejudice, but I am compelled to record the fact
that it is most general, most unanious (sic) and is assuming an
acute stage."

Speer's comments were underscored when, on the day of

the show, the media reported on a potential clash between neo-Nazis and human-rights protesters at a supremacists' rally planned for the weekend in Minden, Ontario. It was an unsettling backdrop to our session, which turned out to be live, slipped between a weather forecast and events around town. True to expectations, we contemplated multiculturalism, immigration, the Canadian soul and other imponderables, all in the allotted time of ten minutes.

Beneath our talk and the events at Minden lay the real problem of Canadian identity: the country's inherent racialization, a key factor underpinning the resistance to Canada's growing ethnic diversity, a cosmopolitanism that had begun when the French and English landed. Or, taking a longer view, that had been going on ever since humans stood on two legs and started walking around in and out of Africa. Or, if you prefer Biblical genealogy, ever since Noah and his offspring began repopulating the earth after the flood. Like Speers in his report, we need to understand this peculiar prejudice.

Race is a European invention that began taking shape in the sixteenth century. It is a system of beliefs that, based on physical appearance, humans can be divided into distinct groups, their physical traits being indicative of qualities such as intelligence, temperament, and moral virtue. The ideology posits that there is a natural ranking and inequality of races, among whom whites stand supreme. Such thinking holds that the totality of one's being is determined by race; it is inheritable – in the blood – and cannot be truly altered.

ANOTHER COMPONENT OF RACIALIZED THINKING IS the concept of purity, which can be diluted or lost through intermixing. This poses no small contradiction when one considers that Europeans are themselves of mixed bloodlines, and that in colonizing the New World they spread their genes around, creating significant populations of mulattos, mestizos and Metis, the result of white unions with Africans and aboriginal peoples.

The ideas that coalesced into the concept of race arose, innocently enough, in the search for identity, the universal need among human tribes to claim a line of descent, a point of origin. Europeans at first found their answer in paganism, then in Christianity which, in its adoption by the Roman Empire, began toppling a vast array of old gods. Christianity brought diverse tribes together under one creator, presenting them with a single cosmogony that explained all human existence in a line beginning with Adam and Eve, then proceeding to Noah and his sons Japheth, Shem, and Ham.

Biblical exegetes deduced that Europeans descended from Japheth, the Semitic peoples from Shem, Africans and other dark-skinned peoples from Ham. According to the Bible, Japheth and Shem were favoured; Ham was cursed when he entered Noah's tent and saw his father's nakedness. Noah's curse fell, in fact, on Ham's fourth son who was doomed to be a "servant of servants" to his brothers. This passage has been cited as Biblical justification for the enslavement of blacks.

The historian Cheikh Anta Diop offers an explanation for this stroke of bad luck. The Hamites were Egyptians who had enslaved the Israelites, authors of the Old Testament and its Book of Genesis, who took the opportunity in their writings to lay down a hex on their former oppressors. There was another unfortunate coincidence for the descendants of Ham: the association of the colour black with evil; white with godliness.

In these revelations I found the answer to a puzzle that had intrigued me for some time: the tribalization of church iconography; the blond depictions of Christ, of angels and saints who populated heavenly scenes and, by deduction, God himself. There were other matters, such as the men who preached hatred while claiming to be defenders of Christianity; the contradiction of white and black churches. It was all too apparent, the extent to which the holy word had been racialized.

For almost a millennium, Europeans delivered the gospel as the Lord's chosen apostles. Then came a seventh-century challenge from an alternative monotheism, Islam. According to historian Bernard Lewis, "Islam was not the first religion whose spokesmen claimed that the truths entrusted to them were not only universal but also exclusive – that they were the sole custodians of God's final revelation which it was their duty to bring to all peoples of the world. But the Muslims were the first to make significant progress in achieving this aim, by creating a religious civilization beyond the limits of a single race or region or culture. The Islamic world in the high Middle Ages was international, multiracial, polyethnic, one might even say intercontinental.... Yet it was the poor, parochial, monochrome culture of Christian Europe that advanced from strength to strength...." Conflict was inevitable. By the will of God, Islam and Christianity became locked in centuries of war during the Crusades.

In a significant Islamic victory, the Moors took Spain, maintaining their presence for some eight hundred years. They were enlightened conquerors for their time, accommodating a remarkable degree of religious and ethnic pluralism. However, the Spaniards were not so inclined. In their Reconquest they set about expelling Moors and Jews. An Inquisition was launched to weed them out, along with those who were converts and not of "pure" Christian lineage. By law, such persons were barred from certain occupations and activities. This led many Spaniards to obtain certificates of *limpieza de sangre,* purity of blood, issued by the church for a fee. The certificates attested that one's genealogy was untainted by Moorish or Jewish blood, relieving the bearers from investigation by the Holy Office. It was an incipient racial ideology in practice, on the eve of the Age of Exploration, by the country that would lead the European charge into the New World.

In the sixteenth century, Europeans sailed into the Americas and extended their explorations of Africa and Asia. Racial ideology took shape in the context of their contact with peoples they had never before encountered, many of whom in terms of material culture and technology were less advanced, without effective countermeasures to muskets, cannon, and the Bible. In particular, it was Africans and their enslavement in the New World that provided Europeans with the terms of their self-definition, and around whom racial ideology would fully develop.

Prominent thinkers would argue that blacks were not human, or just barely so. As such, slavery was their natural condition, one that befitted them. Some of these arguments would be framed not only in the context of the emerging sciences of anthropology and genetics, but also against the realization that the wealth of many European nations was directly linked to their New World colonies. Plantation slavery had become an engine of economic growth, lubricated by the myth of race.

While there were enslaved Africans in Canada from its beginning as a French settlement, the country escaped the large-scale bondage that the French and English established in their southern colonies. Nevertheless, beliefs about the status of blacks in the human family had already infused Canadians. Robin Winks in *The Blacks in Canada: A History,* writes: "The racial prejudice which was beginning to be apparent at the close of the French period, and which intensified greatly in the following decades, appears to have grown independently of ideas relating directly to slavery. Negroes were inferior not because they had been slaves but because they were Negroes."

And there was an emerging quality in the Canadian character: the art of turning the blind eye. The French Revolution, with its ideals of liberty, equality, fraternity, presented immense problems not only for French colonial societies, but also for other slave-holding European powers. But as Winks observes, "...not so in Canada, where the revolutionary ideals took little root. Inaction not égalité aided the Negro...."

The fight against slavery was carried by several distinguished abolitionists, one of whom was Lieutenant-Governor John Simcoe. In celebrating his accomplishments, we should remember that the "abolition" act he spearheaded in September 1793 amounted to a Canadian classic, freeing not a single slave. While no one was to be enslaved after passage of the act, those who were legally slaves would continue as such until death. Children born after the act would be free at the age of twenty-five. It was abolition by attrition, and it arose as a compromise in the face of resistance from a powerful lobby of slaveholders. It was a compromise in the face of the deep-seated corruption that slavery and its underpinning ideas of race exacted upon Canada.

The laws of the state, guaranteeing basic rights to its citizens, treated slaves as movable property, so that the question of slavery became one of the property rights of slaveholders. Slavery commodified humans. In a sense, it was a fundamental dilemma of progress: the choice between profit and doing the right thing, a decision that would be linked to another ideology – capitalism.

In Nova Scotia in 1807, twenty-seven Loyalists owning a total of eighty-four slaves petitioned to have the government either introduce legislation that would keep their property secure, or "in the true interest of Humanity" abolish slavery while paying the owners compensation.

On Canada's religious front, the abolitionist Reverend James MacGregor launched attacks in his sermons and writings. In a public letter of 1788 to a fellow clergyman who owned a slave, MacGregor addressed, among several pro-slavery arguments, the question of colour. As Winks recounts:

"...that black men were creatures of the devil, as shown by their colour, was scarcely true, he (MacGregor) argued, for white men only thought the devil black as an opposite to themselves; in Africa black men thought him white.... Further, 'the devil being a spirit can have no colour, and it is merely by a figure of speech we call him black.'" The voices of churchmen like MacGregor, and the anti-slavery work of countless others, brought Christianity into the light. That was in the past.

The colonial powers have abolished slavery and dismantled their empires. Among world religions, mainstream Christianity has made great strides, standing at the forefront of a wide range of human issues such as social justice, human rights, poverty, and ecumenism. And science has debunked the ideas of race, suggesting that if we wanted to divide humans into valid categories, we could do so on the basis, for example, of the possession of anti-malarial genes. This would place the likes of Yemenites, the Dinkas of Africa, Thais, Italians and Greeks into one race, while northern Europeans like Swedes and Germans, and the Xhosas of South Africa would be grouped into another.

Alternatively, humans could be divided on the basis of the possession of the enzyme lactase, creating a race of milk-drinkers that would include Arabs, India's northerners, the Fulani of Africa, and Europeans. The rest of us would be lactase-negative. But this would ruin the concept entirely, since race isn't about genetic truth, but about maintaining power through a visible form of social stratification.

The fact is that we remain infected by a potent ideology of difference. If you listen, you'll hear it blurted out loud, or slipping from the subconscious, in those wonderful, interminable discussions we like to have about "who we are as Canadians."

WHITE GIRL SCREAMING

Sue Walsh

S A YOUNG GIRL I LAY IN THE DARK AND LISTENED to the whispers. My friend Sharon Bennett lay in the bed nearest the window and told me in hushed but excited tones that a teenage girl she knew had been attacked. Apparently, this girl slept in a bed next to a window and in the middle of the night a strange man reached in through the open glass – or did he smash it? – and held a knife right to her tender throat. From then on, I made sure I slept in the bed farthest from the window. Some nights, I lay half-dreaming, half-waiting, for that arm to come through the burglar bars, for a hand to grip my throat, for the cut of the knife. It went without saying that the hand would be black.

Growing up in white South Africa, a lot of things went without saying. If your house was burgled, it was surely a black man who'd done it. If a murderer's mug shot appeared in the daily paper, his face was often too dark and the print too grainy, to make out individual features. If a white woman was brutally raped, it was a given that the "bastard who'd done it" was some filthy black man after pure white flesh.

As an adult, I have wondered how I came by these givens. Someone must have said something; white folks must have been talking. And were they spreading insidious lies? Yes and no. No, because the majority of criminals stealing, assaulting and murdering in South Africa were, and continue to be, urban black males. Black South Africans outnumber whites five to one, and for every thirty unemployed black men, there are five unemployed whites. Crime in South Africa is, to some degree, a symptom of racialized economics and representative demographics. The haves versus the have-nots. On the other hand, yes. Yes, they are insidious lies because white people in South Africa were, and still are, paralyzed by fear, and fear breeds hatred, lies and more fear.

Not to mention distortion. For many years, whenever I heard of a woman being attacked or a house broken into, there was the immediate fear of the grasp and slice of the knife through that bedroom window. In my mind I would scream. In my mind I do scream. Almost thirty years later, I still have to remind myself that this is a fear largely based on a fiction – on a hearsay passed on from one small girl to another.

The basis for fear is now thousands of miles away. I live in Victoria, British Columbia, a city where black males are in the visible minority. I have replaced fiction with fact and tell myself that most white women raped in Canada are assaulted by white men they know personally – no tall, dark strangers. I listen to the statistics. I take a self-defence course. Yet in my distorted mind's eye, the likelihood of an intruder breaking into my home being black is disproportionately high.

And so I confront racism and prejudice within myself. I try to understand why and how I came to fear this unknown black man. The risk of writing about him – of bringing him out into the supposed "clear light of day" – is that I nourish similar fear in others. I hope I don't. We can talk all we like about the elimination of hate and prejudice, but unless we examine the depth and nature of our individual fears, we change nothing.

I GREW UP JUST OUTSIDE PRETORIA, A PREDOMINANTLY Afrikaner city and South Africa's administrative capital.

Pretoria is also a military settlement, with both national army and airforce headquarters not far from my childhood home. Many of my friends' fathers were military men – men, I thought as a child, who held the weight of the country's "security" on their shoulders. In the evenings they walked home down the hill to their families, sun low on the horizon, military stripes and brass heavy on their chests.

My father sold IBM typewriters. Our family was quintessential middle-class white South Africa. My parents argued about money, but we lived in a comfortable home with a rockery filled with aloes and shrubs, an aviary full of domestic and imported finches, and a swimming pool with a mosaic octopus that my artistic mother designed and pieced together by hand.

It was in this pool, at age six or seven, I first realized that black men were real men, and that there was something sexual and shameful about race. One late afternoon Sharon Bennett and I were splashing around in the shallow end, two small blonde girls skipping in and out, shrieking, the Alsatian barking. Mac the gardener was up at the far end of the pool, pruning the grapevine, not paying us a bit of attention. It is only a snippet of memory: "Hey, garden boy, look!" Sharon flipping up her string bikini top and holding it there. The small flat round nipples like two blind eyes. And my horror at the act. Then her persistence, "Hey, you – garden boy, I said look!" I remember Mac's head turning, the brief look of incomprehension and bewilderment. He turned away quickly. I was so ashamed.

As an adult, I remember now that Mac worked at the airforce base during the day, and did garden work for my parents in the evenings in exchange for the small *khaya* room at the top end of our yard. I remember too that he was an ace soccer player, and that Saturday afternoons he would sit on his haunches in our living room watching the Kaiser Chiefs thrash the Mamelodi Sundowns on TV, he and my mother whistling and hooting for their favourite players. If I think even harder, I remember that he was a tall, handsome man with a shy, young wife and two healthy toddlers. Yet in my mind, there is something shameful about Mac, shameful about Sharon Bennett. Shameful about my own body?

Behind our property was an expanse of open *veld*. Down the side ran a dried-up ravine that flooded every year with the heavy rains. During the dry season, we kids went exploring, crawling on our hands and knees through the twin water tunnels that ran under the bridge on Oslo Road and out the other side just next to our house. At night, the *veld* around this ravine was dark territory; we knew it was dangerous. Black people partied and drank there, building small fires to warm themselves on frosty highveld nights. Men shouted, women shrieked, dogs barked and crickets chirped. We stayed indoors.

I first learned about sex in this ravine. Cheryl Whitfield, who was a few years older and lived next door, insisted she'd seen two black people doing it down in the tunnel. I had no idea what she meant. Her eyes were wide: "There was this black and he was lying on top of this *ousie* girl and they were doing it," she said without breathing once.

Cheryl dragged me down there, through the long grasses, jumping down onto the soft silt and crouching low to look into one of the tunnels. We held our noses because it smelled of pee and stale beer and there were lumps of turd too big to belong to the neighbourhood animals. She pointed to where she'd seen the copulators, the woman lying flat on her back in this mess, the man bearing – no, squashing – down on her. I could barely breathe.

When I passed this story on to my bun-headed ballet friends, Valerie Williet, also a year or two older and wiser, confirmed my worst fears. It was true, she said. Sex meant men lay on top of women, "and then he puts his thing in her thing, and in and out and in and out, and then they have a baby." I thought of the filthy tunnel, the acrid smells, the brutal force. The act seemed savage. It was filthy, and from what I could see in the tunnel, it was black.

I remember also, from these years, the first time a black actor played Othello in South Africa, remember the outrage when the Sunday paper printed a picture of this man kissing his Desdemona. There was a collective gasp. The Immorality Act was still firmly in place, and it was illegal for black and white flesh to mingle.

In retrospect, this racialization of sex seems so absurd. As an adult, I see how ludicrous it was and laugh it off. But as a small girl, I took it for truth, and I must note that millions of young white girls like me grew up to be women – girls whose experience was even more racialized, whose parents were far more prejudiced than my own. Some of these girls were not as protected as I was, and perhaps experienced real-life acts of sex or brutality. And so I see that it is often through these insidious couplings of skin and dirt and sex and fear that racism and prejudice are perpetuated.

As I grew up, the threat to my body and life was always black and always male. Black women were our maids and nannies – women who sang as they carried us on their backs, made us apricot jam sandwiches and cleaned the scum out of our bathtubs. They were second mothers. Black men, on the other hand, were distant and inscrutable – foreign in their strangeness and silence. Black men, we were informed by some kind of dull cultural osmosis, were either lazy or stupid or terribly vicious. They circled on the periphery of white consciousness, like dogs, waiting.

The mid-seventies saw the coming of television to South Africa. Along with the Brady Bunch, "Who shot JR?" and local sports coverage, we were subject to a steady diet of township riots, Communist threat, and terrorist bomb blasts on the evening news. This was the height of *swart gevaar* in white South Africa, the fear being that an army of black guerrillas, armed with Soviet machine guns, would march down the face of Africa to seize power. Whites would be killed in the dark of night and their houses taken from them.

At the same time, I began to see contradictions in these perceptions. I was perhaps only ten years old, but I suspected that these nameless, faceless black shadow men – the fear incarnate – had to be none other than the everyday neighbourhood men who slouched on the corner outside Shorty's Café. Men who glanced balefully at me, a small white girl not wearing her shoes as she slipped by them to get a litre of Coke from the local Fish-and-Chip shop. Men like Koosie, our maid's delinquent lover, who alternately beat her and loved her and sneered at my parents' threats to call the police. We often saw Koosie lounging on the pavement up at Shorty's, and though I was petrified of him, I sensed he and his friends knew something I did not. I understood on some instinctive level that men like Koosie were not stupid.

At thirteen, with my parents just divorced, I moved down to the tropical port city of Durban with my mother and younger brother. In the new verandahed house, with another sparkling pool and surrounded by thick bushes, there was still the unspoken fear of the hand through the window. I mentally calculated whether a man could stand on the slim ledge outside my bedroom and reach in through the burglar bars. We knew people cut through our property in the dead of night and that vagrants slept in the rambling hedges down by the gate. Again, we stayed mostly indoors at night.

At this Durban house, we had a once-a-week gardener called Sipho, a man even more mysterious than Mac because he came, worked and left in absolute silence. He was Zulu and spoke little English. At the outset, my mother laid the water hose in an artful curve where she'd planned flowerbeds. But Sipho defied her designs, chopping flat angular beds longer or wider than she wanted. He also routinely chopped her roof-high poinsettia hedge down to the ground without asking. At fourteen, I began to see the humour in this. Still, I took care not to suntan when Sipho worked in the garden. If I did swim when he was working nearby, I took a breath and did careful lengths underwater. When I came up for breath, I partly expected to see Sharon Bennett flashing her now-matured breasts. "Look, garden boy, look!"

OVER THE YEARS, THE THREAT OF SEX AND DANGER diminished, a creeping realization of South African politics and the imbalance of it all replacing some of the fear. I remember friends coming down on holiday from Pretoria in the mid-80s. Wayne, the eldest son, and I wanted to drive down to Battery Beach for the afternoon; there were water restrictions and we were hot and grubby. The beaches along Durban's Golden Mile had just been de-restricted – no more whites-only, coloureds-only, blacks-only swimming areas. Battery, the nicest beach, was now open to all. My mother flatly refused. The idea of me swimming with blacks was completely unacceptable to her. "I don't want black men staring at you on the beach." I was horrified, a new kind of horror. "But I'm with Wayne! We're just going for a swim!" What did it matter whether a man who stared at me was black or white? She refused. Filled with righteous disgust and indignation, we slammed our car doors and tore off up the hill to buy ice cream cones instead. The fact that Wayne could have driven me anywhere and done anything he pleased didn't seem to occur to her. I sat fuming in the blazing sun.

In some obscure way, my mother might like to know that

her fears were justified. The only time I have been sexually assaulted the perpetrator was a black man. It is a small but vivid memory, an event of indeterminable and ambiguous impact. I was fifteen years old, running down the wide, curving staircase at a discount superstore in downtown Durban. It was near closing time, and the store was almost deserted. I knew that my father, who was visiting at the time, was waiting for me in the checkout line downstairs.

I was late and watching my feet so I did not fall, admiring the new belt I had bought two floors above. Then, on the periphery of my vision, I saw a quick dark shape coming up in the opposite direction. The instant I lifted my head, he reached across the wide stairs, grabbed quickly at my crotch and kept on going. I doubt I screamed, but I did look back and remember a wide, toothy grin, a cheeky smile. Under other circumstances my dad might have called him a chancer.

I could not tell my parents, though. Partly because the act confused and shocked me into silence, partly because it seemed so fleeting and insignificant, partly because he was black. They would be incensed. My mother would blame my father for not being with me, and I would have to explain to my dad in words of sex what had happened. In hindsight, I see that this black man was just a teenage boy taking a chance, climbing a wide, deserted staircase and seeing a white girl coming down the stairs, a girl his own age. The adults wouldn't have seen it that way, and I had no words to explain.

It is difficult to implicate your own parents, harder to expose their prejudices than it is to reveal your own. I imagine my mother's biases must spring from fears similar to my own, from years of being white and woman in a land full of black men, a land that is increasingly violent. She lives alone in Durban, a city where criminals can be desperate, ruthless and callous, where she is always in danger of being robbed, carjacked or shot. Still, living half a world away, and having the luxury to do so, I feel the need to move beyond this fear, both hers and mine.

WHEN I CAME TO CANADA IN THE EARLY NINETIES, I met a whole community of black South Africans, many of them exiled ANC and PAC MEMBERS. For the first time, I saw the individual eyes and ears, the flatter noses and sardonic smiles of South Africa's civil war. I heard real-life stories, both funny and full of terror, from people who had lived it from the other side. My husband David and I met and befriended black men and women, ate and drank wine with them, invited friends over to our home. And yet, I found myself trying to behave normally, to pretend this was nothing out of the ordinary for me, but it was. I remember having an ex-freedom fighter over to stay for the weekend and lying awake that night, some small, irrational part of me quietly screaming, wanting to lock my bedroom door to keep him out – and then the slow resisting of this fear.

In 1995, we travelled back to Southern Africa for the first time. The first multi-racial elections had birthed a "new" South Africa, and the dreaded *swart gevaar* was a thing of the past. Violent crime, though, was on the rise, and it seemed every friend and relative knew someone who'd been held at gunpoint or robbed or carjacked – a new kind of *gevaar*. And so, once again, we stayed mostly indoors at night.

The month we spent with friends in a township in Zimbabwe was altogether different. Here, I was often the only white woman in sight, and yet, I felt perfectly safe walking alone down the dusty street to buy a pint of milk. Once or twice, I brushed off a come-on from a man sitting on the concrete steps outside the café, and smiled to myself. I had travelled a long way.

Finally, there is a long-term friendship with a microbiologist originally from Swaziland, now living in Seattle. He and I flirt at times on the phone, my husband listening in from the kitchen, chuckling and shaking his head as he washes the dishes. This man called Khisi knows very little of where I've come from, but tells me in no uncertain terms just how sexy his black ass is, and that women cannot resist him when he takes his gorgeous son Nathan to the park in his stroller. I know his white wife Julia is rolling her eyes on the other end of the line. I remind him that his child might be gorgeous, but that Nathan's good looks are entirely from his beautiful mother. "Bullshit!" he says, and we laugh. He knows that I am only teasing, for they are both fine-looking people.

These are the triumphs, the moving beyond race and the moving beyond fear. These are the days when the small white girl inside me looms larger than the shadows, and she is cheering.

UNDER MY SKIN

Caterina Edwards

"WHAT DAY IS IT TODAY?"

The three of us are sitting around the kitchen table: the psychiatric nurse, my mother, and I.

"What year is it?" The nurse smiles and nods encouragingly. "What year?" She is radiant in her bright summer dress, radiant with youth and prettiness and health.

"1982," my mother says. The nurse smiles and nods again, as if the answer were the right one.

"Mrs. Edwards, what month is it? Can you tell me the month?"

My mother turns her face to me. I translate the nurse's words into Italian.

"November," she says in a confident voice. "November," I translate, suppressing the urge to supply the right answer.

My mother has failed various parts of the test, and I am embarrassed. She shakes her head when asked her address and telephone number. Wait, I want to say, she knows how much she paid for this tablecloth twenty years ago. She knows the exact age of my children in each of their childhood pictures.... She knows more than you think. Sometimes I do prompt her a bit. Remember I say, and I drop an appropriate hint.

Remember, please –

I know what the nurse will say to me once we stand up and move off to the front door. I know the diagnosis. This is not the first assessment my mother has undergone. Other times, I wasn't allowed to attend, but the doctor has decided I am needed because of "the language problem." I know the nurse will assume a concerned and caring expression; she may touch my hand. "Alzheimer's or senile dementia," she will say. "The results are the same." She has a pile of leaflets from the "coping with caring" office that she will press on me. Tips on feeding, bathing, toileting. How to allay anxiety, how to minimize disorientation and delusion.

Disoriented? Delusional? Let me count the ways: when she doesn't recognize the rooms of her apartment, when she claims that a dark woman broke her watch, that a homecare worker stole her teeth, that a strange man turned on the stove and left it on, when she screams at me, "I know what you want to do to me." Paranoia, hysteria, rage: I have watched my mother suffer through them all.

The test is over. In a moment, the visitor will stand up. In a moment, I will stand and continue coping. Mamma is chatting freely now, throwing out a mixture of Italian and English words. The nurse keeps smiling. "Oh, yes," she says. Usually, I step in and translate, adding a little order and meaning. But suddenly I am exhausted. I cannot move. Or talk. As my eyelids droop, I see the three of us at the table, an illustration of the phases of womanhood, with me in the middle: confused and hovering between confident youth and tremulous age, between sun and shadow. The nurse glows; Mamma's eyes are opaque, her body shrunken. She soaks up my light, pulls me to her darkness. I feel myself growing old, moment by moment.

WHEN I WAS A GIRL, PARTICULARLY WHEN I WAS A teenager, I was convinced my mother was insane. I was waging my war of independence, and though I knew that several of my friends were also in conflict with their parents, I was sure that no one was oppressed as I was. The rules my mother imposed made no sense. No lipstick, no dating, no fashionable clothes, no sports, "they're bad for you," no ballet lessons, no hanging out, straight home after school, no nasty friends no, no, no. No life, I thought. I may as well be dead, I thought. (I always had a melodramatic streak.)

She taught me to starch linen tablecloths, iron sheets, polish silver, and, though I was all thumbs, to embroider. She sent unmusical me to years of piano lessons. She bought me a hope chest that she expected, dreamed, we would fill with Murano-blown glass and sheets and cloths that I had embroidered.

She said: never place a hat on the bed, never open an umbrella in the house, never eat meat on Friday, never put the bread plate on the right, that's where the wineglass goes. She said: never go out without a vest, never let a man touch you...until you're married, never drink juice cold from the fridge, never wash your hair while you are having a period. Each rule was of equal weight and importance. I insisted – truthfully – that none of the other girls had to follow such rules.

"Janice," I would say, "showers during her period all the time. And nothing happens. She's healthier than I am."

My mother would shake her head gloomily. "So far," she would say, and then add her favorite rhetorical question, "if all the other girls threw themselves into the canal, would you?"

Into the canal: that should have been my clue. My mother's frame of reference was Venezia in the twenties and thirties, the time when she was growing up. But then, I persisted in judging the rules as irrational, examples of my mother's delusional vision of the world.

"Why are you wearing that vest thing?" Janice once asked as we changed for gym.

I gave my usual answer: "It's my mother. She won't listen to reason."

Janice's response was also habitual. "She is odd. Really odd."

AS THE YEARS PASSED, SHE HAD TO GIVE IN ON MANY of her rules. My father pressured her. And then, I went away to university, two hundred miles away. She could no longer stop me wearing lipstick, pale and shiny, heavy eye makeup, miniskirts and tight tops. She had not completely stopped me before. I waited until I left the house and then I layered on the black eyeliner and rolled up my waistband. But now I could be more open. "Get real, mother." I no longer had to date on the sly. Mamma had to limit herself to calling me a *puttana* and comparing the young man to a piece of *baccala*.

But the undershirt – that fight went on and on. Mamma would not budge. I had to wear an undershirt, woolen in winter, cotton in summer, or I would catch pneumonia. In this damned climate, it was a matter of life and death. I told her I was willing to take the risk.

"Only grandfathers wear them," I said, echoing the all-knowledgeable Janice. "None of the girls do."

"If they want to throw themselves in the canal?"

"You can't even buy those things here."

Mamma had the woolen undershirts for herself, my father and me sent from Italy. They were of a fine, soft wool, close fitting. But I found them chafing, itchy, humiliating. I was always worried a bit might show at a loose neckline or through a too-sheer blouse. Even if it didn't show, I knew it was there, next to my skin, marking me out as different.

Providentially, I developed an allergy to wool. Mamma added to my pile of sleeveless cotton undershirts. They were less obvious, but still irritating. It was the sixties; the look was sleek, modern and minimal. Three sets of straps from bra, undershirt and slip were too much.

No way: when I went to university, I dropped all three layers. Burn the bra and the undershirt. We argued on each of my trips home. It wasn't decent, not wearing an undershirt. Or a slip. Or –

In Mamma's eyes, I had grown into someone alien, unrecognizable. Ironically, when things between us were at their worst, I started spending more time in Italy. And I quickly discovered that what I had thought were Mamma's private obsessions were actually national myths. Undershirts, for example, were almost universal. And cold drinks, don't even think of it: the dangers were too great.

I also realized that the woman she wanted me to be was not just her particular fantasy. I found the prototype in the nineteenth-century novels – the lady, modest, sheltered and accomplished, the lady, who knew how to run a household, knew how to command servants, who could entertain the dinner guests with a turn at the piano, who could exchange witty conversation with her head bent becomingly over an embroidery ring.

A lady fulfilled by her service to her husband, her children and her aged parents. An outmoded ideal, but prewar it was still potent for the Venetian middle class. Not that my mother was part of that middle class. She was an orphan, forced at the age of ten to leave home and go to work at a bakery in Padova, forced to live in the house of employers and well-off relatives most of her youth. At close quarters she watched how other girls lived and were educated. She aspired. Over the years and miles, the aspiration intensified, refined itself into a fixed purpose. As her only child, I was her outlet and object. She was determined to give me all the guidance she never got.

What a disappointment I have been to her: cold and Canadian.

"*Buona da niente,*" she yelled at me. Good for nothing, she still yells when I try to help her. She has forgotten much, but she insults me in exactly the same way she always has. *"Non diventerai mai donna,"* was one of her favorite phrases. "You'll never become a woman," she tells me repeatedly, shaking her head sadly. "Poor me," she usually adds. "Poor me."

Poor Mamma.

A characteristic of Alzheimer's disease is that those afflicted lose all sense of being at home in the world. They are disoriented, disconnected. Everything seems unfamiliar, strange, uncanny.

Mamma has lived in Canada for forty-one years, but she has always refused to make it her home. She has remained resolutely closed, impervious to this country in both her attitudes and her skills. She never learned to write a cheque, to drive a car or to speak more than rudimentary English. It does not seem odd to her that she does not know her address or phone number. Part of her never knew where she was. Now all of her feels out of place.

"Where are you going?" she asks loudly, anxiously, each time I am about to leave.

When I try to take her out for a doctor's appointment or to the hairdresser's, she stalls and complains. A few times she is so agitated that she flails at me, landing a few ineffective punches. Once, instead of distracting her, as the brochures counsel, I catch her wrist in my hand and hold her arm still. "I am stronger than you," I remind her.

The intensity of her rage was always unusual, surprising. From childhood on, I was determined not to be like her. I trained myself to suppress anger, to control actions and words. My ideal was Canadian: easy does it, don't make a fuss, relax, kick back, play it as it lays. What goes around comes around.

When I was in therapy, dealing with, as the psychologist put it, "issues with my mother," I was encouraged to "face my anger" by hitting a pillow with a tennis racket. I tried, I did, but I never could do it. It felt too silly, too foreign.

Now I am startled not by my mother's anger, but my own. She stalls, and I find myself shrieking and jumping with rage. Like a cartoon character, up, up, I feel jet-propelled, down, thump, and up. I am ashamed and exhilarated. And eventually amused.

You can take the undershirt off, rip it up before you toss it away. But you can't really get rid of it. It stays with you – that sensation of itchy wool – no longer over but under the skin.

When I confess my tantrums to the nurse, she is reassuring, "it's natural. It's very common." Then, with a professional, concerned look. "You don't have to do this, you know. There are alternatives."

"I have to try," I say. "It's the way I was raised," as if I hadn't spent my life resisting that way.

ZAIDA

Joshua Frost

T HE GESTAPO MARCHED INTO RACHOINZ ON *Shabbis* – the day of rest. Row after row of young, clean-cut German soldiers, indistinguishable in the uniform of the Nazi, smug with the virtue of superiority, declared a small *shtetl* in the northeast corner of Poland their own. Mendel Frost left synagogue to see the spectacle but soon returned. Scripture waits for no one.

Yom Kippur, the day of atonement, would be the last time he ever saw that synagogue. The rabbi had explicit orders to discuss only the Torah. Anything political and he would be killed. Mendel fasted, like all Jews on Yom Kippur, and after sunset waited in the square for the Gestapo with the others. The officer in charge ordered the Jews to clean the streets on hands and knees. "If that should be all," Mendel thought, "we are very blessed."

The next day, the Nazis ordered the Jews to gather in the town square once again. The same Gestapo officer laid the rabbi's son on a bench. Mendel watched. The young officer told the rabbi to beat his ten-year-old son. The rabbi, with an open hand, slapped his boy across the chest and on his legs. After each slap the rabbi turned away. The boy remained silent. After ten or fifteen slaps, the officer stopped the charade. The officer loudly declared that the beating was not to Nazi standards. To the delight of the other officers, he beat the rabbi until he could no longer move or breathe. One of the other officers took the still-silent boy away. Nobody knew what happened to the boy; everyone believed that he was killed.

Mendel saw the disbelief, shock and fear in the eyes of every witness.

Mendel watched the rabbi lie still in the middle of the square. Mendel could do nothing. Mendel prayed.

Two days later, the train came for the Jews of Rachoinz. They were sent to the Warsaw Ghetto. Just one stop for Mendel Frost, my *zaida*, on the way to Birkenau.

At age six I rejected faith. God couldn't compete with something more real – television. That day, as on all Yom Kippurs, my parents insisted that I attend synagogue. Since it was a Saturday, all of the best cartoons were on TV, and I didn't want to leave the house. I threw the loudest, most obnoxious temper tantrum this world has ever seen. To no avail; an hour later I was sitting beside my *zaida* in synagogue.

The two worlds sit uncomfortably beside each other. My *zaida*, a man who lived through the horrors of the camps, believes in God. I do not. I am a faithless, secular-culture-loving, twenty-three-year-old Jew and I am not alone. Most Jews in their twenties don't go to synagogue because the Purposeful Maker can't compete with the material world he created.

After barely escaping the Holocaust, the chosen people are choosing to leave the religion. We are assimilating into the larger secular culture with astonishing abandon. One rabbi says that nearly half of all Jews are marrying out of the faith. His synagogue is filled with old people. Soon, there will be almost nobody left to fill the pews on *Shabbis*.

THE JEWISH COMMUNITY LOST A WAR BEFORE IT properly identified the enemy. Rabbis once preached that secular culture should be ignored altogether. The strategy failed.

Secular culture is now explained in a Jewish context, and rabbis will slip a TV or movie reference into conversations with younger Jews. Clearly, the hip-rabbi approach isn't working, either. The community still hasn't admitted to itself the real problem: young Jews don't feel that they need faith.

Many young Jews have too much money. Money facilitates full immersion into secular culture. Secular culture is everything except for God. We are victims of our own success. There is no need to have faith. We already have it all – huge TVs, nice cars and big houses in posh neighbourhoods.

Faith provides answers to questions larger than any one individual, but most young Jews don't think about eternity. Secular culture fulfills desires of the material in the present. God can't compete with secular culture nor should He try. To the believer, faith promises more than instant gratification. Faith promises eternity.

MY *zaida* FINDS IT HARD TO BREATHE – THE START of congenital heart failure. Each time I visit, he wastes a few breaths to ask if I am dating someone. I usually tell him that I am to end the conversation and avoid an argument. I would never say that I date non-Jewish girls. It would break his frail heart to know that I am part of the problem. I am the Jew his rabbi preaches about. I am the Jew with assimilationist fantasies. I am the Jew who would marry a *goy* and never return to my *zaida's* synagogue. I am everything my *zaida* can't understand, but I am also everything that he loves.

About a year ago my *zaida* explained his faith and told me that believing in God is the only way our world can make sense. I agreed with him, but our worlds are not the same. Perhaps God is the only way his world can make sense. I can't understand why he believes in God because I can't make sense of his life – the Holocaust, the hardship and the poverty.

My *zaida* needs faith as he needs air to breathe. After the war, after bearing witness to the coldest, darkest corner of humanity's heart, faith was all that was left. I don't have faith because I don't need my existence explained. Secular culture provides me with a necessary diversion from questions of life and death as the holocaust must provide the impetus to accept God. The comparison is as absurd as trying to understand my life in the context of my *zaida's*.

I AM NOT A SURVIVOR. MY RELATIVE AFFLUENCE IS not a result of some great Herculean trial but of luck. In no way do I deserve the lifestyle I was born into; I haven't earned it. The poverty *zaida* has endured for most of his life is also a result of luck. He was lucky to survive to camps. He has lived an incomprehensible life and in the complexity sees God. The staid and tired colours radiating from the TV screen fill me with feelings of passivity and apathy. God can't be felt by those who don't appreciate anything.

My lack of faith might be a test orchestrated by a perverse God. My *zaida's* test was extreme and vulgar; he escaped not only with his life, but with a love for The Maker. The apathy and dislocation that I feel in the core of my soul could be my personal concentration camp. I must conquer these emotions and replace them with love and deference for God. In the present I can't. I only think of myself and the foolishness of faith. I love my *zaida* dearly but I know when he dies that will be all; I will never see him again. If overcoming secular culture is my trial of faith, I am failing.

I now attend synagogue on Yom Kippur because it pleases my *zaida*. As I sit beside him, I am unable to pray. I think about sex and sports and social plans for the afternoon. My *zaida's* face contorts and twitches in synch with the tone-deaf wails of the cantor. Each prayer, each word and each sound has infinite meaning for Mendel Frost.

The concentration camps ravaged his family – he was the only survivor. Rachoinz no longer exists. Faith, through unimaginable hardship and trial, remains. Now, as the prayers move from irrelevant to sycophantic, my *zaida* starts to cry. Gently at first, but soon he is silently sobbing. The tears roll off his worn face to their final resting place, the prayer book resting on his lap.

I dare not look into his eyes because I know I will cry. I try to turn and face the opposite direction but am unable to escape my thoughts. They entrap me and forcefully return me to him. His life as one giant trial of faith, mine as a testament to ease and affluence. One faith indestructible and another non-existent.

Now I am crying as the cantor continues affirming God's benevolence. My father sees the tears and smiles. He can't wait to tell my mother. She will be so proud. My *zaida* takes no notice of me; he is inside the prayer. The inside must be a different place. I know that it is far away from my cold and polluted world. My *zaida's* cheeks turn red. It must be comfortable and warm inside. I almost feel the warmth sitting next to him.

As the prayer ends, the congregation moans a breathless Amen and the rabbi launches into another irrelevant sermon in Yiddish. My *zaida* stops crying, but his cheeks are still red. He looks into my eyes and sees tears. He touches my arm. In broken English he asks if I am all right. I say nothing and try to compose myself. I wish I knew faith.

MONTREAL SUITE

Rita Donovan

My father presses PAUSE *on the camcorder. The taping stops but the scene keeps moving.*

IT IS A WINDY AUTUMN AFTERNOON THE DAY THE maroon station wagon pulls into the city. For my father it has been a trip across the bridge from the South Shore; for me a journey that has taken me west and east and to Europe and back. Now we are here, finding a side street to park on for free because there will never be enough quarters to pay for this pilgrimage.

Already I have lied, for the journey my father has made is significantly longer than the bumpy ghostly moan across the grating of the Victoria Bridge, a bridge opened by Edward, then Prince of Wales, a bridge that was a triumph of the Empire. Already I have fragmented and figmented that afternoon, the city moaning with spirits, voices of men down on the docks; grunts of the blind buffalo in the basement of Joe Beef's Tavern; the voiceless folding of hands in the walls of the Congregation de Notre Dame, the immured Jeanne le Ber telling her silent beads as her brother lies mortally wounded in an Indian raid near Fort Chambly; wide-eyed, tiny cries of the young daughters of France who have come to meet their fate, and their husbands, in this damp city; the cadence from the pulpit as D'Arcy McGee sits below and to the left, St. Patrick's facing the harbour, facing the old town, its back to the boulevard.

No, my father says. Why don't we start up this way?

There is nowhere to begin.

Nowhere.

As a child I played up at Notre Dame Cemetery, guessing the names, dates of birth and death, of entire family trees. Oh, the fallen angels; I fell asleep thinking of those weighted-down angels carrying lethal family histories on their cold limestone wings. I stood on tiptoe, hanging from the metal latticework, attempting to see into the vault of D'Arcy McGee, pondering how D'Arcy had more space clasped up in his tomb than I did at home with my sister and my brothers. Such is the stuff of Catholic childhood.

The mountain was always a place for me to go, and for my father as a boy. I blink and blur and can see my grandmother, too; she must be about ten or eleven, flying down the toboggan slide, her fair hair streaming behind her. She almost waves but it is not me she is greeting but her younger brother, dust waving across a snow bank to dust.

I think I am standing in Parc Jeanne Mance.

No, says my father. It is Fletcher's Field.

It depends on when you are standing there.

My father wants to put on film the places he lived in as a child. How many, he wonders, are still where they were? I think of what he has said and part of me answers: where else would they be?

My mind is still up on the mountain with Carol and Tony, friends of my best days. And at Auntie Tina's after a movie, the warm gingerbread box of a hillside apartment filled with music from the console hi-fi lined with her collection of Toby mugs. I am still walking with Carol, our India-cotton shirts fluttering as we laugh at absurdities we will one day call our own, with Tony as he turns into a gargoyle on a wall, passersby nodding at the little crust of street theatre thrown their way this early spring day.

I am lying on the grass beside Malcolm, everybody lost in

thought. Remembering that it has only been a year or two at most since the mountain was overrun with military police, since James Cross was taken from the winding road nearby.

Pierre Laporte was found less than ten miles from my home. I remember the helicopters, the searchlights over our house, the warnings to stay inside while they passed by. I remember peering outside at the dark fields suddenly bright, oats and wheat waving up at the whirling blades.

My father is filming nothing in particular, a rundown row house painted an ungodly red. It is only when I see him measuring with his footsteps that I realize I am staring at one of his old homes.

Surely this red...and the video store on the corner, the OUI signs in every window, surely this is not....

This is where Uncle Leslie came to visit the time he chased us all around the house in his gas mask.

My father grew up in the Depression. My grandfather liked words. It was a bad combination. The few jobs the man could ever get were sacrificed every time the city called an election. Grandfather wrote speeches. Eight children did not live well on speeches and relief vouchers, so the family moved a lot.

I am amazed at the compactness of this world he shows me! They moved at least once a year, or whenever they couldn't make the rent, but they never ventured more than five or six blocks in any direction. The world revolved around St. Mike's, the imposing parish that looks surprisingly like a mosque. Here, the world stayed the same for my father. He might turn left to get home, or run down an alley, but in the choir loft of St. Michael's he was comfortingly home.

I know he will be taking a picture of this church. It has as much of a place on this video as any of the other standing buildings. I know, too, that St. Michael's is no longer Irish Catholic. The demographic shift means the parish is now Polish, the masses are in Polish, and, my father supposes, the choir sings in Polish.

I suppress an obvious comment about coincidence and continuity, the fact of my father marrying a woman of Polish descent, the fact of my own bloodline. There is no point in talking of this. St. Mike's is on the film because it was one of the places my father lived. It is as simple as that.

He does not venture up the alley, but I do. The church is of interest but the laneways are where the secrets are, the laundry whipping white in the wind, the crates of beer up on the balcony, the unexplained mattress slouching against the back fence. In this alley, time itself has been forgotten. I wonder why my father doesn't film the alley.

We wander on to the place on St. Viateur where my father was the only *goy* on the street, which garnered him a job turning the lights on in the synagogue. He runs into a woman as he is lining up his camera in front of the grey exterior. She lives somewhere in this walk-up of which my father's home was ground floor, on the end. She is polite and enthusiastic when my father speaks of the old days and tells him that the small backyard he mentions so fondly is still exactly as he describes it. Later my father will comment that he wishes he had gone through to the yard, but for now we stand in front of his old home, number five, or is it number six? Number 11. We stand there in front of the FOR SALE sign – yes, there is even a FOR SALE sign – and my father presses RECORD.

HERE.

Gone.

Here, but changed.

My father goes through the list.

And I am compiling my own mental catalogue and wondering when it became a catalogue and not my life.

Rockhead's Paradise.

Summers of all-night jazz.

Sitting with Annie, with Sadik Hakim, who is trying to explain to me how it takes long years before an artist does really good work. And me so young and stupidly fervent, fly-swatting the table with a copy of college-issue poetry, arguing Coleridge, arguing Keats. Sadik smiling decades into an ash-tray on the table as somebody turns the stagelight on him and he is forced to take a bow.

Countless jobs, babysitting up on the mountain; running credit checks in a dirty little office on de Maisonneuve; working in the accounting department of the *Montreal Star,* my aunt down the hall in Classifieds.

CEGEP. University.

Years spent walking down St. Catherine's.

Oh, I wouldn't film there. It's really shacky now. All strip clubs.

LIKE MY FATHER, I MAKE NOTATIONS.

Rockhead's: gone.

Sadik: gone. Died in New York.

Me: gone. Years and years gone.

We are talking about loss here, or absence.

Absolute.

It is the way I feel whenever a plane is landing, the tarmac stretched before us, the impossibly heavy airplane on its tiny wheels.

Bump.

And it lunges up again.

Bump.

And we are aloft.

We touch down in these tiny moments.

We touch down.

WE ARE GETTING TIRED. WE PASSED A PLACE A while ago I would like to have tried for coffee. It looked from the outside as though nothing had altered it for fifty years. I could see the soldiers spilling off the trains and heading up the street toward home and stopping in for a Coke and a smoke with the guy who ran that diner. Yet I am probably wrong and, besides, it is too far to go back.

When I refuse the obvious doughnut-chain on the corner, my father realizes, I think, that we are going to be winding this down. He has one more place, he says, that he must get to; we agree that we will head home from there.

Circle past Luke Callaghan School; my father's childhood. Past the row houses, tenements, until we are standing before a duplex no better, no worse, than any other on this Montreal street.

That, he tells me, his eye in the lens on the camera, *that is the last family home I lived in.*

Returning from the war, duffel bag, gunner's wing, returning to this house where his mother and brothers and sisters live upstairs, where his father sleeps on a couch downstairs in the landlord's unit because there is no room, there is simply not enough room, for them to live together any more.

Mom said she always felt bad she didn't see the way his arms were getting thin. That's what she said at the hospital. How his arms had gotten so thin. She thought, maybe if she'd been with him every night, you know, she might have noticed.

The Irish treasures preserved from the boat, from the days in County Cork, are gone, put in storage during the war because there was no room, and then no money to reclaim them. Trunks of family history rotting in a warehouse that itself will disappear.

And my father's father, my grandfather, a couple of years later, dying in the hospital in the printed robe his own daughter died in a few years earlier, watching patiently as the sunlight moved down the tiled hall, his Latin book of psalms by his side.

Yes.

This is the last place I want to look at, too.

We move through the streets in silence, awash in the muted whisperings. He holds the camcorder so protectively, the way he used to hold me. When we get to the car, we note that two cars in front of us someone has a ticket. I almost comment on our luck. He lets me hold the camera on my lap.

We drive through the banners, the OUI signs of Montreal East, wordlessly pointing out one or two NON. We drive through traffic we didn't notice when we were out walking, and we use our horn just like everybody else.

I wonder about his driving, now that he wears two hearing aids. Especially since he's admitted he usually turns them off. He won't drive at night any more, that is true. Not unless he has to. I notice his Saint Christopher is still taped to the car even though, as I recall, the patron saint of travellers was bumped from saint status. Or perhaps it was some other saint. I really do not know.

My father is thanking me for coming along for the ride. He says when the film is full he will transfer the contents to another tape.

You can't leave it all in the camera, he explains.

WRESTLING THE ALLIGATOR

Barry McKinnon

I'M NOT A BIG FAN OF TRAVELLING BY GREYHOUND even though bus travel has improved since my regular bus sojourns in the 1960s. In those days there was always one smoking and drinking rowdy who kept everyone wide awake with loud questions about how long until the next rest stop, or why the girl across the aisle wouldn't marry him.

The bus I took in September from Prince George to Smithers*, to visit my old friends Ken and Alice Belford at their wilderness fishing camp in northern British Columbia, was a much different experience. This bus was "comfort controlled," complete with a full-length movie that took my eyes from the autumn reds and yellows swishing by. I'd rather watch the leaves and the quiet reflection they inspire, but the *Uncle Buck* movie kept sneaking into my periphery. I started to feel a little bus sick with all the conflicting motion of the Hound whizzing along Highway 16 West, and the mini-TV screens placed overhead every six feet. I wished that the driver would turn the screens off so I could read a book, or think about Blackwater Lake and the experience ahead of me.

---

* Prince George is in the centre of BC. Smithers is 371 kilometres to the northwest. The Belford camp, accessed only by float plane or helicopter, is an hour and one-half northwest of Smithers toward the headwaters of the Nass River.

After the supper stop at the Tastee Freez in Burns Lake, I didn't feel much better. My Tasteeburger looked just like the one in the menu picture (usually a bad sign) and the french fries had an anemic watery consistency that begged the question: are these real potatoes or some kind of junk food concoction invented for astronauts? I couldn't wait for Alice's real down-to-earth camp kitchen cooking.

My last touch with the modern world was a little rundown room for thirty-seven dollars at the Twin Valley Motel next to the bus depot in Smithers. I turned on the TV set and chose one of the fifteen channels hoping to miss the one that might be playing *Uncle Buck*. I got Larry King interviewing Latoya Jackson about her life with brother Michael. "Would you like to give the name again of your exercise video?" Larry asks. "Yessss Larrry, I'm really very very excited by my new exercise video that you can get for $29.95 right now if you call the toll-free number on the screen," she says in a sexy, throaty whisper. A good promotional trade-off: gossip about Michael, just what the world *really* wants to hear, for Latoya's increased sales of a moondancing weight-loss video.

Soon I'd be chopping wood. But for now, bus-weary, I fall asleep on the saggy motel bed, and dream about Latoya and I making a weight-loss video up at Blackwater Lake – all sweated up and clutching our crotches in a tribal moondance around an axe hopelessly stuck in a pine knot.

Morning, September 18: Everything in Smithers is brilliant, a town glazed by sunrise and autumn frost. I wait in the parking lot for Hannah, Ken and Alice's eighteen-year-old daughter and expediter, who will drive us to the lake and the waiting Cessna 185. Hannah pulls up in an old faded green van and introduces me to Jim and Norm, two serious steelheaders from Denver – nice sixtyish guys colour coordinated from socks to hats like two male models in an L.L. Bean catalogue, and geared up to climb the north face of K2 or Anna

Purna. By contrast, I'm in my fifteen-year-old hiking boots, well-worn jeans, a Pioneer grease-stained jacket, a ratty ball cap my kid lent me, a mummy bag good for plus five degrees celsius, and a packsack full of beer – a college teacher who gets outdoors only every ten years or so – the guy who always looks a bit altitude sick at base camp.

Jim says, "Hannah's bin tellin' us a feeew good stories about yuu n Ken."

"I was hoping no one would find out! You boys from the South?" I ask – a question that could include any place from 100 Mile House, to the tip of South America and beyond. But I figure small talk about origins and nationality is a good place to start when you meet strangers. "You sound Texan," I say to Jim.

"Well hell yaas, I wuuz pretty much born and raised there, but weee've bin in Denver ever since, but Norm here's originallly from Neew Yeork."

"Hell," I say, "I love Manhattan, but the fishing's lousy." A little warm-up laughter as we drive to the lake.

I get scared shitless on small bush planes. Ken's stories about pilots and their fate aren't far-fetched tales told around campfires or a beer table, and not at all funny. These brave men who fly become friends to the guides they serve, and that makes their deaths all the harder to take. My friend Bill, an experienced northern outdoorsman, gave me a simple warning before I left Prince George: "if the pontoons are below water, she's overloaded. *Don't get on the goddamn plane!"*

BUT I BEGIN TO FEEL CONFIDENT WITH JOE, OUR PILOT. Joe tells us it's an old plane, but well maintained. He's in his fifties and assures us he wants to live a little longer. He ain't the young daredevil type who's going to take any chances. I glance at the pontoons, a good few inches above water, and believe him, and then thank Bacchus and Al Purdy (or whoever the god of beer is) that my forty pounds of Black Label doesn't have to be jettisoned as non-essential weight.

Now I'm happy as we plow against the gravity of lake and air. Then Swooosh, we're airborne, suspended in the clear blue mountain sky, headed northwest for the next hour and fifteen minutes to Blackwater Lake. Jim adjusts the earphones and speaker volume and begins to chatter to the pilot as the Bulkley Valley disappears behind us. It turns out he's a pilot too.

"Joe.... Yuu know I crashed wunnove these baabies once!" he says. Why do pilots talk about flying and crashing when they're flying? I think about my wife and kids and my untimely but spectacular romantic ending. Headline: College teacher dies in small plane on way to fishing camp.... American passengers found alive...survived on beer...ate college instructor....

But Joe safely and skilfully manoeuvres the plane through the pockets of mountain turbulence and glides us smoothly down to the lake right on schedule. Ken is on the dock to greet us, looking like a mountain guide should. Big. Six feet, two hundred pounds, bearlike, dressed more like me than L.L. Bean. He's a man who exudes a solid confidence about his outdoor knowledge and abilities. He's been out in all kinds of weather. Ken and I embrace in a bear hug. We've been friends for twenty-five years bound in a long conversation about poetry, sex, chainsaw repair, fly cast technique, ecology, the fate of man, health, exercise and vitamin dosages, the complexities and follies of human behaviour, and just about anything under the sun. Compulsive talkers. And what stories! I've snorted beer out my nose laughing about the characters he's known, like old trapper Ron and his famous no-vegetable stew – the whole damn moose boiling away for months – a stinking pot full of breakfast, lunch, and supper, complete with tufts of hair, guts, lips and eyes. It's a good story around the supper table while we dig into our third and fourth helpings of Alice's great grub.

Alice, unlike Ron the trapper, *is* a great cook, but she isn't always trapped in the kitchen. The mix of duties in camp aren't carried out in terms of the old male/female role structures. Over the week Ken and I sweep, do dishes, laundry – a range of camp chores – while Alice fires up the generators, chops wood, or canoes down to the river to guide the fishermen.

Ken and Alice share an equality you don't often find. These two wilderness caretakers in their long thirty-year partnership, are intelligent and sensitive to the world around them. And they've made a happy place in a crazy world that can reduce most people to idiocy. At Blackwater you can't click through forty TV channels, or mindlessly drool on yourself while peddling a stationary bike, or flabbily bound around out of breath to Latoya's moondance video. At Blackwater it's a life of natural health and balance that tunes into the pleasures, rhythms, and lessons of mother nature.

Catching fish is one of the ancient pleasures, and why most people come to Blackwater. Norm and Jim, however, serious members of the steelheader brotherhood, got skunked in the next six days of dawn till dusk fishing. They caught salmon, dollys, and trout, *but only one steelhead*, so they looked a bit sad-assed around camp, failures of sorts in this obsessive brotherhood. I'm not as serious about fishing, but like the rest of the camp, hoped for a good heavy rain so the river would rise enough so the steelhead could swim the holes and migration channels to their breeding grounds and journey's end.

"Ken, thar ain't no daamn steelhead in thaat daamn river," exclaim the Yankee clients who've paid a good few thousand bucks to come here. It's a statement that gets us into much talk around the kitchen table about wilderness ecology, weather, and "fisherman's luck." Questions about dwindling fish stocks in the northern river systems are thick in the air without clear answers. One thing is clear: there aren't as many of the big steelhead any more, which might partly explain the number of interest groups, biologists and bureaucrats who are descending almost daily on camps like Blackwater. They are high-tech and serious. Some kind of big trouble is going on – the depleting fish as measure of serious change and much of the change, seemingly, man-made.

One morning the lake resembled a wilderness version of O'Hare airport. The normal silence of the lake, occasionally pierced by a loon's cry, or a fish flop, or a flock of mergansers dancing the waves, was displaced by a helicopter and a Beaver loaded with a menagerie of outsiders hired to study, map, and measure. Alice wisely disappeared while Ken answered questions about aboriginal trails in the territory, the number of fish in the river, and, "what the hell do you think we can do about all this Ken?" Ken, like everyone else, has his theories; he and Alice have read, studied on their hands and knees first-hand, and written clear intelligent lobbies with the thesis: *protect and take care of these dwindling places and the wildlife that inhabits them.* One agent at the table that morning, a spokesman for the intense but quiet young native leader with him, felt that a special university to train native people in the skills they've lost might provide one "solution" for these lost tribes. He thought Ken, for instance, an experienced white outdoorsman, could become an important part of this process and help to teach these age-old survival skills. The young native, maybe sensing the overall irony, stayed mysteriously quiet, smoked half a pack of Players and let the hired pro do the talking. The biologist with a three-hundred-page report full of graphs, tables, line charts, and statistical numbers with more decimal points than the fish in the last salmon run, asked us the questions that you'd hope his ongoing study might someday answer: *where* are the salmon and steelhead, *how* many are there and *what* natural or unnatural conditions have affected their complex cycle?

Too much coffee, too much talk, too much abstraction and a too-intense barrage of details I can't or don't have the energy to understand. This high-level confab reminded me of the junior college – an institutional world of stress and tension I'm trying to escape for a few days. I take a walk up the path behind the cabin to my wall tent, sweep the floor, and as a distraction from the morning's activity, invent more ways to keep two summer nylon bags stuck on top of each other so that I don't freeze another night. I think about Velcro, safety pins, bed straps, or keeping a steadier night vigil on the stove fire, until an answer finally hits me: put one bag *inside* the other, dumbo! Maybe some of the ecological solutions will come to us this way if we're fast enough, smart enough, and cold enough.

When the pros and experts leave, the camp returns to a normal routine: breakfast at 8:30, and table talk – the wish for better luck on the river over last cups of hot coffee. By 10, James, Ken's young talented guide, loads the canoe and paddles the length of the lake to the river. It's quiet except for the static chatter over the radio phone: *how are you? over, squawk. real gooood! squawwk.* Ken and Alice and I wash and dry dishes and talk until we exhaust ourselves with conversation; it's quiet again. Time to go chop some wood, or canoe over to the creek to catch fish for supper, or watch a local grizzly amble along the west shore, or count eagles and otters, or listen to a far off moose in rut – these wonderful aspects of Blackwater – this multitude of species living in an ecological soup that inspires a sense of contemplation and questions about one's own place in it. You don't really come here just to fish. It's more about ritual and activity that, like poetry, can give a sense of the mysterious whole if you're open to it. It's an experience that humbles you. I'm thankful for a chance to be within this bounty of natural elements.

Ken and I like to log for firewood, another way to experience the elements, the woods and weather, and sweat a little. The forest is dark, full of fresh smells; the air has a texture; the ancient trees groan in the upper breeze. We pick out the right tree, and Ken makes the cut. "Do you know what a widow-maker is?" Ken calmly asks, then tells me about a couple of his friends who have been killed logging like this, and then goes on to explain the physics of our tree hopelessly hung up against another spruce.

These are some great outdoor tools: chainsaw, peavey, and come-a-long winch. What's that old line? Give me a lever and I'll move the world. I'm about as scared of felling a big tree as I am flying when pilots tell their crash stories, but Ken is careful, methodical and he knows how to winch and shift these hung-up tons. I trust him. Concerned for my safety, he tells me to take cover behind another tree ten yards away. A half hour later and the monster crashes to the ground Wwwwwhuuuumpphhhhh. We cut and stack our load into the twelve-foot aluminum boat until she sinks to the gunnels, perch masthead dog Heidi on top of the bolts, start the trusty Honda 12, and head back to the dock.

Having to haul fifty-pound chunks of wood up a greasy path to a woodshed might have inspired an engineer at Honda to design a motorized cart with rubber tank treads – a machine that will go anywhere and travel over any *thing,* including the driver if not careful. I named it "the alligator" – a good description of the way it moved and also of its temperament.

Ken gave me the job of hauling our cord up the trail in this innocent looking all-terrain, an experience that got me thinking about two good safety rules for desk-bound college teachers too old to moondance: never give them a chainsaw, and never let them wrestle with alligators. The Honda cart is a marvel, no doubt, that some have tamed and mastered with correct technique: hold the left brake lever down and the right tread turns on itself so you turn left – or is it right? No time, however, to figure out these mechanics as I chug near the cliff-edge of the path (sweating more from fear than exertion), frantically pulling every lever in sight until I find the right combination that will tame and redirect this slow toppling ton. But now the alligator is on the edge, wobbling like a tightrope walker with baskets on his feet. I pull right and it goes left! I pull left and it goes right! I'd let out a sport fanatic's YEEEES! and pull a clenched arm down in triumphant exclamation, but my own fear and diffidence won't let me. I know if I let go for a second I might end up as a graphic example in a first aid text, or an obituary about a sudden passing: college teacher runs over self...crushed by load of wood...eaten by cart....

Instead, I give a quick pheeew of relief, keep both hands on the controls, and I get back on the path – sweating now from fear *and* physical exertion, but with only one big hump in the path ahead of me. The grinding rubber treads eat their way to the crest and begin to climb, pointing up almost ninety degrees until the weight of the load topples the cart back and jams the levers into the dirt. I find REVERSE, pull GAS and start to move hopelessly backward to the cliff I just escaped. Going forward is difficult, but *now* I must figure out the lever action in *reverse* order. My foot's over the cliff. Holeeeee Jeeeeesus! I grab the FORWARD gear just in time and seesaw back up the trail to the crest I just backed away from, and get hung up again in *exactly* the same way. I think it was then that I heard the alligator whisper something in Japanese: "give up Charley boy...turn this sucker off before you kill yourself." I leave the cart stalled, pointed skyward, and haplessly head for my stash of Black Label, sensing defeat and disgrace – the whole camp laughing while I tremble and gulp a can of beer.

Soon the magical days at Blackwater have come and gone. It's our last day, clouds drifting thick above the lake. Jim, Norm and I begin packing up, our chatter mixed with the radio phone in the backdrop: *What's the ceiling? Will we get out today? Jeez, I slept warm like a baby last night. Gotta be in Frisco for a meeting. Hello, Burns Lake, come in. Pilot's on his way – a little clearer over here. OK. Will the taxi be there? Squawk. Over and out.*

Airborne: Blackwater Lake begins to disappear. Ken, Alice, and James, dots on the dock, wave farewell. The wings wave back. Minutes after the climb, the engine drone becomes steady and familiar. The old Cessna scoots southeast, along forest valleys, around mountains and glaciers and through the northern air. Rectangular blockcuts, clearcuts and denuded lakeshores forty-five minutes south signal the raw and brutal commerce of the outer world. The pilot wonders out loud: "I don't understand why the forest companies couldn't leave ten feet of trees between the cut and the lakeshore." Is the simple answer in profit and loss economics versus the aesthetics of a mountain lake? I wonder too: how long before the logging and mining spreads up the valleys to the places we just hiked and fished? For some, territories like Blackwater may be no more than a resource on a map, or a pristine reserve for silly outdoor indulgences – a place that exists only for its potential as "resource development." Does that make those who want to protect and sensitively manage the animals, rivers and forests out-of-touch dreamers, negative thinkers out to wreck the economy? I think about Alcan's Kemano Completion Project, and how it represents the corporate ethos that supports progress and profit at any social and ecological cost. I think about the euphemism "completion" and its other meanings: *finished, the end, over.* If the project isn't stopped, according to the brave and outspoken biologists who haven't been muzzled, and the other hard-fighting lay people and experts alike who form the coalition to save the river, the proposed massive flow reductions and altered water temperatures will destroy one of the world's most important salmon runs, and adversely affect *all* aspects of life along the river. I hate to believe that the Nechako River I walk along daily is at stake for beer cans (and God knows, I've snapped my share), electrical power, and more drained-off profit. These activities in the name of progress, are part of the continuing sad story and legacy of the

North and its diminishing resources. But the urgent question doesn't change: can these giant corporate powers, their share-holders, the government, and the diverse interest groups – natives, foresters, miners, farmers, ranchers, commercial and sport fishers, guides and outfitters – also with much at stake, negotiate and compromise within these extremes of attitude, approach, and investment? The alligator is large and complex.

The pontoons hit and soon I'm on the Greyhound for home. I've left Blackwater with a sense of renewal, but also worry about *our* fate as a species. Where are we going? Are we already there? My hope is that the Blackwater territory will *always* be a place *and* a measure, untouched – that little cabin on a lake with my friends Ken and Alice or the next genera-tion of Ken and Alices, guiding in the largest sense by loving and caring for the place they inhabit, and by resisting the forces and processes that could change or destroy it.

Tonight, the movie screens on the bus are blank overhead. I should be tired and sleeping, but I'm wide awake. The Hound heads east in the dark.

POSTSCRIPT

This piece was written in the fall of 1995 for a guide magazine Ken Belford was editing at the time. I hardly ever write jour-nalism and had never written a travel piece, but took on the task at Ken's request to see if I could write the specifics of my experience in Ken and Alice's camp, and to say something about environmental issues that affect the north and the province of British Columbia as a whole. I wanted to ask a few questions clichéd or not, that swim around in most northern-ers' heads. Ken gave up the editing job that year and the essay was never published.

I've felt more successful as a poet when writing about the

social world. Poetry cannot prove anything, but it can peel away at the thin veils that often keep us from seeing or caring about the reality about us. In 1969 when I got to Prince George, the veil was thick with a common ethos: progress and prosperity. The nauseous and toxic pulp stink was locally described as "the smell of gold." End of discourse and analysis. Recently one of the wealthy old-time mill owners who wanted to build a fibreboard plant within the city limits, bragged at a council meeting that PCB emissions wouldn't be a danger to the air quality or the population: he'd lived here all his life and lookit him – seventy years old and healthy as a moose, living medical proof! The scant studies, however, relating overall health to the polluted air in Prince George, prove him wrong.

What has changed is a more informed public willing to confront social and environmental issues if their livelihoods, families, or lands are threatened. This process takes place within a complex spectrum: loggers and logging companies want to survive and will fight the tree-huggers and/or government stumpage policies that threaten the industry. Residents along the Nechako River who might ordinarily support industrial progress flocked to the Kemano Completion Project[1] public hearings held in 1995, and made a convincing case to stop it; likewise, high-level lawyers, biologists, company officials and managers countered these folks with a boatload of technical data and euphemistic assurances to argue that progress, in both the short and long run, is for the betterment of all.

But the Kemano Completion Project, according to its critics, was mostly a grab for profitable electrical power. They rightly claimed that the project would create very few jobs; fish would disappear; water levels would rise and fall based primarily on the needs of the company and not the fish or the communities flooded or dried-out down below. The Cheslatta Indians who were flooded out and evacuated with only hours of notice in 1952, have a deep and bitter understanding of the company that displaced them, and their story acts as a dark measure of unbelievable corporate ruthlessness. Mike Harcourt's NDP government was legally hog-tied by near-sighted contracts signed with Alcan from the '50s and into the '80s. But after all of the evidence was in, the disastrous dimensions of this project became too obvious. The NDP government cancelled the Kemano project in January of 1995 and began negotiating a compensation package to stop the half-finished $1.3-billion project.

The alligator appears pinned for now: Alive. Resting.

---

[1]Bev Christensen's book *Too Good to be True* (Vancouver: Talonbooks, 1995) gives an excellent critical account of Alcan's history in the Northwest. As the book blurb says: "This book is must reading for those who wish to remain informed on the question of who is to control North America's vital water and power resources in the 21st Century."

BREATHING

SPACES

ACTS OF LOVE

Pat Krause

FRAGMENTS OF FATS WALLER'S "HONEY HUSH" litter my widow's web of memory. A mishmash of threads crisscross the music and lyrics at random angles and planes. It isn't easy to untangle them by myself. I have to try.

It wasn't our song, romantically. It was our song because of an event only Frank's younger brother remembers. One drink too many at family gatherings, and Stan would swear that in 1947, the night Frank started going steady with me again, we borrowed his 78 rpm record of "Honey Hush" to take to a party and broke it.

"We? Include me out," I used to reply to his accusation for decades, and sing the first verse.

Then the others joined in and I led a family singalong. The kids loved it. Frank and Stan demonstrated their brotherly love by standing shoulder to shoulder and doing an off-key duet. For the finale, I always sang the fourth verse solo so I could imitate Fats Waller's trilly birdlike whistle at the end of the second line, "Oh, how I love you honey hush / My heart is singing like a thrush...."

But that was in another life. I couldn't even remember enough of the tune to hum it when the audio tape arrived in the mail out of the blue. There was just the small package addressed to Mr. & Mrs. and the two business envelopes for Frank. That was it. Queen Victoria propped Prince Albert's clothes on his chair after he died so she could feel he was there. I didn't have to go that far. I felt Frank watching over my shoulder.

The first envelope, from the Centre of Agricultural Medicine, Royal University Hospital, was full of graphs, stats, a six-page questionnaire and a form letter thanking him for his continued participation in their survey of the long-term health effects of common urban pesticides.

The second, Hospitals of Regina Foundation envelope – addressed to Rev. instead of Mr. – enclosed an appeal for a "generous" donation. I decided to send them a generous list of reasons why, in the age of do-it-yourself medical care, my husband chose to die at home twenty-two months ago.

I thought the package was C.S. Lewis's journal, *A Grief Observed*. I couldn't remember ordering another copy, but mine was getting messy. On one of the dog-eared pages, Lewis describes his lover's absence as being, "...like the sky, spread over everything," and I've changed absence to presence. Finding a tape inside the box was a big surprise.

Wrapped around the cassette, there was a handwritten letter from the man in Kingston, New York, who'd sent it. "I'm sorry it took me so long to respond to your ad in the January '95 issue of *The Good Old Days* magazine. I think you'll both agree this copy of my pristine record of Fats Waller playing and singing "Honey Hush," his classic stride piano composition, is close to concert hall quality. Listen and enjoy all those memories a special song arouses."

In a postscript, he wrote, "I joined the R.C.A.F. in World War II before the US got in and trained at Yorkton. I'd sure like to come back. Any chance of a Fats Waller revival up there at your famous Saskatoon Jazz Festival?"

I opened the cassette case and stared at "Time: 3:07" neatly printed on the tape's label. An ad in *The Good Old Days*? A final arrangement I didn't have a clue my old high school sweetheart was making. Does Frank want me to listen to three minutes and seven seconds of music and unravel fifty years of memories we made together all alone? Give the tape to Stan as a *mea culpa* for something we didn't do?

If I concentrate, can I summon him back to give me some answers? Hang onto him until he does? While he was dictating his obituary to me, he paused, smiled, and said, "When I return after I'm gone, please detain me so I'll be here when I get back." I wrote it down in my journal.

Sometimes, when I awake under the 4 a.m. avalanche of sadness, he reaches across my shoulder and places his hand on my face. I stay curled on my side of the bed, my back to his empty pillow, hoping he'll reply, "Love you, too, hon," when I tell him I love him so much it hurts. But he's silent. A warm presence. He doesn't speak or give advice.

So where to begin? Another decision to make on my own.

I'm sixty-six years old and this is the first time in my life I've lived alone. I can't believe how much trouble I am to look after. Busy, busy, busy. So much to do. Accept every invitation. Be cheerful. Nobody likes a black widow with an hourglass frown tattooed on her forehead.

Shop for groceries, pay the household bills, run my own errands, load the dishwasher, vacuum, put out the garbage and Blue Box, use the old soup pot to carry eight loads of salt crystals from the 20-kilo bag in the trunk of the car down the basement to fill the water softener. Climb the aluminum ladder with no one to hold it steady to change a smoke alarm battery or to try and twist fluorescent light tubes into slots I can't see looking up through bifocals.

Cope as each change of season adds another partition between then and now. Sweep the gravel off the driveway, hook up the hose, take the tarp off the air conditioner, cut the grass, rake the leaves, put the tarp back on again, wash the furnace filters, reset the outdoor light timers for longer nights, dig through the stuff in the shed for the plastic snow shovel – done today, just in time.

It's Saturday, October 19, 1996, almost midnight, and a heavy wet snow is falling. I light a three-hour log in the fireplace. Play the tape. Listen to Fats Waller whisper, "Honey hush," after his final riff on the piano, hug myself, and make up my mind where to start.

These three excerpts from the research I've done about widowhood and Waller fit together best to set the mood.

In his memoir "A Death In The Family" in the December 1995 *Harper's* magazine, poet and Michigan undertaker Thomas Lynch, says, "...mourning is a romance in reverse."

Webster's Dictionary: romance, Mus. a short, simple melody, vocal or instrumental, of tender character.

"He could make a song and the piano couple in the act of love," biographer Joel Vance says in *Fats Waller: His Life and Times*.

Metal strings struck by felt-covered hammers coupled with tender words. Me, alone, remembering what?

That my lighthearted efforts to flick Stan's stuck needle forward with family songfests didn't work forever? The exchanges of snide remarks over a broken record?

It took Stan three decades to recall that the party Frank and I went to was on the Ides of March. He claimed it was a Saturday night sock hop on the badminton court of my hoity-toity Wascana Winter Club where I'd won a silver cup bashing around birds. "Shuttlecocks!" I said, emphasizing the last syllable. I didn't have to check my diary to know he was wrong. Just me and my shadow were going steady until my prayers were answered Sunday night.

After that, Stan just had to look morosely into his refilled glass and swirl the ice cubes around with his finger to trigger my solo of Fats Waller's "Your Feets Too Big" while I did the jitterbug out of earshot.

All of our sporadic attempts to find Stan another '78 failed. The late '60s phone calls to Library Information Services for who'd recorded it – Victor or Bluebird? RCA or Bulldog? – only established that "Honey Hush" wasn't listed in either of their Fats Waller discographies. Several letters to CBC Radio's Clyde Gilmour in the '70s and '80s weren't answered. Searches of vintage vinyl stores in the early '90s turned up some of his Hit Parade tunes, but it wasn't on the flip side of "Honeysuckle Rose" or "Ain't Misbehavin'" or "Jitterbug Waltz."

Now, here it is. "Honey Hush." A single. On tape.

A good old days theme for reverse romance. Not just one more sympathy card message that says – oh, so pitifully rhymed – the comfort of memories can keep a loved one close forever. Forget it. Ask any widow. Memories are history. Mirages from the past. Puddles on the road ahead that are tears still unshed. Where's the damn magic?

I punch the rewind button on the Sony, and Fats Waller appears, large as life, in the archway at the far end of the living room. I almost fall off the loveseat.

Fats Waller? In person?

He wriggles his caterpillar eyebrows, rolls his big pixie starshine eyes, and repeats the only line he had in the 1943 movie, *Stormy Weather,* "One never knows, do one?"

Oh, yes I do. It's him. I saw that movie when I was thirteen, an indelible age, and recorded it in my diary. Saturday, December 18, 1943: A gang of us went to see Lena Horne in *Stormy Weather.* Went to The Winter Club after and talked about life instead of playing badminton. Everybody said it really felt strange to see Fats Waller jazzing it up on the screen when we'd heard on the radio he died three days ago at age thirty-nine. I got a good quip in, for once. Too old to live fast, die young, and have a good-looking corpse, I said, one never knows, do one? It got a good laugh.

This week, I borrowed a video of the movie from the

library and watched it again. It's an old-fashioned musical loosely based on the story of Bojangles Robinson. There's hardly any dialogue. The first time Fats Waller delivers that one-liner, it's one of a string of ad libs he was famous for making while he played a blues or jazz number he found less than inspiring. A female singer is belting out the lyrics of "That Ain't Right," and he's responding as if he's the no-good man she's berating. In his only scene away from a piano, he pauses at Lena Horne's dressing-room door, looks down at the rival dancer Bojangles has just laid out with a punch, and says it again.

On December 15, 1943, on a train going to another gig, he died of pneumonia somewhere near Kansas City, Missouri, and it became his epitaph.

Fats Waller is dead. Long gone to the great beyond. I'm not on the Hollywood set of a crowded Beale Street bistro in an old black-and-white movie. He's not standing there waiting for me to invite him into my living room.

"Baby, baby, say what you sees. Lay on no lies or prefabrications, sweet woman, shoot me the truth," the figment of too much research says.

The truth is, the wrong man has joined me tonight. I'm hallucinating. It's not right.

"Beef to me, mamma, beef to me, I don't like pork no how." He does one of his sent eyeball rolls.

Frank had a trick like that he did with his eyes. It was a hit in high school. He closed one eye, rolled the other eye up, said it was glass, and pretended to pluck it out. Gruesome was his game. Girls got hysterical, squirmed and squealed, covered their eyes and loved it.

Everyone called him Eyeball, later shortened to Eye. When Stan started Grade Nine two years behind Frank, he was stuck with the nickname Eye Junior. Beside Frank's graduation year picture in *Ye Flame,* Central's yearbook, it says: "A sport. The

Eye is our foremost author of topical and horror shorts. Donned blades for this year's ice squad. Curly will likely major in hair dressing."

For me, Frank's sent eyeball rolls were love signals, before and after. I smile.

The ad lib maestro winks a fringed-awning eyelid at me. Then he ambles over to the floor-to-ceiling bookcase, sits down on a nonexistent piano stool, pokes his butt, and says, "You all on there, Fats? Yes, sees you is."

That's what he did on opening night at the London Palladium in 1938. His manager was worried about his hangover from alcohol, not what hung over the stool.

He wags his head. Says, "Suffer, excess baggage, suffer." Tips back his hat. Flexes his fingers, runs them back and forth across a shelf of Saskatchewan prose and poetry, and begins to play "Honey Hush."

The spines of the books sing like birds at sunrise. Sweet as summer. Notes flutter. Kiss my ears lightly. Tinkling trills, plaintive burbles, buoyant warbles; soft, sweet, and tumbling together exuberantly.

I hear what Fats Waller heard after a night of insomnia and woke his manager at dawn to help him write. The spiel Fats used to get him out of bed was, "I was just walking around in the park and the birds were singing so pretty they sang me a tune and I want to get it down on paper before it does like a bird and flies away on me."

I watch as his right hand plays the melody and his left delivers the rhythm. See his fingers fly. Recognize stride piano. The successor to ragtime. Jazz, blues and torch song, played by a wizard in a derby hat. It's magic.

I shut my eyes. Carefully, gently, not too fast, I press the last images of us together in my mind again.

Frank's sitting up on his side of the bed, his swollen feet on the floor, puffed fingers holding his penis to pee. I'm kneeling beside him holding the curved plastic bottle. His head is bent. The curls of his new growth of hair are as soft as snowflakes on my forehead.

We murmur like mourning doves about the level of pain, more morphine, sips of water, the comfort of his pillows, sleeping soundly, sweet dreams, loving each other. I blow softly in his ear. He smiles, remembering the promise he made. It's carved in stone in my diary: *Sunday, March 16, 1947: Old lover boy Eye's back! Maybe "I'm All Dressed Up With A Broken Heart" won't be my permanent theme song. He says he and the vixen are just like two gloves that don't match no matter how often they try. He hinted they'd had a fight, called it quits for good last night. I heard it was a dull party. A basketball court sock hop for R.C. guys only, held by boy crazy girls at Sacred Heart Academy? Nuns measuring the distance between dancers with their big iron crosses turned lengthwise? I said, I know I match you and you match me. He said, blow in my ear and I'll follow you anywhere. I did. We necked for awhile and agreed to go steady again.*

Scheming my schemes, dreaming my dreams, I wish it would work now if Frank blew in my ear.

"When do you get to sleep?" Frank asks as I get him settled propped up against the pillows.

I lie down beside him. Listen to him breathe. Stay wide awake, listening.

The pair of glossy blue ceramic mourning doves look down on us from the top shelf of the white wicker bookcase. We bought them in Sarasota, Florida, soon after seeing an accident that affected us both deeply.

We were driving down Stickney Point Road when we saw the mourning doves. One of them was trying desperately to pull its wounded mate off the narrow highway into the ditch. Frank was driving. He swerved sharply to miss them. There wasn't any oncoming traffic, but there were lots of cars behind us. We pressed the levers that rolled down our windows, waved our arms wildly back at the birds, and yelled, "Swerve-swerve-swerve!" at the topsy-coiffured head barely visible above the steering wheel of the creeping black Lincoln. The stupid woman hit them. She was going about fifteen miles an hour and she ran over both of them.

There was a sharp edge of solace in seeing them killed together. One bird didn't watch its mate die.

But, as Jesse Jackson said, "Death is certain and life is uncertain." I have to stay alert. Awake. Listen.

I lie on my left side and watch the covers rise and fall slightly with each of his shallow, fluidy, breaths. Unlike the cancer, pneumonia is his friend. He knows that.

At 4 a.m., Frank suddenly sits bolt upright without my help. *Hey, what're you doing?* I ask. He says he's going down to the kitchen for a soft drink and tries to stand. Wait, wait, I cry as I'm running around the end of the bed to hold the glass and the oversized straw so he can sip some Gatorade. I'm there, picking up the glass on his bedside table, and he falls back across the bed in slow motion. Rolls his eyes one last time. Stops breathing. We are both motionless for a long time. I don't know how long.

I've never seen anyone die before. I hold him. Kiss his closed eyelids and his dry lips. Whisper in his ear. Remove the oxygen tubes from his nose. Leave him briefly to switch off the tank. Lift his legs back up on the bed. Turn him so his head is on the pillows again.

Tonight, I let myself circle around the lingering sounds of the Gregorian chant and hissing oxygen tank. Breathe deeply and replace the hospital smell of medicines with the scent of the blueberry candles on the dresser. Hear Frank say, "We both look nice in blue," after we've put on our new emergency pyjamas. Feel his hand lift my chin and his lips against mine. Suspend the scenes in one of those lacy nets of concentric ladders orb weavers spin.

And I listen as Fats plays and sings "Honey Hush."

Hear each note and word. Shyly, lip-sync the lyrics I knew off by heart half a century ago and didn't really forget. Sing aloud. Harmonize. Be-bop a little bit – shades of Ella. Swing my hips. Do the trilly bird whistle.

Glide smoothly with Fats into the last verse. "Your eyes shine like stars up above/making me know that I'm in love/Oh my sweet, don't do this to me/tell me you'll be, always with me."

And slowly dance backwards.

THE BALLAD OF FRANK LITTLE

Myrna Kostash

OR MOST OF MY LIFE I HAVE LIVED WITH THE conceit of Albertans that we have more in common with Americans to the south of us – that would be the Montanans – than with our fellow Canadians to the east and west. I decided to test the contention by driving around Montana for a couple of weeks to see just how related I felt to these folks of the Rocky Mountains, cattle ranges, and Blackfoot reserves, of the mission where Louis Riel taught for a time and the boneyards of Custer's Army and the Nez Perces, of boosterish towns strung along a highway just south of the border I took to calling the Medicine Line.

The history and landscape were awesome, but I did not want to be "related." There was too much in them of American hubris often run amok. But when I got to Butte, the legendary mining town that shared, briefly and violently, a labour history with Alberta, I stopped resisting. For I was led straight into a story that I would have told, had it been mine to dream up.

Kings Of The Hill, Butte

In the beginning was a gold rush which begat the investors in gold and silver mines who were duly rewarded: Montana had its first millionaires by the late 1870s. In its potted history of frontier capitalism, the Butte Chamber of Commerce's *Visitor's Guide* tells us that Butte sat on "the richest hill on earth," two billion dollars' worth of copper, gold, silver and zinc, exploited by the "colourful characters" known as the Copper Kings.

William A. Clark amassed a collection of European Old Masters for his Fifth Avenue mansion in New York and bought himself a seat in the United States Senate. Augustus Heinze profited by $10 million when he sold his Butte interests in 1906. Marcus Daly, who at least stayed in Montana, built a baronial manor in the Bitterroot Valley and amused himself in the raising of race horses.

In 1899 Daly merged his company with William Rockefeller's Standard Oil to create Amalgamated Copper Mining Company which held, in addition to mines, smelters, lumber and railway operations, coalfields and Montana's major daily newspapers. By 1910, having absorbed more companies, the ACMC became the Anaconda Copper Mining Company or "the Company," evidence by epithet that Montana had become a "company state," and the curse of the working class.

Of the workers' crammed and sloping hillside communities – Dublin Gulch, Finntown, Meaderville, Chinatown, Parrot Flat and Cork Town – almost nothing remains. They were gobbled up by the expanding crater of the open-pit mine that in 1955 replaced the mile-deep mining shafts. Around their hulking black headframes the neighbourhoods had been built cheek by jowl with the mine yards.

This "nightmare network of trestles, railroad tracks, scaffolds, wooden buttresses, crazy stairs, bunkers, fences, houses, rusty iron pipes, electric transmission lines, hoists, buildings black and red – a cosmic junk heap [...] this Dantesque waste land, where no flower blossoms, no seed grows [...] It is burnt-out, ravaged, raped and discarded...."

– a traveller's description, quoted in Joseph Howard Kinsey's *Montana: High, Wide and Handsome.*

Kinsey thinks the author too impressionable, but he lacks all imagination not to see the infernal in the slough of black smoke swilling out the bowl of the valley, the spears of flame shooting a fiery light from the chimneys into the darkened skies, and the molten, sludgy advance of the slag heaps across the hill.

The Chamber of Commerce takes considerable pride in Butte's reputation as the "Gibraltar of Unionism," and in the toughened, courageous and martyred heroes of labour who took on the "kings of the Hill" and their goon squads, their militias, their complaisant police chiefs. But when Anaconda abandoned labour-intensive underground mining for the more cost-efficient open-pit method of extraction and when in 1970 its holdings in Chile were seized by a socialist government, labour's doom in Butte was sealed.

Now the Town of Butte welcomes the visitor to its golf courses, its World Museum of Mining, its St. Patrick's Day parade and Gun, Knife and Antique Show, its abandoned pit and its historic uptown. Teddy Roosevelt ate lunch at the Thornton Hotel in 1908 while an appreciative public gaped through the open drapes. A new endurance record for non-stop dancing was set in 1909 at the old Renshaw Dance Hall; the Butte-Silver Bow courthouse was used as a barracks in 1914 when the city was put under martial law during labour strife; and on Granite Street William A. Clark built himself a thirty-four room house. One day, the Chamber of Commerce hopes, Butte will put up a statue to another of its famous sons, Evel Knievel, who in 1975 gloriously leapt in his motorcycle over thirteen buses in Ohio.

Don't Mourn, Organize!

> *The working class and the employing class have nothing*
> *in common. There can be no peace so long as hunger and*
> *want are found among millions of working people and the*
> *few, who make up the employing class, have all the good*
> *things of life.*
> – from the Preamble, IWW Constitution

The largest delegation of workers to the founding convention of the Industrial Workers of the World (IWW or Wobblies) in Chicago in 1905 came from Butte. Eugene Debs of the Socialist Party was there too, and Big Bill Haywood of the Western Federation of Miners, and Mother Mary Jones, white-haired septuagenarian organizer for the United Mine Workers of America.

"Fellow workers," Haywood boomed, whacking a table with a board to bring the convention to order, "this is the Continental Congress of the working-class. We are here to confederate the workers of this country into a working-class movement that shall have for its purpose the emancipation of the working-class from the slave bondage of capitalism." His own union, the WFM, would eventually bolt from the IWW, but other members would go on to cover themselves in a kind of lunatic glory battling for the destruction of capitalism and the creation of a co-operative commonwealth managed by workers.

By 1917, only twelve years after their founding, the Wobblies were a shattered force. Against their uncompromising militancy and impressive solidarity, the bosses and their mobs, the newspapers, and the state with its courts and police had thrown their awesome resources.

But labour had put up a very good fight. Never more than 10,000 strong at a time (many were unemployed or migrant workers), the IWW "travelled everywhere...they organized, wrote, spoke, sang, spread their message and their spirit," writes Howard Zinn in *A People's History of the United States.* "In jail they sang, they shouted, they made speeches through the bars to groups that gathered outside the prison." They were involved in an astonishing series of struggles for freedom of speech, in Spokane, Washington; in San Diego, California; in Missoula, Montana; in Calgary, Alberta, where they flooded in by the hundreds and thousands in boxcars to challenge ordinances preventing them from speaking and to spend weeks in jail, taking turns lecturing about the class struggle and singing Wobbly songs.

> *"The Copper Bosses killed you, Joe,*
> *They shot you, Joe," says I.*
> *"Takes more than guns to kill a man,"*
> *Says Joe. "I didn't die."*

The Wobblies organized railway navvies and construction and lumber workers and coal miners in Alberta and British Columbia, although in the coalfields of Alberta the Western Federation of Miners got there first, still tough and militant at the turn of the century. By 1905, the WFM had withdrawn from Alberta and was replaced by the more moderate United Mine Workers of America which in turn was thrown over, in 1919, by 95 per cent of miners voting them out at the Western Labour Conference: "Never again shall we belong to that rotten international!" Many of the defectors, with revolutionary zeal, endorsed the principle of "proletarian dictatorship," sent fraternal greetings to the Bolshevik Party in Russia and joined up with the One Big Union, Canada's own home-grown anarcho-syndicalist movement that would outlive the IWW by only three years. A vigilante squad dragged OBU organizer John Sullivan out of his bed in Drumheller during the general strike in 1919 and beat him up while others vandalized the striking miners' shanties and hunted down those who had fled into the bush. Owners employed returned war veterans to keep their mines open. Special constables, sworn in by the mine operators to protect their property, hauled OBU militants to kangaroo court and rode them out of town.

In July 1919 the OBU showed up in Butte, holding a convention through which they hoped to attract union affiliates in the American northwest. They got one, Mine Metal Workers of America Local #1 of OBU, "a long title for an almost moribund organization," writes Montana State University political scientist Jerry Calvert in his book, *The Gibraltar,* about socialism and labour in Butte. When the Supreme Court of Canada issued an injunction in 1920 against the OBU to cease its activities, it was all over for the union.

On The Road: Richard Roeder, Helena

He's weak and miserable, recuperating from major surgery, but he'll see me anyway, this professor emeritus of history, co-author of *Montana: A History of Two Centuries,* wrapped up in blankets and wheezing in the overheated air of his living room. His house is a substantial suburban bungalow, but there is a strong atmosphere of the bachelor's digs in the mismatched clutter of the furnishings, something of the discarded in the coffee table wrapped in veneer and in the crocheted doilies no man would acquire on his own initiative. The pitiless late-morning sun beats down on us through the picture window – the whole room lies in the glare of radiant heat – but the professor only pulls the blankets closer. He would make me tea but excuses himself; on canes and in bedroom slippers, he can only make a few steps and then must rest again. I've come to get a point of view on working-class radicalism in Butte, and I do get it, occasionally irascible and drifting in and out of focus, as the post-surgical medications take their toll on his memory, and, yawning hugely, he loses the drift of his stories.

The Song of Professor Roeder

"Montana is a labour state. If you don't believe it, think of Wyoming – that prehistoric society, a cowboy state. Cattlemen are always S.O.B.S. Anyone who grows up in the animal industry is cruel – tough, mean and ornery. Unionize there, and you bring out the hired guns. This kind of violence – the lynchers – you don't find in the industrial centres. The model in Butte wasn't in the vigilante squads of cattlemen but in the goldfields of California, and the Wobblies. I can't imagine young workers now rallying around the union like so many Pete Seegers. But they used to. Seeger didn't make those songs up.

"The first wave of miners were Irish and Cornish ("Cousin Jacks"), and Butte still is essentially an Irish town. After industrialization, you get the north Italians, Croatians, some Serbs, as underground miners, Germans as bakers, carpenters and brewmasters. Between 7,000 and 8,000 Chinese worked building the Northern Pacific line. What's left of them in Butte is the Pekin Noodle Parlour.

"People say too fast that we had company unionism here. We never had unions under the direct aegis of the corporation. True, there were union elements very cosy with the companies and a conservative impulse in older workers who didn't want to fight the company. Too much to lose – their own proletarian prosperity. They were smart; they didn't want to get hurt.

"Companies were able to stir up anti-Bolshevik fear among the middle class but how much they themselves believed in the power of union radicalism is an open question. As is the extent to which radicals were Communists. What made characters like Burton K. Wheeler, the liberal district attorney, and Jeannette Rankin, the populist suffragette, so scary was that they were people around whom a farm-labour movement could have coalesced. 'Bolshevik Burt' Wheeler was backed by the Progressives and Rankin by the Butte workers, but their failure hinged in the end on the bourgeois attitude of the farmer. The price of grain goes down, he's a radical; it goes up, he's a conservative.

"Now the mines are owned by out-of-state interests, unions have lost clout and the whole of western Montana is controlled by absentee landlords, the movie-star celebrities who put land out of reach of local farmers whenever they come into town and pay big. (Ted Turner and Jane Fonda own about three counties.) And watch the struggle for the development of the Sweetgrass Hills. To the Indians, it's sacred ground. To the industrialists, there is gold in the ground."

Butte was Local Number One of the Western Federation of Miners, one-third of all union men in the Butte district. In this "black heart of Montana," Howard writes, in vivid apotheosis, "the miners have risen in wrath and smitten the Lords of the Hill, and struck, and fought again; and they have been betrayed and defeated, and driven back into their holes." On June 13, 1914, the annual Miner's Union Day parade – the largest union celebration in the state – was attacked by a mob, setting off a riot which spent itself in the sacking of Miners' Union Hall, the police nowhere to be seen. Ten days later, in a confrontation at the beleaguered Hall between WFM loyalists and the pro-Wobbly Butte Mine Workers' Union, two workers died in a furious discharge of gunfire. After the crowd had dispersed, the Hall itself exploded from the force of twenty-five dynamite blasts all night long, the handsome structure finally a pile of shredded lumber, charred window frames and tin roofing falling into the crater of the building like a disintegrating stage curtain. The police had locked themselves into the station house.

At the end of August ACMC's Parrot mine fortuitously blew

up, providing the authorities all the excuse they needed to place Butte under martial law, occupy it with National Guardsmen and lock union workers out of the pits. There is a photograph of five Guardsmen lounging around a field gun in downtown Butte, as though they were at the front, holding back the Boche. For the next three years, there would be no miners' unions at all in Butte.

Then on June 8, 1917, fire broke out in the Speculator mine. Ignited by a carbide lamp, it sent gas and smoke belching through the shafts, and flames shooting 2,400 feet up to the surface, cremating men in the lifting cages caught in the incinerating fire at the pithead. The heat was too intense to allow rescuers to get to the trapped miners. Of the 164 who died, many were found heaped together against the cement bulkheads between tunnels, their fingers worn to the bone in their death panic to claw through the walls. A state law requiring doors to be built in bulkheads had never been enforced.

Three days later, on June 11, the miners downed their tools and walked off "the hill." Unperturbed, the Company refused to negotiate and instead sent hired gunmen, goon squads swaggering through the streets. The fear of summary deportation, of random, murderous violence, clogged the sulphuric air. There were at this time as many detectives as Wobblies in Butte.

On July 18 or 20 Frank Little came to town.

An injury to one is an injury to all! So all together, you diggers and muckers...[f]orce the bosses off your backs, put them to work down in the hole...hand them their muck sticks and make them earn a living for a change.
– Frank Little, *Solidarity* newspaper, July 21 1917

As with Joe Hill, it is the manner of Frank Little's dying that has signalized his life story among the thousands it otherwise resembles in the radical working-class movements of North America. Masses of men and women in Butte alone led dramatic and sometimes tragic lives in their confrontation with capital, but it is Frank Little who has the monument in the cemetery.

An account of events leading to the death of Frank Little, as distilled from several sober histories of Montana:

A member of the IWW's General Executive Board, Little arrived in strikebound Butte hoping to win workers over to the Wobblies and away from the nascent Metal Mine Workers. (Only one account, the most recent, in Michael Malone's *Montana: A History of Two Centuries*, mentions that he was of mixed-blood Indian ancestry. I came across no photograph of Little that would help confirm the description.) He appeared at several meetings in town – for example, at the ballpark, at an open meeting of the Metal Mine Workers, and at the Finlander Hall – but is nowhere quoted verbatim. Only the editorial responses of the newspapers give some idea of what he was saying, as in this bellicose comment from the *Anaconda Standard:*

> *The Industrial Workers of the World has arrayed itself in open rebellion to our country and our government. It is against America, it is against the institutions of this land.... The leaders, by their acts and utterances, have placed themselves outside consideration as American citizens.... As enemies of this country they should be given the consideration and treatment to which enemies are entitled and no more.*

The liberal-minded US District Attorney Burton K. Wheeler

came under intense pressure from the politicians and Company to "do something" about Little, but even after reviewing the 1917 federal Espionage Act, Wheeler could find him in no violation of the law. Ironically, if Wheeler had ordered Little's detention or arrest, he might have saved his life.

In the early hours of August 1, six men (in some accounts masked) pulled up to the boarding house where Little was staying and, presenting themselves as "officers," intimidated Mrs. Nora Byrne, landlady, into disclosing his room number. Having dragged Little out of bed, clad only in his underwear, past a "terrified" Mrs. Byrne, they shoved him into their car – recovering from a broken leg, he offered little resistance – and "roared away in the night."

They drove only a short way, then stopped, hauled Little out of the car, tied him to the rear bumper, and dragged him over the pavement for several blocks. In one account, the dragging scraped his kneecaps off. When they stopped again, it was to beat him up, shove him bleeding and helpless back into the car, speed over to the Milwaukee bridge, there to hang him from a trestle. A workman found him in the morning. A card had been pinned to his undershirt (in another version, a placard was hanging around his neck): "Others take notice...first and last warning, 3-7-77." It was the vigilante calling card: the enigmatic numerals of Stuart's Stranglers of 1884.

The coroner's jury concluded that Little had been murdered by "persons unknown." No one has ever been indicted. At various times, his death was rumoured to have been the work of Company agents, rival union militants or outraged patriots. On December 20, 1917, the Metal Mine Workers' Union officially declared its strike was over, acknowledging a *fait accompli*: demoralized smeltermen and strikebreakers were keeping the smelters working, and it was business as usual again for the Company.

FRANK LITTLE 1879 – 1917
SLAIN BY CAPITALIST INTERESTS
FOR ORGANIZING AND INSPIRING HIS FELLOW MEN

The young man conducting tours of historical Butte told us exactly where we would find Little's grave in Mountain View Cemetery. It was easy to spot among the bare and scrubby plots: a grey granite headstone adorned with a vivid cluster of red poppies and a bouquet of red and white paper roses. By the inscription, Frank Little's admirers, at least, were unambiguous about who they thought his killers were.

In the photograph, six pallbearers stand outside Duggan the Undertaker's premises. Perhaps that is Duggan himself at the doorway in a frock coat, holding his top hat upright by the brim, a more formal figure than the men bearing the coffin. They wear their best Sunday suits, hats in their hands, and red sashes stamped with the words, "Martyr for," the rest of the imprint disappearing around their waists. We see them again later at the graveside, kneeling by the coffin and surrounded by some of the 6,800 mourning men, women and children present for the burial. Because there had been no family or kin to claim his body, his remains belonged now to the working people of Butte. Seventy-six years later they were still bringing flowers to his grave.

I suppose there is anthropology to explain the grip on a community's imagination of the tale of the sacrificial hero, especially one who arrives with only agit-propaganda for a past and who dies violently in their midst for the people's own good. But there is also erotic excitement in the figure of the unmarried, childless male, boundlessly available to those around him, the weaker ones, who long to be drawn into his field of energy but who are in awe of him as well: they knew who Frank Little hated, but who did he love?

In 1931, the prolific (but now virtually forgotten) Montana

novelist Myron Brinig published *Wide Open Town,* a thinly disguised account of a socially tumultuous and politically com-
bative Butte in 1917. Near the end, he tells the story of Phil
Whipple, the "extraordinary" strike leader from the IWW who
the reader understands to be Frank Little. Brinig's portrait of
him is both spiritualized and sexualized, this Revolutionist
whose followers compare him to Jesus Christ and who form an
"adoring bodyguard" wherever he goes, helping the Master
perform his miracles "on the docks of San Francisco and
Seattle...in the lumber camps of Washington...in the sweat-
shop strikes in New York City." Of course, he is strikingly
handsome as well as politically astute, tall and well-propor-
tioned, desired by women of means and taste, but it was said
of Phil Whipple that he never touched women. "This was
strange, for when you looked at Phil, you saw him as sexually
magnetic, vivid and sensuous in his body." The magnetism
and sensuality were animated by pure idea, however; by
Revolution: what excited Phil about women was that he
believed in their "full emancipation."

He lodged in a modest room, the ascetic among the artifacts of nonchalant need: the cracked water pitcher, the army
cot, the well-thumbed edition of Marx read by candlelight.
Into this sanctuary Brinig brings *thirty* masked men crashing, splitting his door in twin with an axe (the terrified landlady has disappeared from this scenario). Phil Whittle,
unlike Frank Little, is dressed in corduroy pants as well as
the undershirt that reveals his shapely, muscular arms. Like
Little, he does not resist his tormentors. But Little had a broken leg and was severely beaten and dragged about. Whittle
goes calmly, murmuring "Finis," as the masked men drive
him in silence to the trestle bridge and his hanging.
Unbolted, he is even allowed to make a speech: "I salute the
workers of the world and I say, 'Keep on my brothers! Do not
despair!'" And then helpfully steps up on the wooden box

and places the noose about his own neck.

As he twisted in the air of the night, from darkness to moonlight and back to darkness again, "[h]is lithe form looked delicate and wistful swinging back and forth without effort or strain." It is the revolutionary's gift to his lovers: fertilizer for the struggle.

On The Road: Roland Maw, Lethbridge

I'm on the way home now, crossing the border back into Alberta at Manyberries, and, by way of "round up," I call on a professor of environmental science who grew up on a ranch in Dillon, near Butte, Montana. He's middle-aged and lives in a big and comfortable house with big furniture. He's been in southern Alberta for years and years – he married and had children here – but he is fluent and vivacious with the anecdotes of his Montanan beginnings. He is almost ferocious with his feeling of belonging to his birthplace, in the sense of his own right to have had his sources there: he reminds me that the Blackfoot arrived on the open plain *after* some of the cattle ranches had already been set up in Montana.

This "special relationship" of the white Montanan to the land he occupies was "engraved in grade school," from the recital of the exploits of Lewis and Clark to the family stories of hardship overcome on the ranch, in the mine, on the railroad.

"This was more than a history lesson. This was about people's *lives* being bonded to the land. We read Charlie Russell's *Trails Ploughed Under,* not *Ivanhoe.*"

As school kids they studied all of Lewis and Clark's trails and were taken to the sites of some their caches. "The last place Lewis and Clark saw a grizzly bear before going on to the coast was a spot that's now on our ranch at Dillon." This oft-told tale of an expedition in 1805 along the Missouri to its headwaters in the Rockies is the true story of Maw's beginnings which lie, not in some remote ethnic conclave in a forsaken Old World, but in the place where they first became Americans, or at least Montanans.

Nor was there much interest, he admits, in communities wider than the local. Structures, institutions and stories that engaged lives beyond the neighbourhood were "alien," belonging to someone you had never met and never would. Even politicians from Helena, 120 miles away, were "alien."

Maw left the ranch to go to high school in Butte in the 1960s. At this point his story intersects with that of the working class bonded not to land and herd but to the memory of its own brawny genius.

"Boy, were those kids from the mining families tough. They carried knives and brass knuckles and beat up on the Catholics. And vice versa."

There were strikes in 1960 and 1961 that dragged on for months. Maw was aware that strikers' kids were stealing his lunch out of his locker, prising open the door with a crowbar. "They were literally starving." Maw went to complain to the vice-principal. The vice-principal replied, "There are people who don't live like you do," and wept.

That's Maw's story for me about the time he spent in Butte. It's haunted him for thirty years and now it haunts me.

A SCHOONER IN MEMORY

Don Gayton

T HOMAS GAYTON WAS BORN IN IRELAND. WHEN he was twelve, his parents shipped him to Nova Scotia, under some form of indenture. That was in 1805. Thomas's life thereafter was tied to ships, first fishing off the coast of Newfoundland, then working in the Halifax dockyards, and finally as master of a schooner based near Yarmouth, on Nova Scotia's South Shore. His ship plied the Maritime and New England coasts until he died in 1858. A life in place, summed within the confines of a paragraph.

OUR TRIP TO FIND THIS THOMAS BEGAN IN HALIFAX. After an exhausting flight across the country, I arrived at the airport late in the afternoon. Since there was time to kill – Dad wasn't due in until the next morning – I started walking to the hotel, a few kilometres away. A busy freeway overpass loomed in front of me, and I realized it had no sidewalk. For me, overpasses are among the most inhospitable structures on the planet, and I felt an old and rancid alienation rising as I walked across this one. Thomas, my great-great-great-grandfather, had to deal with a hostile ocean, and lost a son and a nephew to it, in fact, but never had to deal with toxic structures like this, ones of our own making. This overpass would have been a flagrant denial of my pedestrian rights, in the old days. Now I found it simply unpleasant, and hurried across.

The anonymous hotel was curled in the concrete embrace of a cloverleaf. Right after checking in, I went outside to run. I wanted to shed the alienation three airports and an overpass had created, and get a small foretaste of the landscapes we would see on our journey to the South Shore. The famous fogs of Halifax dictated that its airport was fifty kilometres out of town, and I realized now that the whole complex of airport, interchange and hotel were just a small enclave surrounded by forest. The paved road I ran on angled inland, away from hotel and freeway. Very soon pavement switched to gravel. There were no houses, and the road was dead straight and lonesome, a road built for exploiting resources or maybe dumping bodies. The forest on either side of me was more engaging – a mix of second-growth white spruce, tamarack, and the odd white pine. The tallest trees barely reached thirty feet, and the spruces had heavy, clumped tops. There were pockets where the trees were only a few feet high and widely scattered, and in those areas, undergrowth took over. A shrub I didn't know showed off white blossoms, like an apple tree. Labrador tea competed in places with rhododendron. Exotic white branching lichens reached all the way up to the shrub layer. The ground was patterned into humps and valleys. The tamaracks, or what I as a Westerner am pleased to call larches, heralded the oncoming spring by turning out their incomparably green sprays of needles. Passing a boggy spot, I saw the classic unfolding fiddlehead ferns, looking like the necks of green violins. At a road cut, I dug my fingers for the first time into the yielding red clay of the ancestral Atlantic.

I ran for forty-five minutes, slowly, slowing occasionally to look at plants, and finally stopped at the crest of a long hill. This odd subboreal forest stretched away indefinitely to the west, and a low ceiling of braided cloud rolled overhead. What a sight it must have been, all this unclaimed expanse, for the twelve-year-old born to a country as land-hungry as Ireland.

Turning back, I mulled over the logic for my being here. Neither Dad nor I had ever been to Nova Scotia, but we had discussed a roots trip off and on for probably twenty years. I reminded myself that genealogy is a clever trap, waiting to snare the writer into thinking his material is inherently interesting and important. Dad and I might have been better off picking some town in Iowa or Manitoba, and researching a historical family chosen at random. Furthermore, I saw genealogy as linear, patriarchal thinking; the tyranny of the surname means that women's contributions are automatically downgraded. Family history seems most often invoked to show some splendidly early arrival date or a connection to the famous. On balance though, genealogy does provide a crack in the present, I reasoned, giving access and a legitimate reason to reinvent the past.

Dad arrived the next morning. Somehow, he could arrive from California in a few hours whereas from British Columbia it had taken me all day. We hugged warmly, but he was preoccupied: his suitcase had not arrived. The people at the check-in desk assured him it would be in on the noon flight. If he would leave the key with them, they would clear it through customs and send it on by cab to us in Halifax. I hadn't seen my father in a couple of years and I watched his grave and massive presence as he talked with the ticket agent. The weatherbeaten skin of his neck was the colour of old, dark wood, and his close-cropped beard alternated brown and silver. We left, but Dad was worried about his pyjamas, which were in the suitcase. I granted him that mundane worry; at seventy-five he was entitled. I had reached the age where I was beginning to accept our similarities.

We splurged on a full-size rental, rationalizing that both of us were six feet four, and that father/son tours of ancestral Nova Scotia came only once in a lifetime. We drove in state down to Halifax harbour, where young Thomas Gayton had helped repair the British boats *Shannon* and *Chesapeake* during the War of 1812. I remarked how curious it was that Thomas aided England, but his grandson and great-grandson – who both grew up in New England – harboured the traditional Yankee dislike for the British, whom they referred to as "the bloody lobsterbacks."

This Thomas we were going to find was also a minor participant in that finest hour of Canadian entrepreneurship, the great clipper ship trading era. Between 1786 and 1920, some four thousand wooden ships of over five hundred tons draft were built in the Canadian Maritimes. They sailed the seven seas, moving fish, lumber, gypsum, salt, molasses and a hundred other commodities. Yarmouth at one time had the second largest fleet registry in Canada, second only to Halifax, and the ships of Nova Scotia's South Shore competed head-to-head with ships from Boston and Liverpool. Nova Scotia produced the greatest designer of the clipper ship era, Donald Mackay, as well as its greatest sailor, Joshua Slocum.

Thomas sailed a two-masted schooner, with sails facing fore and aft. The schooner was a New World innovation, born along the North America's eastern seaboard, where crews were scarce and coastlines serrated. The schooner's fore-and-aft sails could be raised and lowered right from the deck, with a much smaller crew than the traditional square-rigged ships required, and they could also tack more easily and go farther "into the wind." The sons and nephews of Thomas gravitated to the transatlantic trade, which was dominated by the bigger, square-rigged barques and brigantines.

Nova Scotia ships were built as a community enterprise. Two or three families in places like Meteghan, or Port Greville, or Barrington would pool labour and capital, set up a shipyard, and begin hauling logs from the forests behind. Meanwhile, a tabletop scale model of the ship's hull would be in preparation, sculpted and resculpted based on tradition, the ship's intended use (heavy ore cargoes, for instance, required broader beams and sturdier construction), and always a leaven of innovation.

Once the model was completed to everyone's satisfaction, dimensions were scaled up to full size, and work began in earnest. Sawyers produced the dimensional lumber. Tamarack, spruce, pine, oak and fir were all used, each for a particular application. The keel would be laid, and a small steam plant would be set up to bend the various hull components to the right curvature. Metal fittings, rope and canvas would be ordered from Halifax. The "ways," complex tracks that would carry the completed ship on its only terrestrial journey, from the yard into the water, were also constructed.

It is sobering to think that the vast quantities of information and technology required to design, build and launch a seaworthy schooner, to sail it along poorly marked coasts and unpredictable seas, and to run it as a business, all resided in these tiny, isolated communities of Nova Scotia's South Shore.

DAD'S SUITCASE FINALLY ARRIVED, MINUS ITS KEY, and we drove south down the coast, passing Lunenburg and then Shelburne. Before we checked in to our hotel in Yarmouth, we stopped at a hardware store and bought a key blank and a file, to reproduce the childishly simple suitcase key that had gone astray. As Dad worked on the key, I fiddled with the suitcase, idly spinning the tumblers to a combination lock that apparently provided an additional level of security. Dad soon had both the key locks open but was stunned when the suitcase remained shut.

"Did you fool with the combination lock?" he asked, accusingly.

"Well, yes, but don't you know the combination?"

He shook his head slowly. "It's your grandfather's suitcase, and I've never used the combination lock. I've always simply left it unlocked and used the key locks instead."

The pyjamas again became theoretical. I busied myself with the lock, turning the tumblers with my ear pressed against them, hoping for some telltale click.

Dad began examining the side of the suitcase. "That's it, Black Horse!" he said excitedly, and pointed to the letters ACO printed in small letters on the side.

"What on earth do ACO and Black Horse mean?" I said.

Dad was busy counting on his fingers: "Never mind, try 347."

I stared at him blankly.

"Never mind, just try it."

I dialed in the numbers, and the suitcase popped open. I looked at Dad with some amazement.

"It's a mnemonic, you see. Pop wanted a way to remember combinations, so he dreamed this up years ago. You find a ten-letter word or a phrase that has no letters repeated, and you assign a number to each letter. With Black Horse, B stands for one, L for two, A for three, and so on. Then you write the letter equivalent to the combination right near the lock somewhere, and all you have to remember is Black Horse."

He took out his pyjamas triumphantly.

Genealogy is definitely a trap, I thought to myself. There was the grandfather, Donald the First, who dreamt up alphanumeric mnemonics and built clocks from scratch. There was the father, Donald the Second, who can arrive at pi from a dozen different mathematical pathways, and the son, Donald the Third, horrified yet fascinated, who stands to inherit the mnemonic suitcase, plus a set of yet unknown obsessions. Donald, Donald, Donald. I named my first child Ivan, trying to put an emphatic end to this blood-and-fathers nonsense, but already I see traces: my son builds guitars with fret placements honed to the third decimal place. That night I fell asleep wondering what threads might be woven all the way forward from Thomas.

AFTER HIS STINT IN THE HALIFAX SHIPYARDS, YOUNG Thomas was sent to the South Shore community of Argyle, between Yarmouth and Cape Sable, to work as a sailor on a schooner belonging to one Isaac Spinney. Thomas married Spinney's daughter Anne, took up two hundred acres of land somewhere along the Tusket River, and sailed for the rest of his life, becoming the master of at least one ship, the schooner *Armenia,* of fifty tons capacity. His wife Anne bore eight children.

The man Thomas Gayton died in 1858, leaving few marks on the landscape and none on a sea that will not allow them. He was not alone in his invisibility; of the 238 people claiming occupation in the 1861 census of the Argyle District, 34 were mariners, and 38 were fishermen, all most notable by their absence from terrestrial record. A few of these people left memoirs, as did Captain Benjamin Doane of nearby Barrington, but most, including Thomas, did not. Lives such as these can be expanded slightly by inferential research, but far more substantially by a kind of geographically-centred imagination. The true biographer of Thomas and his kind would have to be a novelist.

The next morning Dad and I had a leisurely breakfast at a restaurant overlooking Yarmouth harbor. It was pleasant to be beyond the bitter political arguments that had poisoned our relationship for so long. We sipped coffee and watched the ocean-going ferry arrive on its overnight run from Portland, Maine. I asked Dad to go over the familiar ground of his childhood again, in the small deepwater port of Tiverton, Rhode Island. He grew up surrounded by maritime tradition and, as a boy, spent much of his time either at the docks or at his uncle's sail loft, taking in the fading sights and smells of the clipper ship era. By the time he left Tiverton, most of those ships had either been beached and abandoned, or converted to pleasure craft for wealthy Bostonians. My father's Tiverton experience gave him a direct tie to the language and culture of the Nova Scotia clipper ships. I, on the other hand, grew up as a drylander and didn't know a mainsail from a marlinspike, but was sure I could feel the impetus of our previous maritime generations, like one feels an onshore wind.

After breakfast, we drove to the Yarmouth County Archives, situated in an elegant old stone church. We had phoned in advance, and the archivist met us with stacks of information. For the next three hours we fossicked through genealogies, land titles, censuses, records of shipping, maps and diaries, coming away with a raft of notes. One of our objectives was to find Thomas's grave. The archivist gave us a photocopied document listing surnames in the graveyards of Kemptville, and Gayton was among them. This was odd, since everything we had read associated the family with Argyle, on the coast, and Kemptville was several kilometres inland. How little is written down about an ordinary person's life.

We folded ourselves into the big Buick and drove toward Kemptville. I soon discovered that in this part of the Maritimes there are at least three different routes leading to the same place, none of them very direct. I also learned you must be quite specific about the community you are traveling to. As for our destination, there was Kemptville Corner, East Kemptville, and North Kemptville to choose from. The nearby Pubnicos offered the choice of West, Middle West, Lower West, East, Middle East, and plain Pubnico. These were communities all right, but not in the sense that you could always identify when you were at their centre. Some would have a gas station or a church; others were simply collections of widely spaced houses and small farms.

Kemptville Corner lay in rolling terrain and Acadian scrub forest. The cemetery yielded the grave of one Havey Gayton who died in 1866 at age one, and clouds of blackflies, but no Thomas or Anne. The surnames of Nickerson, Crowell, Spinney, Ryder and Goodwin abounded though, and we knew these people to be contemporaries and relatives of Thomas and his descendants. I stopped at a country store and asked about other cemeteries in the immediate area, and the teenage girl at the counter drew an excellent map showing the locations of two others. We scouted both of those, to no avail. We decided to try the Argyle area, even though there was no graveyard list to work from.

Argyle Sound is a long, open bay cutting into the Nova Scotia coastline, ending at Argyle Head. The other Argyles were ranged further down the Sound. We started with the big cemetery at Argyle Head. Again, we found contemporaries of Thomas and Anne, but not those two. Next we tried the cemetery at Central Argyle, again with no luck. To be so concerned with finding graves was silly, since they would give us no more information than we already knew, yet somehow it was important. Thomas was unique in our ancestry as one who chose a place as a young man and stayed rooted there until he died. His grave would celebrate that fact as well as his person.

The community of Lower Argyle came next. Dense second-growth tamarack, white spruce and alder came right down to the shore. A few of the houses looked ancestral, but there were others from every era right up to the present. How many groups had stormed or slunk on to this storied and rocky coast, I wondered: Vikings, Mi'kmaq, Acadians, Planters, Loyalists, freed slaves, Novascotiamen, draft dodgers (from more than one war) rum-runners, American tourists.

We took a break from our graveyard tour and stopped for a moment on a nearby beach. There was no sand, just gravel and bedrock. Among the wrack at the tide line was a smashed lobster pot and a great curved chunk of wood, its graceful arc plainly of nautical origin. In the days of the schooners, pieces like these were cut entire from the curving trunks and roots of old-growth spruce trees.

The peaceful water of Argyle Sound in front of us was dotted with islands, where some of the French Acadians hid during the brutal Expulsion of 1755.

AN EXAMINATION OF ROOTS ULTIMATELY BECOMES an examination of landscape, and as we sat on a driftwood log, I made a comparison between the imagined landscape I had created for Thomas and the real one. What I had envisioned was a broader band of coastal vegetation, with windswept trees and beach grass. Instead, the forest was dense and boreal right to within a few feet of shore. Of course I had imagined the upright, two-story white clapboard houses with long windows facing the sea, of which there were a few, but my imagination had made no room for the ordinary bungalows, the designer beach homes and the comfortable farmhouses that were also scattered along the road. What I had intuited correctly though, was the feel of the air. My imagined Argyle also came complete with compass directions, which turned out to be quite correct.

This sound we stared at had witnessed fifty-six oceangoing ships built and launched between 1800 and 1895. Now it was a quiet backwater. Even Yarmouth, at one time a key port on the international shipping lanes, now had only a few fishing boats and the ocean ferry.

We got back in the car and resumed our search, both now somewhat skeptical of ever finding the graves. We knew Thomas and Anne lived in the Argyles for some time, but that was all. They could have moved to a different community toward the end of their lives, or become indigent, unable to afford headstones. And Jackson Ricker's *Historical Sketches of Glenwood and the Argyles,* one of our sources, spoke ominously of abandoned graveyards in the area.

Lower Argyle's cemetery turned out to be right by the road, a small, treeless plot of ground tucked in between two farmhouses, a few hundred yards up from the beach. How different these were from Western Canadian graveyards, I thought, which only had to accommodate barely a hundred years of history. By now, we had a drill established: Dad took the right, I took the left, and we slowly worked our way along the rows of headstones. Some of the older ones were almost undecipherable. It was as if the letters were wounds on the stone that, over the decades, had healed. Just as the injured body carries an image of itself that is a blueprint for healing, these old stones seemed compelled to return to their original mute, smooth surfaces.

Dad let out a shout, and I knew immediately that he had found the graves. The day brightened, going from humdrum back to adventure again. It was actually a single bronze, four-sided family memorial. One side had an anchor on it, and read:

> *Thomas Gayton*
> *A Native of Ireland*
> *Died Oct. 10, 1858*
> *Aged 64 Years*
> *At Rest*

The next side was Anne's, reading:

> *Anne*
> *Beloved Wife of Thomas Gayton*
> *Died May 3, 1857*
> *Aged 64 Years*

The third side read:

> *Jeremiah*
> *Youngest Son of Thomas and Anne Gayton*
> *Died At Sea*
> *April 7, 1880*
> *Aged 49 Years*

We had gleaned a bit of cryptic information on this son Jeremiah from Ricker's book: "Mr. Jeremiah Gayton of Lower Argyle who had been away from home for twenty years and was returning home as one of the crew of the barque *Clydesdale*, fell from aloft and was instantly killed."

We looked further into the graveyard and found the markers of two other sons of Thomas and Anne, plus a grand-nephew, a James who died at sea at age twenty-six. Of this James, the genealogy said: "James Gayton, son of James, of Argyle, died at sea in 1878, being drowned on board the schooner *Moero*, himself the captain, on a voyage from Yarmouth, N.S. to St. Kitts, West Indies. In a heavy gale of wind the vessel was thrown on her beam ends, dismasted and waterlogged. Only two of the crew survived." We looked for another nephew, Jeremiah Gayton, whom Ricker had listed as the Captain of the four-masted brigantine the *Gypsum Empress*, but he was not to be found.

We used an adjacent gravestone as a camera rest and took photographs of ourselves next to the cenotaph, each vying, as always, for the highest ground so as to appear the tallest. We nudged and jostled and mugged for the camera, trying on the piercing seaward gazes each thought might be worthy of this ancestor. Even though we came to it from different directions, it was a fine moment.

Driving on beyond the cemetery, we saw the Lower Argyle dock, which was crowded with the broad, squat lobster boats.

By mutual, if silent, agreement, we got out and wandered slowly along the dock, feeling a bit self-conscious in tourist clothes. This was not a tourist dock. A short, powerful man in T-shirt and baseball cap said hello, and we stopped to chat. He said the three-week lobster season was about half over and the catch had been good so far. To my ear, untrained to these Eastern accents, his could pass for that of a slightly faded Irishman. He introduced himself as Nathan Goodwin, and he recognized our surname, even though all the Argyle Gaytons had either departed or died one hundred years ago. We concluded that we were probably distant relatives, and enjoyed the brief moment without further entanglements. After saying goodbye, Dad said that was enough for one day, and we drove slowly back to the hotel.

That night, after Dad went to bed, I borrowed his long black raincoat and walked the streets of Yarmouth. So I had finally captured Argyle, this place of personal and historical and imagined dimensions, a balance point on my family heart-line, one that my grandfather first told me about when I was ten or eleven. Argyle was presented to me then as a kind of unblemished Anglo-Saxon verity, which I subsequently rejected for two decades, but which now presented itself as real place, a backwater of mildly turbulent, mildly romantic history, where my great-great-great-grandfather chose, or perhaps was told, to live and die.

A great welter of impressions awaited sorting and reflection. Now I had the flesh and blood of Argyle, the stony beach and subdued forest, and a place for Thomas. I could see him there on a Sunday afternoon, on an infrequent home stay. Church and meal are over and there is the pleasant hum and rhythm of children. He leaves the house and goes slowly down the path to the dock and the schooner, to check on some inconsequential matter. His black suit catches the summer sun, and unaccustomed warmth spreads pleasantly across his shoulders.

The shingle rock crunches underfoot as he steps on to the empty beach, now midway on the path between schooner and home. The water of Argyle Sound sparkles, the breeze has dropped to cat's-paws, and the whole earth seems to be on a long afternoon nap. This Argyle was given to him as place; it was unavoidable. He must do everything, to bend himself to relation with this place, become a father of many, perhaps to replace the one who gave him away. Destiny or random economics had casually given him this spot, which he must passionately embrace. Thomas, with his mandates, indentures, and memories of Ireland in the way, will find this difficult. The land and the ocean, for their part, will do nothing, save to embrace him in the end. His finished work of person-in-place, of Thomas-of-Argyle, would not be for him to appreciate, but for his itinerant great-great-great-grandson to see and envy.

When I travel, I don't seem to need much sleep, and nervous energy accumulates. Walking at night has always been a way to drain off some of that energy, and that night I walked for hours, down Yarmouth's huddled streets and lanes. Dad's black raincoat reminded me of a photograph I had once seen of Loren Eiseley, another insomniac, wearing a similar coat as he walked the night streets of Philadelphia.

The memory of our visit to the dock bothered me, and I turned the scene over and over as I walked. A walk down a picturesque dock crowded with lobster boats on a sunny Nova Scotia afternoon is not normal cause for concern. I had no idea of the condition of the lobster fishery, but my gut reaction was that virtually every resource extraction that we do – from logging to fishing to farming to lobster harvesting – was in some kind of trouble, and this one would be no exception. The docks and boats and river drives and lumber camps and farm fields that we have invested with nostalgic romanticism are now all faintly suspect. Is the lobster fishery sustainable in the long term? Are we simply equitably dividing up a steadily diminishing remainder until the last one is gone? Did my ancestors set a pattern of selfish resource extraction that we carry on, but on a much grander scale? In his memoir *Following the Sea,* Benjamin Doane, a contemporary of Thomas, describes a telling encounter with an albatross during a whaling expedition:

> *Not only for the purposes of food, however, were gooneys [albatrosses] killed, but often merely to gratify that savage instinct which sometimes possesses men to kill for the sake of killing and to gloat upon scenes of suffering. That tendency in me received one day a check, the influence of which has never left me. It was when the sharks were thick about the carcase of a whale which we had alongside, and I was chopping at them with the spade. A large gooney scaled down to pick up a sliver that lay drifting in the sleek water. A sudden thoughtless impulse made me strike at him, and the keen edge of the spade gave him a glancing blow upon the neck. He trailed away, mortally wounded, his snowy breast reddening with blood, his reproachful eyes upon me as they glazed in death.*

In Doane's mind, there was a clear separation between his random and purposeless killing of an albatross and his systematic and purposeful slaughter of whales. Could he have any inkling of where his profession of whaling was headed? Perhaps even more than the western cowboy or the old-time logger, the whaler has traditionally been the ultimate romantic male professional. Yet now, whalers are virtual pariahs, operating in a kind of moral shadowland between ignorance of ecology and contempt for it.

Ruthless extraction of resources is done exclusively by males, often in very intimate, almost tribal situations, of which Doane's whaling crew was a classic example. The biological horror of what they did – kill huge mammals for a few barrels of oil – was diffused over a group of men rather than resting on the shoulders of one individual. Recruits into these male guilds are often very young (as Benjamin Doane was) and any moral revulsions to the nature of their work are overridden by their intense desire to become an accepted part of the guild.

Still I am not sure that I can indict Thomas and his contemporaries. They came to Nova Scotia with rudimentary technologies of fishing, agriculture, timber harvesting and commerce. Their forefathers had evicted the Acadians (I would not be surprised to find the land that Thomas bought once belonged to an Acadian), and they had a very limited understanding of the complex terrestrial and marine ecosystems they imposed themselves on. These people were no more or less farsighted then we are, plus they inured themselves to maritime death tolls that broke over them like the waves of an endless storm. Their saving graces were perhaps the scale and capacity of their works, neither of which were very large. If I indict Thomas, I must also indict myself. We know more, but we also destroy more.

Thomas and Anne Gayton endured, and had eight children. Their firstborn, John, became a sailor like his father, and married Abigail Smith from nearby Barrington. John and Abigail in turn produced eight children, as well as adopting a boy named Manassah Spinney. As a young woman, this Abigail started writing a journal on New Year's Day of 1840, and she penned the last entry – in the same book – in 1896. Abigail was a tough woman. Her implacable ally was the Baptist Church; her implacable enemy was the sea, which kept her an agonized single parent for most of her married life. As her five sons grew, she formed a powerful resolution to keep them away from seafaring. Again, using Benjamin Doane as interlocutor, we get a sense of the Maritime mother's lot as the young son prepares to leave home on a three-year whaling voyage:

At home, mother sat knitting and though she said little, I
knew that her chief thoughts and all her hopes and fears
were for me. Three of her sons had gone away to sea,
never to return in life. Now I, her youngest was about to
go on a long and dangerous voyage, and she was old, and
feared she would never see me again.

Abigail was more outspoken than Benjamin Doane's
mother. Anyone who keeps a journal in the same book for
fifty-six years has some measure of persistence, and Abigail
finally won her battle with the sea. Early in the spring of 1862,
their lives more than half over, John, Abigail, their children
and a number of other families chartered a vessel to take them
to St. John, New Brunswick, thence up the St. John River to
Hartland, and then overland to a place in the forest they chris-
tened Knowlesville, in honour of the Baptist minister who led
them there. Abigail knew the soils of Lower Argyle, as an alternative to the sea, were just thick enough to go broke on. The
deeper soils of their new home in New Brunswick were somewhat more productive, and after a brutal decade of clearing
land, stumping and building fences, they had a farm.

Abigail was a passionate Baptist; I think her ultimate triumph, even greater than that of vanquishing the sea, would
have been to have her menfolk throw themselves down in
front of another male, the Minister, and say "I believe." From
her journal, it is obvious she was not successful. Subsequent
Gayton menfolk seem to have carried this skeptical tradition
forward.

DAD AND I CHECKED OUT OF OUR MOTEL THE NEXT
morning, and drove through Lower Argyle once more, just to
fix the place in memory. I wanted to see more of the South
Shore, so after leaving Lower Argyle we stayed off the highway,

following the coast road through the Pubnicos, Woods Harbour, Shag Harbour, Doctor's Cove and then Barrington, where Abigail and Benjamin Doane grew up.

Getting back on to the highway at Shelburne, I began to look more critically at the forests around me. This was obviously not the same forest that produced thousands of wooden ships. This was not the same forest in which every oak over twenty inches in diameter was marked with a Broad Arrow and was the property of the British Navy. In fact, I saw no oaks at all. This was not the same forest in which the old-timers recall never felling a hemlock of less than twenty-four inches diameter on the butt. This was not the same forest that produced trees big enough for the masts of a Novascotiaman. I found out later that the forests looked stunted and boreal not by nature, but because of historical overcutting coupled with inappropriate burning.

We detoured off the highway once more to Lunenburg, the Canadian equivalent of Mecca, the home of the schooner *Bluenose*. My American father knew of the Bluenose, but couldn't understand all the hype and hoopla surrounding this particular schooner. I showed him our dime and explained that it was the fastest schooner ever built and a kind of Canadian Liberty Bell, the only difference being we probably wouldn't go to war over it. The ship was graceful and beautiful, even while moored at the edge of a crowded parking lot with all its sails furled. Sailboats verge on the biological; I see them as part organism.

I knew the ship was actually the *Bluenose II*, a modern replica, the original having been destroyed in a case of unconscionable national negligence. Pursuing this connection between landscape and local industry, I asked the interpretive guide where the masts for the new ship came from. The fellow replied, with misplaced patriotic pride, that they were made from Douglas fir that came all the way from British Columbia.

I was beginning to get the picture.

John and Abigail's first son, Ebenezer Crowell Gayton, my great-grandfather, left the New Brunswick farm as soon as he could for upstate New York, to work in the brand new petroleum industry (so our lamps could be lit by fossil life instead of live whales) and eventually become the fire chief in the small town of Gowanda. Evidently Knowlesville soils weren't thick enough to hold him. A forester colleague of mine, who worked around Knowlesville, told me that in the middle of mature forest, he would often stumble on to old furrows from abandoned farm fields. No Gaytons remain in Knowlesville, either.

Among the family odds and ends I have a copy of Ebenezer's 1894 US citizenship certificate, which demands that he "renounce and abjure all allegiance and fidelity to every Foreign Prince, Potentate, State or Sovereignty, and particularly to the Queen of the Kingdom of Great Britain, of whom he was then a subject." When I became a Canadian in the early seventies, I was asked to swear the reverse, but crossed fingers behind my back when it came to the part about the Queen.

Families were getting smaller now; Donald Vince Gayton, the First, was one of only five children fathered by Ebenezer Crowell Gayton. Donald the First moved to easy California as soon as he was able. He and his first son, Donald the Second, then pursued a distant but binary relationship all up and down the West Coast, bestowing on the present first son all the geographical and national ambiguity that has carried forward since Thomas.

Periodically I build fascinations, and another one, now completed, has slid down its ways into my mental waters: to establish the link between the evolution of forest landscapes and historical shipbuilding on Nova Scotia's South Shore. To have that link firmly in mind would seem to me to be very valuable. Place and landscape and vegetation have obvious influence on history only occasionally, but to know of these instances can give us the feeling, whether it is illusion or not, that we are actually rooted to the earth, and even have a crack at sustainability.

Back in Halifax, my father and I said our goodbyes, and winged our separate ways across four time zones, each to his own home. When I arrived, I rooted around in a storage closet until I found an old cedar cigar box I had saved from childhood. This was my talisman box, containing objects that were fiercely important to me at one time: arrowheads, rusted square nails, old foreign coins, agates from trips to the desert, wisps of snakeskin, a petrified shark's tooth dredged from one of old Ebenezer's oil wells. Among them was Thomas's pocket compass, given to me by my grandfather at the height of my talismanic age.

The small compass is from France, and its casing is the particular rich, burnished colour unique to old brass. The rose is badly oxidized and the glass is not removable, so the last few nights I have been injecting various solvents through a pinhole opening in the side of the casing, trying to clean it. By inserting a fine needle wrapped with thread, I have been able to clean off the cardinal points, but not the degrees. Symbolic objects like the compass don't move me as much any more, and I clean it more from a sense of historical duty. If I am to have a talisman at all, it will be the memory of that ship's rib, that aged and graceful meeting of spruce and artifice, on the beach at Lower Argyle.

STRIP-MINING THE LAND OF SORROW

Ann Charney

I N THE VESTIBULE OF THE STARONOVA SYNAGOGUE
in Prague, "the oldest functioning synagogue in Europe,"
an elderly Czech woman and her grandson run a lively
little concession, worthy of the new spirit of free enterprise.
The hands of the woman and the young boy are kept busy sta-
pling together semicircles of cardboard, which they sell as
skullcaps to tourists visiting the synagogue. Even in the dark
off-season days of winter, there are many visitors and the head
coverings, at forty korunas (about $1.75), sell briskly. The stiff
cardboard caps, reminiscent of children's party hats with their
brightly coloured designs, appear oddly frivolous against the
somber vaulted Gothic interior, like Frisbees at a funeral.

There are numerous tourist attractions in Prague. Its richly
decorated palaces, churches and squares have survived for the
last six hundred years, untouched by natural disaster, the
wrath of war, or the perils of postwar redevelopment. But no
part of its historic legacy is more vigorously promoted than the
ruins of a phantom civilization – "Jewish Prague" – a community founded in the tenth century and now vanished. Dead
Jews are proving to be a highly profitable commodity for the
Czech people in the post-Communist, entrepreneurial age.

Czech treatment of Jews throughout history predictably
resembled that of its Central European neighbours – pogroms,
persecution, restrictive laws, and the innovative introduction

of an obligatory yellow circle to be worn by Jews as a form of identification, long before the Nazis imposed the yellow Star of David. Of the 55,000 Jews who lived in Prague when Hitler occupied the city in 1939, 36,000 were killed in the camps. Fewer than 2,000 of these original inhabitants remain in the city today. The Jews may be gone, but their spirit is kept alive by a kind of Disneyland theme park recreation of the past, attracting crowds and foreign currency to the shaky, new Czech economy.

Prague is particularly fortunate in possessing a rich variety of Jewish relics which lend themselves to this sort of illusory reconstruction. While traces of Jewish existence were scrupulously eradicated in other Central and Eastern European cities, Prague inspired Hitler with a different solution. Instead of razing the Jewish ghetto here, Hitler chose to preserve it. Cleansed of its inhabitants who were transported to the nearby camp in Terezín, the ghetto was designated as the site for an eventual "Exotic Museum of An Extinct Race." The Museum was to house one of the richest collections of Judaica – Jewish artifacts, looted from all over Europe and shipped to Prague. Czech authorities, reluctant to see this treasury dispersed, have resisted attempts by Jewish groups to reclaim their property.

Time ran out for Hitler before his plan could be fully realized, but a good idea never dies. The Führer was right in assuming there was an audience for his ghoulish display. Today, the ways of merchandising a vanished people have become increasingly varied and compelling as our distance from their disappearance grows and memory fades.

In Prague, you can buy large-sized pop-up cards of the ancient Jewish cemetery that open to reveal a selection of tombstones leaning towards you in picturesque disorder. On every street corner of the Old City sellers are hawking reproductions of the "art" created by the inmates of Terezín, stark images bleached of significance by this cheerful and relentless marketing, their dark origins as remote as those of the cave paintings at Lescaux.

Prague's most famous Jewish citizen, Franz Kafka, is omnipresent as well. The Kafka industry – museum, monument, grave, books, T-shirts, coffee mugs, baseball caps, postcards – is a lucrative sideline of the dead-Jews trade. Like his fellow writer and outcast James Joyce, Kafka has been rehabilitated in his native land and elevated to a place of honour. In the years after his death, Kafka's works were banned by the Nazis and mostly ignored by nationalist Czechs since he wrote in the wrong language, German. His claustrophobic depiction of the individual's helplessness in a brutal world dominated by bureaucratic power did not endear him to Communist rulers either.

Now, all is forgotten and forgiven. The Czechs' pride in their native son rivals the admiration of the Irish for Joyce. A tour of Kafka's Prague tends to be a little more solemn than a Joycean pub crawl in Dublin, with helpful guides offering a variety of explanations for Kafka's notorious angst. The most plausible analysis suggests that he was deeply affected as a child watching the destruction of the Jewish quarter – a "sanitation" process that saw the worst slums of the ghetto and their inhabitants replaced by elegant *fin-de-siècle* apartment blocks. As a German among Czechs, a Jew among Germans, an agnostic among believers, Kafka had much to fear in later years as well. But time has redeemed not only his reputation as a writer but also his miserable life. The anguish, the ostracism, the lovelessness, the untimely death have all been mythologized and woven into a rich narrative which draws admirers from afar to the city he immortalized.

AT MAKESHIFT SOUVENIR STANDS, IN BETWEEN THE Baroque statues lining the medieval Charles bridge, you can buy figurines of another extraordinary figure – Yossel the Golem – the mythic creature of the ghetto. Forged from the mud of the Vltava river, the Golem was brought to life by the famous sixteenth-century theologian, Rabbi Löw, using the mystical texts of the Cabbala. The Golem, the Rabbi's personal servant, eventually rebelled and ran amok in a frenzy of mischief, forcing his creator to render him lifeless again. Today, the clay giant is once more demonstrating his utility. Replicas of the Golem in different sizes compete well against nesting Russian dolls, featuring a smiling Bill Clinton and a melancholy George Bush. Tourists of a more serious bent can purchase at these same kiosks compact disks of classical music performed by the inmates of Terezín and books in all languages on the intricacies of Prague's Jewish history.

For the visitor with an inclination to explore the countryside outside of Prague, the American Express on Venceslas Square, site of the mass demonstrations that heralded the "Velvet Revolution," offers outings to the celebrated spas of Karlsbad (now Karlovy Vary) and Marienbad (Mariánské Lázne). But the site of Jewish extermination is proving to be as alluring a destination as the former pleasure grounds of kings and courtesans. There are regular group excursions or private ones with chauffeur and guide to Terezín which include a tour of the notorious concentration camp, a visit to the Memorial of National Martyrdom, the Small Fortress with the crematorium, and the Museum. The price of the trip includes lunch served on the premises of the Memorial.

The more adventurous can travel independently by bus from the Florenc bus station to the Terezín ghetto to visit the Theresienstadt Museum where a new exhibition details the small Czech town's conversion to Nazi "model ghetto" during the war, as well as a display of artworks by the presumably model prisoners. The eye-catching flyer for this trip is in bright yellow, with black Hebraic-like script spelling out the word *Jude* inside the Star of David. Obviously, no effort has been spared in achieving a facsimile of realism.

As you make your way through the congested streets of Josefov – the name given to the ghetto at the end of the eighteenth century in honour of the Austro-Hungarian emperor Joseph II's magnanimous treatment of Jews – or take your place in the long enthusiastic queues before three-star attractions, or fight crowds at the cemetery for a view of the ancient tombstones, an inevitable conclusion comes to mind: Czech Jews have never been as popular as now, when they are dead and gone.

Merchandising misfortune is of course by no means limited to the Czech. Strip-mining the land of sorrow is now a global concern. Individual anguish is regularly harvested in memoirs, talk shows, therapist couches, support groups, survivor websites, each tale replenishing the Holy Sacrament of Victimhood. Communal disasters have proven to be equally profitable, none more so than the mass destruction of the Jews, which has given rise to a veritable growth industry. In the name of keeping memory alive and preserving the lessons of the past, an ever-expanding range of products – films, books, TV soap operas, artworks, comic books, memorials, avant-garde museums – offer an emotional catharsis for audiences in search of quick redemption. And as these representations of the past become more real than the events that inspired them, there appear to be no limits to the inventiveness of the Holocaust industry. European Jews could have scarcely imagined that their suffering and dying would come to this.

BREATHING SPACES

Merilyn Simonds

Beep. Take a breath and hold it.
That is all.
Beep. Take a breath and hold it.
That is all.
Beep. Take a breath and hold it.

T HE MACHINE GIVES THE COMMAND AND I OBEY,
sucking in air as if through a straw. But have I taken in
enough? My lungs are so full they quiver. Perhaps I
have taken too much.

It is in my nature to follow orders, though lately, I find com-
pliance troublesome. I long for the simple directives of childhood. Take your elbows off the table. Go to your room. Comb
your hair. Demands that are easily met. As an adult, I stumble
over questions of interpretation. How large a breath, exactly?
Starting when? Hold it how long: ten seconds, fifty, a hundred?
I have learned that for every action there is a reaction, rarely
equal and never opposite, consequences falling like dominoes
from the flick of a finger, however innocent and thoughtless.
And so I stay on my guard. I try my best at all times. I purse my
lips together, locking in the breath, worrying that I haven't got
it right, although it strikes me even as I think it, how silly this
thought is. What kind of punishment do I expect?

That is all.

The voice of the machine is measured, breathy. Young, but
not childish. It has a certain authority despite its youth. A
voice one yearns to please. My body jerks a fraction deeper

into the machine. It is a human voice, a female voice, not a digitally arranged assortment of electronic pulses. I imagine women gathering in an anteroom for auditions, stay-at-home mothers wilfully breaking their routines, young actresses on their way up, old ones on their way down, breasts and bellies sagging but their voices still firm, each of the women silently spending the windfall payment a dozen different ways as they wait. One by one the women breathe the nine words into the microphone, the judges on the panel close their eyes as they listen, leaning back, then gravely shake their heads, conferring, finally nodding, yes, yes, this is the one.

Take a breath and hold it. That is all.

ROSS MUST HAVE RIDDEN A MACHINE LIKE THIS ONE, listened to the same measured voice. One young woman speaking the same firm soft orders across the country, throughout the continent, around the world. Or does each machine have its own voice? Is there a cadre of such women? Training schools, perhaps, where they stand in formation, mouthing the perfect vowels. Reunions where they chant the words together, in unison, marvelling at the differences, admiring the subtleties in each other's tones.

I remember the day a young woman with straight dark hair that fit her like a skullcap came to teach Ross how to breathe.

Once every half-hour, five deep breaths, she says, inhaling so deeply her nostrils fare. Like this: in...then out. Slowly. She presses her painted lips together and releases tiny kisses into the empty spaces above his bed.

And every hour, I want you to cough three times. Cough for me, she says, and he coughs, one, two, three.

Good. Do it just like that. Then she leaves the room, her white coat dusting the frame as she moves past the door.

Ross coughs three times and takes a deep breath, blows it

out hard and fast, sucks in again, coughing.

That's good, I say, smoothing the sheet across his chest. Now rest. We'll do it again later.

But he won't stop. He shakes his head and coughs again. And again. He grabs at the air and spits it out in gusts, coughing and gasping, his eyes wild, trying to get it right.

I can hear the young woman giving orders in the hall.

My uncle doesn't understand, I say, touching her sleeve. She is half my age and shorter than I, yet the way she looks at me makes me feel like an insolent child. I hear the whine in my voice as I say, You have to tell him to stop.

She looks back through the door to the old man wheezing and sputtering on the bed.

Oh, I see. It's all right. You can tell him he doesn't have to do as I said.

She doesn't understand. She gave the order, so only she can take it back. My father said, Do it this way, and though my friends, my lovers, my sons tell me it doesn't matter, still I take a breath and hold it, knowing there is a volume of air of a certain size and a way of clasping it in the alveoli of my lungs that I must strive for, until I get it precisely, perfectly right.

That is all.

The voice is preceded by a short, sharp beep. I imagine a red light flashing on, it's that sort of sound. Although we've built up a rhythm now, the machine and I, the beep, the voice, the whirr of some moving part, the voice again, the slight jolt as I move deeper into the ring of invisible light, and although the rhythm should make the beep so predictable that the woman's command comes at just the right moment when I would naturally take a fresh breath, still, the sound startles me every time.

Beep. Take a breath and hold it.

The voice is soothing but the words strike me as ominous. Breaths are not meant to be taken in the singular, one breath here, another there, like a child plucking apples off a tree, random and chaotic. Surely there is danger in learning to breathe on command. Of all things, the taking in and out of air should be automatic, unconscious of desire or need. A matted knob of nerves no bigger than a cyst nestled at the base of my brain regulates the smooth rise and fall of my chest, twelve breaths a minute, a new half-litre of air every five seconds. To hold a breath, catch a breath, bated breath, breathlessness: these are acts of fear, surpise and wonder. What if she forgets to order the next? And why doesn't she say, Exhale, Breathe out, or, Let it go. Why does she say, so casually, with such finality, *That is all*.

The table I am lying on pulls me forward again. I wonder how far apart the notches are, how thin the segments of my body that are being observed. Once, during a tour of a medical laboratory, a doctor showed me the body of a man, sliced into inch-thick slabs, head to toe, each preserved like an enormous steak. The pieces were arranged in order in a vertical metal rack, so that it seemed as if the man still stood upright in the lab's cold green light. The doctor pulled out a chest slab and handed it to me, pointing out the white knob of spine, the pink sponge of lung, the gaping holes of severed veins. The words used to describe the whole of the body – handsome, elegant, homely, gaunt – have no meaning when applied to its parts. The flesh I held was healthy or diseased, the bone fractured or whole, the arteries ragged with plaque or running free.

Beep. Take a breath and hold it.

Hanging on the wall beside the sliced man were half a dozen breasts. Not the preserved breasts of real women, but soft plastic replicas the colour of doll's flesh, the surfaces lumpy, distorted, smooth. On an examining table nearby lay the plastic torso of a woman with collapsed flaps of surrogate skin on her chest.

The doctor took one of the breasts off the wall and inserted it under the flap on one side of the female chest. He slipped another into the other side, then he ran his fingers over the swellings, his touch light as a lover's. Though I knew his eyes were glazed with imagined disease, my own nipples grew erect under my shirt.

That is all.

I chide myself for neglecting to count the beeps. If I could remember the position of my body when the first alarm sounded, note the number of beeps and where my body is aligned at the end, I could calculate the interval between the x-ray scans. I try to reconstruct. Five beeps? Ten? I may have dozed: the voice is that hypnotic. I may have taken a hundred breaths, a thousand inhalations, the rays slicing my chest into rounds as thin as silver dollars, as thin as windowpanes, then what would they see?

Beep. Take a breath and hold it.

From the rollaway bed by the door, I listened to Ross breathe, a noisy drawing in, then the long, dreadful pause as stale hospital air edged past the tumours that crouched where his trachea split into bronchi, obstructing the passage into the starving sacs of his lungs.

Near the end, he rarely sleeps, especially at night. He jerks awake, his hand flailing out. Calling, Are you there?

I'm here, I say softly, bending to kiss his forehead, the skin all but transparent and powdery dry, like phyllo pastry, I think, recoiling form the image, tasting his flesh in my mouth.

His eyelids flutter open, drift closed again, the flicker of his watery blue eyes holding me to his side.

Other times, he locks his bony fingers on my wrist.

Shove a knife in me, he screams. Throw me in the street. Throw me out with the garbage. Go on. Do it. I've had enough! Kill me, please just kill me. Pleading, don't leave me, his fingers bruising my flesh. Don't let me out of your sight. His eyes rolling back in their sockets. Oh God please let me die. Help me, help me, help me. Whispering, can't you let me go? Why won't you let me go?

And now and again, long precious moments when I ease away from his bed and lie down on the cot by the door, curling tightly on top of the covers, eyes wide, listening for the raked-in breath to be let go. Counting the seconds. Thinking, no one can hold a breath this long. Raising myself off the bed, my feet touching the floor, composing myself to believe this, finally, is the last, and then he exhales once more, the air escaping his lips as if tumbling through a great wall of tears, a long, burbling breath that roils across the gap between our beds.

That is all.

My arms are raised above my head, as the x-ray technician has directed. Though my wrists are crossed, I remember to keep my hands relaxed, the fingers falling open and apart, like supplicants. I often sleep like this. Sometimes I make love like this. The technician sits in another room, behind a row of machines. He watches me through the glass, I think, though I cannot see him: I face the white hole that sucks in my body by degrees. Does the machine take all his attention, I wonder? Or does he stand idly by, glancing down now and then at the blinking lights and ghostly shapes, pondering the patients he guides inside the machine, noting who goes willingly, who with curiosity, who in fear. Who among them twitches and rustles on the narrow bench. Who holds their arms open above their head, as if a knife is at their backs, and who crosses their wrists in bondage, one pulsing vein exposed.

Beep. Take a breath and hold it.

Some thoughts never fully form. They twist like ether through the brain, a miasma of the mind that almost takes on substance but when confronted, dissipates, though never quite disappears. I lie on the table, inching into the machine, a solitary breath straining at my lungs, and I chase down the thought like a hound in a swamp.

I didn't know it could be done. To unhook the intravenous, turn off the oxygen tap. To leave it to the tumours to decide.

Early in the evening, his eyes flutter open. Well, that's all

262

then, bye now, he says, his voice clear and firm, a little impatient, as if a social call has gone on too long.

I'm not leaving. I'll be right here all night, don't worry. The words slide out, automatic as breath.

Well, take care. His smile is insistent. He closes his eyes.

I lie on my bed, measuring his breaths with my own, a syncopated rhythm, two of mine to each of his, a susurration that softens the viscous drum roll in his chest.

It's the smell that lifts me off the bed. So heavy and sweet it suffocates me. I edge toward the door. Something overripe has burst, exploding its spores into the room, swelling and pressing against the walls. I gasp, sucking in the rank, sinister smell.

My hand is on the doorknob when I notice. No sound comes from the bed. I wait, holding the fetid breath until I can hold it no longer, breathing in quickly again, pushing the foul air deeper into the tissues of my lungs.

When I touch his face, it feels warm. I lift his hand. It falls back across his chest as if blood were still pulsing through the veins. I stare in the half-light at his chest, convinced it wavers with subtle exhalations. He stares at me with liquid eyes, his jaw slack, as it has been for days. I put my fingers on his eyelids, but they cannot be closed. I dig in my pockets for pennies. How does one do right by the dead?

I put my hands on the window and push the sash as high as it will go. Flakes of snow settle on the sill. I cross his hands on his chest and pull the covers up to his chin. The overbearing fragrance sweeps out of the room and into the night, all but what remains lodged in my lungs, what filters out of my mouth, month after month, what lies there still, for all I know, invisible to the touch, invisible even to this machine whose prying rays expose secrets of human flesh I only imagine, invisible to everyone but me for I took the breath and I held it.

That is all.

HEART FAILURE

Wayne Grady

I AM ON A TRAIN TRAVELLING FROM BOSTON TO New Haven, Connecticut, and my father is in a hospital in North Bay, Ontario, dying of heart failure. I am hoping he will last another two days, enough time to get me through my meetings and take a plane from Hartford to Toronto and a bus from Toronto back to North Bay. But the phone calls have not been encouraging. He was holding steady when I left, but at the Boston station I called and learned that his signs are becoming less and less vital. His blood pressure is down to 80 over 38. His kidneys are secreting medication, and his skin is turning yellow. I should be with him now. The fact that I am not is a puzzle to me, and I can't help thinking that it, too, is a failure of the heart.

I make it through half the meetings and then excuse myself, call a cab, and ten hours later get off a bus in front of the old Empire Hotel in North Bay. The temperature is minus thirty-one. Four years ago we staged a surprise fiftieth anniversary party for my parents in this hotel. We told them we were taking them somewhere fancy for lunch, and when we arrived at the hotel, a faded landmark from North Bay's more prosperous railway days, a hundred of their friends were waiting in one of the banquet rooms, some they hadn't seen for years, including an old Navy buddy who had been their Best Man in St. John's, Newfoundland, in 1945.

Now the Empire has been converted into a retirement

home; the door is locked, and a security guard stares dully at me from his desk in what used to be the hotel's chandeliered lobby. I drag my luggage two blocks through the snow to a pay phone to call a cab to take me to the hospital.

MY PARENTS MOVED TO NORTH BAY THE YEAR I LEFT home to go to university. I spent two summers here, working to pay my tuition, then gradually found excuses for not coming back at all; a better job in Ottawa, a girlfriend, a summer course. I've been back more often in recent years, since my father's heart trouble, but too late to form any kind of attachment to the city, to think of it as home. The cab takes me east along McIntyre Street, deserted at this late hour, and turns north onto Algonquin. The driver asks me why I'm going to the hospital, and I tell him. He nods. "Blood is thicker than water," he says. I nod, but think: That's the problem. My father is being given drugs to thin his blood; ideally, his blood ought to be thinner than water.

His eyes open when I enter his room and he starts like a small, frightened animal. He does this every time he sees me, and each time I think he's going to have another heart atttack. Then he smiles and relaxes. His head seems very large for the body outlined under the thin, green hospital sheet. An oxygen tube passes behind his ears and under his nose, and a plastic identification bracelet is tangled in his watch strap. He has been lying on his back for three weeks, his white hair now grows forward from a point at the back of his head, giving him a kind of Roman senator look. He needs a shave.

"How're you doing?" I ask, taking his hand.

"Not too bad," he says, breathing between each word. He seems not to remember that I have been away. "Maybe you could pour me a little water." When I reach for a plastic jug on his bedtable, he says, Not that one – that's my pee bottle," and we both laugh. Then he starts to cough, deep, lung-wracking coughs that convulse in his chest and end in loud, liquid hawkings into Kleenex.

We don't talk much after that. I sit in a chair at the foot of his bed; he lies back staring at the clock on the wall above my head. Every now and then our eyes meet and we smile. "You must be tired of looking at that clock," I say. "Not really," he says. I stay for an hour, watching him sleep. His chest rises uncertainly, flutters at its apex and then sinks alarmingly into the bedclothes. The oxygen gurgles and hisses. He passes his tongue over his lips and clears his throat in his sleep. He is curled on his side; with his large head and small body, he looks like a comma, not so much fetal as embryonic.

THE TALK IN NORTH BAY IS ALL ABOUT ICE FISHING and the spring bear hunt. The next day, before going back to the hospital, I drive my mother to visit her friend who owns a motel on Lakeshore Drive. My mother is collecting for the Heart and Stroke Foundation this weekend, and her friend has promised to make a donation. It's the last weekend for ice fishing, and every unit in the motel is full of fishermen. The friend's husband and their son take them out onto Lake Nipissing every morning in the motel's two Bombardiers, to a veritable village of ice-fishing shacks the motel maintains a few kilometres out on the ice. Her friend is sorting laundry when we arrive.

"The government's cut two weeks off the season," she says as she works. "It started a week late in December, and now it's ending a week early. That's a lot of revenue lost for us. Not enough ice, they said. Well, look at the lake! There's more ice out there now than there was last month. Twenty-two inches! And this morning when I got up at 4 o'clock the temperature was minus twenty-eight. We could get another two, three weeks in if it wasn't for Mike Harris!"

North Bay is Premier Harris's home riding. His mother goes to my mother's church, except she doesn't show up very often these days, perhaps because she is tired of hearing everyone gripe about her son. Curtailling the fishing season and cancelling the spring bear hunt, which he did a week ago, caving in to pressure from environmental groups in the south, were just about the best things he could have done if he wanted to test his popularity in North Bay. Once the site of a large Air Force base and a major railway hub for Canadian Pacific and Canadian National lines going east and west, and Ontario Northland lines going north and south, the city has had to switch to tourism to avoid disappearing altogether. Not easy for a place that is two hours north of the Muskoka Lakes District, Toronto's vacation playground. North Bay is the near north, a different climatic zone, a different cultural region; it is cold and rough, and its heart has been scoured out by gigantic shopping malls on the outskirts that have sucked the people and the money out of the downtown core. The death of the railways and the withdrawal of the military have buried its arteries and lifelines under mountains of snow. It can afford to think only of winter tourists, which means ice fishermen and bear hunters.

A large elderly woman is having coffee and a cigarette at a table in the dining area while we wait for my mother's friend to write out a cheque. "We'll get rid of him next election," she says. "We'll cook his goose."

"How's Al?" my mother's friend asks.

"About the same," says my mother, making out a receipt. "You know."

WE CAN SEE THE MOTEL'S FISHING HUTS ON THE lake from my father's hospital window, a sprinkling of black dots on a wide expanse of white snow. Wind has patterned the surface into wavelets, and the harsh winter sunlight playing over the ripples makes it look dark and shimmering in places.

"I always think I'm looking at open water," my father says, following my gaze. "I could almost swear I can see currents."

"It's ice all right," says the nurse, bustling into the room. "My husband and I were out on it yesterday. We only got our licence at the end of January, and now we have to bring in our hut by Sunday. It wasn't worth it."

"Did you catch any fish?" my father gasps.

"I got a few perch and six pickerel," she says, fluffing his pillow. "How are we today? Do you want your morphine now?"

"Not now," my father says. "It makes me feel drowsy. I don't want to fall asleep when my son's here."

"Well, then, how did we do with our lunch? Didn't eat the chicken, I see."

My father makes a long face at her. "It was too dry and too tough to cut." The hospital meals are made in Ottawa and shipped to North Bay, part of the government's new centralization policy.

"Well, don't complain to me," the nurse says lightheartedly. "Complain to Mike Harris."

When she leaves, he begins to fuss with his oxygen tube, coiling it and uncoiling it, coiling it again. He does this maybe a hundred times while I watch. Then he pulls the tube away from his face, wipes it and his nose with a Kleenex, and lies back on the pillow without replacing the tube. He sighs and looks helplessly at me. I reach over and put the tube back in his nose, and he takes a few deep breaths. Then he folds his sheet down to his waist and pulls his gown from under his hip and straightens it over the sheet. Then he tucks the gown in again. He does this a few dozen times. "I can't seem to get comfortable," he tells me each time. Then he sinks back, exhausted, and tells me again that the nurse washed his hair last night, that he woke up at 3 a.m. and ate a cookie, that he finished all his breakfast.

"Porridge and cereal and potato salad and mashed potatoes," he says. "Tell Mom I ate everything. She worries about my eating."

He begins adjusting his bedclothes again, and I see his thin white legs when he lifts the sheet to spread it out before folding it. His legs were always pale and skinny, like tendrils of plants that grow deep in the woods, or under boards, starved for light. In his youth, his arms were muscular and deeply tanned in summer, but he never wore shorts and the whiteness of his legs when we were at the beach was accentuated by long, black, sparse hair. I remember him standing over me as I splashed about in the shallow water, his knobby knees at the level of my eyes. I even seem to remember them underwater, where they took on a vaguely repellent greenish tinge, not unlike the colour of his hospital gown. I remember thinking that if I started to drown I'd have to try to swim toward them. He couldn't swim a stroke. "That's why I got out of the Navy," he told me once. "They'd throw me overboard and I'd just sink like a stone. They had to send someone in to save me."

In the water, he would show me how he couldn't swim. He'd launch himself like a white torpedo, arms stretched out in front of his head, and glide for six or seven feet along the surface and then sink like a submarine. He would even lie flat on the bottom until he had to stand up for air, to prove that he wasn't faking. I would watch him, annoyed and fascinated, thinking this was some kind of failing. Fill your lungs with air first, I would tell him, kick your legs. I do, he would say. It doesn't help.

Later, when I took swimming lessons at a downtown pool in Windsor, the instructor would give us white styrofoam wafers to hold onto. We'd stretch them out in front of us and kick our feet behind, like ducklings holding onto slices of bread. I never did become much of a swimmer. I didn't sink like a stone, exactly, but I had to work very hard at not sinking. And I still don't like being in water. I've never seen much point in it. I suppose I see that as some kind of failing, too.

Sunlight pours in through the hospital window and spreads like lava across his bed. It occurs to me that we are both waiting for him to die. Only I am the impatient one. I keep hoping he will turn to me at the final moment with a revelation, some blinding truth that has come to him with his last tremulous heartbeat. I long for this. He will look at me and all pretense will fall away. He will not tell me that the food is inedible, or that the air in here is so dry. We will have a real conversation.

There are questions that run through me like fire as I'm sitting here, questions I have tried to ask him, on and off, for years. I want to know about our family. Why, for instance, did my cousins live with my grandmother after their mother married her second husband? Why did Great-uncle Leason move out of Uncle Art's house and live in a hotel for the last year of his life? Why didn't my father go to his sister's funeral? My father always ducked these questions. Because my grandmother would have missed having them around, he would say, or because Art and Uncle Leason didn't get along. The questions revolve around a bigger mystery to me, a deeper evasion: why are we not a close family? What collapse at the heart of our family sent each of us spinning off on our own, like planets from some distant, silent, cosmic star? I always told myself there would be time to bring the questions up again. Now that there is no time, I want him to come clean.

"Dad," I begin, "why did Joyce and Jimmy stay with Grandma?"

"What?"

"Why didn't they move in with their mother and Benny?"

He is lying on his back, looking up at the ceiling, not trying to remember or to formulate an answer. He is willing his mind to drift out over the lake, across the frozen, wind-scoured currents and curiously bobbing huts. There are fish swimming under the clear ice; he can see them in the green water as he picks up speed and sweeps over the sparsely wooded shore.

"I'm very tired," he says finally. "Would you mind if I just closed my eyes for a few minutes?"

I have always thought of death as a simplification, a reduction, something hot that sears away inessentials and leaves answers sticking up through the rubble like stone chimneys after a fire. But as he sleeps, his face becomes more and more complicated, more anxious than I've ever seen it, as though he is trying to puzzle something out, as though some vitally important thing is eluding him. As though he has suddenly realized that he doesn't know something he thought he knew all along. Or it may be that what I, here among the living, have assumed to be essentials, will turn out in death to be without significance at all. Perhaps it isn't swimming that matters as much as simply being in water. I watch his features crease with pain, frown with sorrow, soften with regret, and I know I will never learn from him whatever it is I think I need to know.

contributors:

VEN BEGAMUDRÉ's latest book is *Isaac Brock: Larger Than Life* which he swears is creative non-fiction. His creation, "Benny Hits His Stride" appeared in a special *Descant* issue about writers who are changing the form of the short story. His newest projects include a first collection of poetry and a fantasy novel for adults and young adults.

KATE BRAID has published three award-winning books of poetry and two books of non-fiction, the most recent of which is *Emily Carr: Rebel Artist*. She teaches creative writing at Malaspina University College on Vancouver Island and lives in Burnaby, on the BC Mainland. She loves the "Fast Ferry."

ANN CHARNEY was born in Poland and raised in Montreal. Educated at McGill and the Sorbonne, she has published, and won awards, for both fiction and non-fiction. She has been a political columnist for *Maclean's* and a contributor to *Saturday Night* and other leading publications. Some of her recent books include *Le Jardin de Rousseau, Dobryd,* and *Defiance in Their Eyes: True Stories from the Margins.*

DANIEL COLEMAN teaches in the Department of English at McMaster University. His essay "The Babies in the Colonial Washtub" (*The New Quarterly*, 1998) won a National Magazine Award. He has experimented with interweaving academic criticism with creative non-fiction in "Masculine Migrations: Reading the Postcolonial Male" in *New Canadian Narratives*.

NIGEL DARBASIE was born in Trinidad, West Indies. In 1969 he moved to Canada, settling in Edmonton. He is perhaps best known as a poet, his work having been published in anthologies and high school textbooks, and broadcast on the CBC. His latest collection, *A Map of the Island*, is due to be released in 2001.

RITA DONOVAN is a freelance writer, editor and speech writer. She is the author of five novels, a number of short stories, works of criticism, reviews and essays. *Dark Jewels* won the 1991 Ottawa-Carleton Book Award and *Daisy Circus* won the award again in 1993. *Landed* won the Canadian Authors Association/Chapters Award for Fiction in 1998. A non-fiction book, *As for the Canadians: The Remarkable Story of the RCAF's "Guinea Pigs" of World War II* is to be published in the fall of 2000.

CATERINA EDWARDS has published a novel, *The Lion's Mouth*, a play, *Homeground*, and a collection of two novellas, *Whiter Shade of Pale/Becoming Emma*. Her collection of short stories, *Island of the Nightingales* will be published in 2000. "Under My Skin" is part of a longer work of creative non-fiction called "Not Home: An Istrian Story."

JOSH FROST recently graduated with a journalism degree from Ryerson University.

DON GAYTON is an ecologist and writer from Nelson, BC. His most recent book, *Landscapes of the Interior*, won the US National Outdoor Book Award. His previous book, *The Wheatgrass Mechanism*, is an enduring collection of essays about the Western Canadian prairies. His work has appeared in *Equinox*, *Harrowsmith*, *Canadian Geographic*, and *Books in Canada*.

WAYNE GRADY has been a freelance magazine writer since 1981. He is the author of seven books, the editor of six literary anthologies, and an award-winning translator. Formerly the editor of *Harrowsmith*, he is now the science editor for *Equinox*. His recent publications include *Chasing the Chinook: On the Trail of Canadian Words and Culture* and *The Quiet Limit of the World: A Journey to the North Pole to Investigate Global Warming*.

KRISTJANA GUNNARS is a writer and professor at the University of Alberta who divides her time between Edmonton and the Sunshine Coast of BC. She is the author of six books of poetry, two collections of short stories and four books of cross-genre fiction and non-fiction. She has translated two books from the Icelandic and edited a collection of essays on Margaret Laurence and one on diasporic short fiction. Her latest book is the novel *Night Train to Nykobing*, released in the fall of 1998. Her book *Zero Hour* was nominated for the Governor General's Award for Fiction.

LOUISE BERNICE HALFE, whose Cree name translates roughly as Sky Dancer, was born in Two Hills, Alberta. She was raised on the Saddle Lake Indian Reserve and attended the Blue Quills Residential School. She has a Social Work degree from the University of Regina and certificates in addictions counselling from the Nechi Institute. Her first book of poetry, *Bear Bones & Feathers,* won the Milton Acorn People's Poetry Prize in 1996. Louise's second book of poetry, *Blue Marrow*, a mixture of prose and poetry, was short-listed for the 1998 Governor General's Award.

PAULINE HOLDSTOCK has published novels, poetry and short fiction in Canada, the United Kingdom and Germany. Her most recent book is *The Turning*, a novel set in France. Her work has appeared in numerous literary magazines and can be found in the anthologies, *Snapshots: The New Canadian Fiction; Moosemilk: The Best of Moosehead*; and *Valentine's Day*. She is the 2000 winner of the *Prairie Fire* Personal Journalism Contest.

MARGARET HOLLINGSWORTH is a playwright who grew up in England but has made her home in Canada since the 1960s. Her most recent play is "Commonwealth Games." The book *Willful Acts* is an updated collection of her best-known plays, including "The Apple in the Eye," "Ever Loving," "Diving," "Islands" and "War Babies" (nominated for a Governor General's Award). She also writes fiction and is currently working on a new novel.

MYRNA KOSTASH is the author of *All of Baba's Children, Long Way From Home: The Story of the Sixties Generation in Canada, No Kidding: Inside the World of Teenage Girls, Bloodlines: A Journey into Eastern Europe*, and *The Doomed Bridegroom: A Memoir*, which was one of *The Globe and Mail's* notable books of 1999. Her essays and magazine articles have appeared in many anthologies. She has been the chair of the Writers Union of Canada and serves on the executive committee of the Canadian Conference of the Arts. Her latest book is *The Next Canada: In Search of our Future Nation*.

PAT KRAUSE is a Regina writer whose fiction has appeared in *Grain, Prism International* and a number of anthologies. Her most recent book is *Best Kept Secrets*. "Acts of Love" is part of a personal journalism manuscript in progress; it was one of the three winners of the 1998 *Event* creative non-fiction contest, and a finalist in the Personal Journalism category of the National Magazine Awards.

RITA MOIR lives in the Slocan Valley in British Columbia. Her creative non-fiction book, *Buffalo Jump: A Woman's Travels* received both the BC Book Prize's Hubert Evans Award for Non-fiction and the VanCity Book Prize for 2000. Her previous book, *Survival Gear*, was short-listed for the national Edna Staebler Award for creative non-fiction and the City of Dartmouth Book Award. Her award-winning story "Leave Taking," about preparing a body for burial, was recently included in the BC non-fiction anthology *Genius of Place*.

NANCY MATTSON is an Albertan who now lives in London. Her 1989 publication *Maria Breaks Her Silence*, was shortlisted by the League of Canadian Poets for best first book of poetry. She has recently begun publishing poetry in UK magazines. Her manuscript "One True Lightbulb" was shortlisted for the 1997 Canadian Literary Awards.

BARRY MCKINNON grew up in Calgary, Alberta, has studied poetry with Irving Layton and has a master's degree in English from the University of British Columbia. He teaches English at the College of New Caledonia in Prince George, BC, where he has lived since 1969. He has published more than a dozen books, and is active as an editor and publisher. His collection *Pulp Log* won the Dorothy Livesay Poetry Award and *Arrhythmia* won the bp nichol Chapbook Award.

EILEEN DELEHANTY PEARKES spent her childhood in the golden hills of California but has lived most of her adult life among British Columbia's "stiff blue folds." Trained as a teacher, editor and technical writer, she now works as a mother, artist and creative writer. Two of her articles recently appeared in *The Globe and Mail*, and she publishes chapbooks on the indigenous culture and history of the West Kootenay.

SHIRLEY SCOTT-BRUISED HEAD is a member of the Blackfoot Confederacy, Peigan Nation. She has a Bachelor's degree in English from the University of Alberta and has published a short story called "An Afternoon in Bright Sunlight" and several poems, including "From Scott's Coulee" and "Sentinals." She works with Alberta Community Development Historic Sites at Head-Smashed-In Buffalo Jump Interpretive Centre as an education officer.

MERILYN SIMONDS is the author of Governor General's Award finalist *The Convict Lover* and a collection of stories, *The Lion in the Room Next Door.* She is an editor, writer and teacher interested in the continually-overlapping boundaries between fiction and non-fiction.

SUE WALSH is originally from Durban, South Africa. She has a degree in writing and English from the University of Victoria. She has received a number of awards, including the 1998 *Prism International* Fiction Award. "White Girl Screaming" is her first published non-fiction.

CAROLINE WOODWARD is the author of *Disturbing the Peace,* a short story collection, *Alaska Highway Two-Step,* a mystery novel, *A Blue Fable,* self-published in Nepal, and *Work is a 4-letter Word,* a collection of illustrated short stories for adult learners.

BETTY JANE WYLIE was first a poet, published in *Fiddlehead* and *Canadian Forum* in the early '60s. She also has three dozen plays to her credit, with productions in Canada, the United States, Britain and New Zealand. After her husband's death in 1973, Wylie turned to journalism and non-fiction to support her four children. She has published thirty-five books, including *Letters to Icelanders: Exploring the Northern Soul, The Write Track: How to Succeed as a Freelance Writer in Canada,* and *Beginnings: A Book for Widows,* which has been in print since 1977. She was a founding member of both The Playwrights' Union of Canada and the Periodical Writers' Association of Canada and is a past chair of the Writers' Union of Canada.

acknowledgements:

"Benny Hits the Big Four-Oh, Or, Aren't You Rather Young to Be Writing Your Memoirs?" (a work in progress) in *West Coast Line*, nos. 26 & 27, Fall-Winter 1998-99 ("Here and There: Between South Asias"), Simon Fraser University, Burnaby [distributed in India by Seagull Press].

"Strip-Mining the Land of Sorrow" by Ann Charney appeared in a briefer format in *Saturday Night Magazine*, July/August 1993 and was reprinted in the *Utne Reader*, Jan/Feb. 1994.

"A Guest of Karen Blixen" was published in two parts in *Logberg-Heimskringla*, the Icelandic Canadian Weekly, July 13 and July 20, 1990.

about the editor

LYNNE VAN LUVEN is ideally positioned to assess the "magpie prose" in this collection, drawing as she does on experience in many areas of the literary arts. Lynne has a PH.D. in Canadian Literature from the University of Alberta, and has been a journalist since 1968. She worked as the books editor for the *Edmonton Journal,* and teaches journalism and non-fiction – first at Carleton University and currently at the University of Victoria. She is the co-editor of *Pop Can: Popular Culture in Canada*, published in 1999 by Prentice Hall Canada.

GO some PLACE further

with these Coteau books by authors who appear in GOING some PLACE:

BUFFALO JUMP: A WOMAN'S TRAVELS
— *Rita Moir*

Hubert Evans Non-Fiction Prize,
BC Book Prizes
VanCity Book Prize for
best book on women's lives

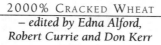

2000% CRACKED WHEAT
— *edited by Edna Alford,
Robert Currie and Don Kerr*

Coteau humour anthology,
including works by Ven Begamudré,
Kate Braid, Pat Krause

OUT OF PLACE
— *Ven Begamudré, co-editor*

Stories and poems about dislocation
and our changing sense of place

EXILES AMONG YOU
— *Kristjana Gunnars*

Poetry from the award-winning
novelist and poet

BEAR BONES AND FEATHERS
— *Louise Bernice Halfe*

People's Poet Award;
Saskatchewan Book Awards finalist

BEST KEPT SECRETS
— *Pat Krause*

Fine short fiction collection

Find these and other fabulous titles at:

COTEAU BOOKS
www.coteaubooks.com

AGMV Marquis

MEMBRE DU GROUPE SCABRINI

Québec, Canada
2000